Contributions to Economics

For further volumes:
http://www.springer.com/series/1262

Giorgio Calcagnini · Ilario Favaretto
Editors

The Economics of Small Businesses

An International Perspective

Physica-Verlag

Editors
Prof. Giorgio Calcagnini
Prof. Ilario Favaretto
Università di Urbino "Carlo Bo"
Department of Economics and Quantitative
   Methods
Via Saffi 42
61029 Urbino, Italy
giorgio.calcagnini@uniurb.it
ilario.favaretto@uniurb.it

ISSN 1431-1933
ISBN 978-3-7908-2622-7			e-ISBN 978-3-7908-2623-4
DOI 10.1007/978-3-7908-2623-4
Springer Heidelberg Dordrecht London New York

© Springer-Verlag Berlin Heidelberg 2011
This work is subject to copyright. All rights are reserved, whether the whole or part of the material is concerned, specifically the rights of translation, reprinting, reuse of illustrations, recitation, broadcasting reproduction on microfilm or in any other way, and storage in data banks. Duplication of this publication or parts thereof is permitted only under the provisions of the German Copyright Law of September 9, 1965, in its current version, and permission for use must always be obtained from Springer. Violations are liable to prosecution under the German Copyright Law.
The use of general descriptive names, registered names, trademarks, etc. in this publication does not imply, even in the absence of a specific statement, that such names are exempt from the relevant protective laws and regulations and therefore free for general use.

Cover design: SPI Publisher Services

Printed on acid-free paper

Physica-Verlag is a brand of Springer-Verlag Berlin Heidelberg
Springer-Verlag is part of Springer Science+Business Media (www.springer.com)

*This book is dedicated to Catherine,
Chiara-Shannon, Dina, Federico, Martina*

Preface

This book is the product of two international conferences held at the Università di Urbino "Carlo Bo" in April 2008 and 2009. When we planned the conferences we wanted to bring together in Urbino scholars from different countries to discuss an issue that traditionally has been faced at the domestic level. Indeed, many times in our talks we had the feeling that the common view, at least in Italian academic circles, was that every economy has its own type of small business. Therefore, policies in favor of small businesses also had specificities depending on the country under consideration. After the two conferences, during which we analyzed case studies in Italy, the EU and the US, we are now more confident that our search for internationally common features in small business economies was worth pursuing. Up to now we had concentrated our attention on comparing the size of small business economies, the policies to support small businesses, innovative small businesses and their financial structures. However we are already working on a 2010 conference that will focus on the effects of the ongoing economic and financial crisis on small businesses.

We wish to thank all participants at the two conferences for their invaluable contributions and their courage in joining us in Urbino. Sergio Arzeni, Charles Ou and Bob Strom deserve special thanks for their continuous support and help in setting up an international network and finalizing the conference programmes. Germana Giombini, who collaborated with us in carrying out research and all conference phases, has made irreplaceable contributions to this project. Finally, we are especially grateful to UBI-Banca Popolare di Ancona, the Pesaro-Urbino Chamber of Commerce, the Marche Region, the C.N.A. – Italia and Marche, and the Svim – Sviluppo Marche S.p.A. for their financial support that made the two conferences possible.

Urbino, Italy　　　　　　　　　　　　　　　　　　　　　　　　　Giorgio Calcagnini
June 2010　　　　　　　　　　　　　　　　　　　　　　　　　　　Ilario Favaretto

Introduction

This volume contains eleven articles on the economics of small businesses (SB). Most of them were presented at two international conferences held at the Università di Urbino "Carlo Bo" in 2008 and 2009. The conferences aimed at analyzing the role of small-sized firms from an international perspective. Traditionally, though not exclusively, SBs have been analyzed "locally": their small size makes it easier to think of them as economic actors associated with a local economic context (a province or a region), as opposed to larger companies which are natural global players. However, when small firms are looked at as a whole their weight critically affects the economic performance of national economies. In Italy, in 2005, 95% of the total number of firms had fewer than 10 employees, while those with between 10 and 49 employees hold a share of 4.5%. Therefore, almost 99% of Italian firms had fewer than 50 employees.

In the same year, at the European Union-26 level (i.e., the European Union-27 minus Italy), the numbers were not so different from those of Italy when we consider both size cohorts of firms (micro- and small-sized firms). However, 7.6% of firms had between 10 and 49 employees, i.e. around 3 percentage points higher than in Italy.[1]

Comparing Italy and the U.S. complicates the picture because of the different breakdowns of firms by number of employees used in those two economies. If we limit our analysis to the class of firms with fewer than 10 employees, their weight within the U.S. economy is significantly smaller (79%) than that observed in Italy (95%). However, when U.S. firms with employees are summed with sole-proprietor (nonemployer) businesses, their share is similar to the Italian (and the European) one. The average size of firms is what differs among the three economic areas. Indeed, while in Italy almost 50% of employment exists in businesses with fewer than 10 employees, and only 18% in large-sized firms, in the rest of Europe those numbers are respectively 27 and 35%. In the U.S. the situation is at odds with respect

---

[1] See Calcagnini and Favaretto (2009), p. 65 and Davis and Lunati in this book.

to Italy: micro-sized businesses make up 11% of total employment and large-sized firms 50%.[2]

At the time of this writing it seems natural to ask: Is there a relationship between the average size of firms and the way economies are responding to the ongoing crisis?[3] We understand that such a question does not have a clear-cut answer. The identification of a relationship likely requires many conditions and is beyond the scope of this Introduction. Notwithstanding, some back-of-the-envelope calculations or graphs may shed some light on the answer.

We will limit our analysis to the current recession, reasoning that it may be more informative than taking into consideration a longer time period characterized by ups and downs in economic activity. Indeed, during phases of positive GDP growth rates economies find it easier to exploit all business opportunities, apart from their industrial organization. Expanding demand makes it viable even for marginal (and often very small-sized) firms to profitably participate in the market.[4] However, during economic recessions only well organized firms, which had invested in innovation and in human capital, are able to compete and survive. Both types of investment are not a prerogative of large-sized companies and, among other things, depend upon the policies and institutional (domestic and international) contexts within which firms operate.

Italy is a good case study to clarify the role of SBs within developed economies and the changes that may occur over time.

In Italy, the current economic crisis may be comparable to the one experienced in the mid-Seventies, even though both 2009 GDP and industrial production fell twice as much as in 1975: −4.7 and −18.4%, −2.2 and −9.2%, respectively. In those days, the crisis was the result of changes in the relative prices that favored raw materials, oil and labor. The reaction of the Italian economy to these shocks was the beginning of a restructuring process that brought about a decentralization of production processes and firm downsizing. Thus, small-sized firms were able to absorb those shocks more easily than larger firms and adapt to the new domestic and international economic environment. Small businesses aimed to control as many employees as possible without negatively affecting labor productivity by substituting firm organization based on Taylorism with a more direct and meticulous control of employees. However, SBs initially appeared to be the outcome of short-term decisions that resulted in the spread of production outside large-sized firms and the planning of economic development not unaccompanied by an increase in firm size.[5]

---

[2] See Calcagnini and Favaretto (2009), pp. 66 and 69. Indeed, the share of employment in large-sized firms would be larger than 50% if we used the definition of large-sized firms utilized in Europe, i.e., firms with more than 250 employees.

[3] Duval and Vogel (2008) examine the impact of a range of structural policies on the resilience of economies to shocks.

[4] See Schmiemann (2009).

[5] See Favaretto (1995), p. 111.

Introduction xi

Those were the years of "small is beautiful",[6] a slogan that – not surprisingly – became popular among Italian academics, commentators and politicians.

The downsizing process of Italian firms went hand in hand with technological innovations available at that time that made the minimum size necessary for firms to be efficient smaller than in the past, and encouraged the adoption of new information technologies that favored the decentralization of industrial processes. The result of this restructuring process was a flexible productive system that was tailored to variegated demand patterns and markets.

Small-sized firms also provided comparative advantages over large firms with respect to labor costs (a) thanks to a larger share of employees with lower professional qualifications, (b) given that wages kept close to their minimum level, (c) due to a lower degree of labor absenteeism, conflicts, and worktime discontinuity. However, the decentralization process was not the only possible solution to the structural changes that occurred in the Seventies. Indeed, it was seen as the most natural result of the inadequacy of the entrepreneurial class, the lack of a national industrial policy, and commercial and financial partners that could have oriented Italian firms towards different patterns of industrial organization.[7]

During the second part of the Seventies the decentralization process and the specialization of SBs into specific production phases and functions – a response that large-sized firms adopted to overcome the effects of the economic crisis – lost their business-cycle characterization. Instead, they became a structural component of the Italian productive structure.

Nowadays the lack of large-sized firms is what makes the Italian economy different from other developed economies, not its large share of small businesses. Indeed, with the exception of a limited number of cases, the downsizing of Italian firms went along with the progressive disappearance of large industrial companies. In 2005, only 3,215 large-sized firms were present in the Italian economy, i.e., 0.1% of all firms. Further, Italian large-sized firms only employed 18.3% of all employees.[8]

To shed some light on the effects of shocks on economies characterized by firms of different average size, we perform a simple analysis. In doing this we implicitly followed the three-stage framework proposed by Davis and Lunati (in this book) to analyze the entrepreneurship process: (1) SB *determinants*, which policy can affect and which in turn influence (2) SB *performance*, (3) and the final *impact* of SBs on economic growth. Specifically, we calculated the cross-country correlation between the per-firm average number of employees and the average GDP growth rate in 2008–2009 for a group of European countries plus the U.S.. We wanted to test the hypothesis of a relationship between the average firm size and the impact of the

---

[6]The quotation is the first part of the title of Schumacher's book "Small is Beautiful: Economics as if People Mattered", (1973).

[7]See Caselli (1974).

[8]In Europe (and by excluding Italy) figures are 0.2 and 35.1%, respectively. See Calcagnini and Favaretto (2009), pp. 65–66.

recent economic recession on GDP.[9] Since the shock that created the recession is common to all countries, differences in GDP growth rates across economies may be accounted for by differences in their economic structures and institutions. To control for differences in institutions we used two variables, the employment protection legislation index (EPL) and the capital access index (CAI).[10] We did not have any prior expectations before running the analysis: a positive or a negative relationship, as well as no relationship at all could come out.

Our simple analysis is graphically represented in Fig. 1. The figure clearly shows a positive correlation between the average firm size and the average GDP growth rate in 2008–2009 for a group of countries that includes Austria, Belgium, Germany, Italy, the Netherlands, Sweden, the U.K., and the U.S.. The value of the correlation coefficient is 0.46. Furthermore, Fig. 1 supports the idea that countries with small-sized firms are more vulnerable to shocks than countries where the average size of businesses is larger.[11]

To better understand this result, we must report that initially we started with a larger group of countries that also included France, Norway, Portugal and Spain. For the expanded group of countries the relationship between firm size and GDP growth is much less strong (0.11), and probably not statistically significant, than the one shown in Fig. 1. We found an explanation for the two results in the different institutions that characterize the countries in our sample. Specifically, we focused our attention on employment protection legislation and access to capital.

We split our sample into two groups on the basis, first, of the average (or median) EPL value and, secondly, of the average (or median) CAI value.[12] On one hand we included countries with lower-than-average EPL values (we defined these countries as more market-oriented, MMO), and on the other hand countries with higher-than-average EPL values (we defined these countries as less market-oriented, LMO). We repeated the same exercise by means of the capital access index, keeping in mind that larger CAI values correspond to countries with better capital access (or MMO countries).

Figure 1 shows the correlation between firm size and GDP growth rates for the group of MMO countries defined on the basis of their EPL value in 2003. Further, this correlation increases from 0.46 to 0.65 if limited to the four countries with the lowest EPL values. In other words, countries with smaller firms are more sensitive to (negative) shocks the more flexible their labor markets are.

This relationship between firm size and GDP growth is still robust when the ordering of countries is made based on the capital access index: the correlation

---

[9] See O.E.C.D. (2009) for an analysis of the impact of the economic crisis on SMEs.

[10] For our empirical analysis we used the OECD EPL index, Version 1, (OECD, 2004), while the CAI is from the Milken Institute (Barth et al., 2008, p. 6.).

[11] This positive relationship between firm size and GDP growth rates reflects a positive and strong correlation between firm size and countries' competitiveness. When the latter is measured by means of the IMD World Competitiveness index (IMD, 2010) the correlation index for all twelve countries is 0.64.

[12] There are no significant differences in our results by using either the average, or the median.

Introduction

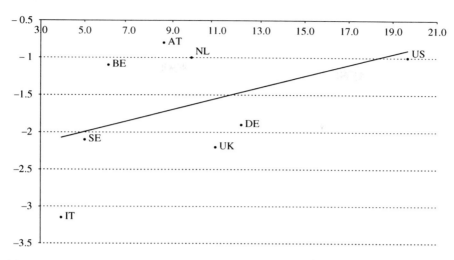

Fig. 1 Relationship between GDP growth rates (*vertical axis*) and firm size (*horizontal axis*)

coefficient for the group of LMO countries is 0.67.[13] In the presence of imperfect capital markets, shocks hit economies harder where firms are smaller. The latter is not a surprising result given the extensive economic literature on the opaqueness of small-sized firms and their difficulties in accessing external finance. This is especially true in less efficient financial markets and during a financial crisis that induces a credit crunch in the form of a contraction in the supply of credit.[14]

A third (political) variable may be called upon in the analysis of the relationship between firm size and GDP growth rates, i.e., the amount of fiscal stimulus. In countries where firms are relatively larger, *ceteris paribus*, one could expect industry associations to be in a better position while trying to organize firm consensus and have more power in influencing government economic policy. During a recession, economies with more large-sized firms will experience larger fiscal stimulus packages and lower GDP decreases. To avoid bias due to the presence in our sample of countries adopting the euro together with countries not belonging to the euro area, we limited the correlation analysis only to the former group. Results showed a positive, but not very strong (0.26), correlation between firm size and GDP growth rates. Thus we decided to not pursue the issue any further.

Overall, our empirical analysis shows that countries where firms are, on average, relatively smaller were hit more severely by the economic recession than countries with larger firms. We pointed out two possible explanations for these results related

---

[13] In this group only entered six countries: Belgium, Austria, France, Italy, Portugal and Spain. These countries are not necessarily those included in the LMO group defined on the base of the EPL index. Only France, Portugal and Spain are contemporaneously in the two LMO groups.

[14] See Udell's article in this volume.

to labor and financial markets.[15] With a flexible labor market, small firms decide to fire their employees and exit the market when the economy is hit by a negative shock. Differently, larger firms likely reduce their production and employment levels less than they would find optimal, besides not laying off redundant workers to ensure that skilled and experienced workers are available after the recession. Indeed, even in countries with low EPL levels, larger firms face higher sunk costs than smaller ones that generate inertia.[16] In countries with a regulated labor market, sunk costs increase for all firms but inertia is still relatively larger among large-sized firms. Therefore, we expect that during a recession GDP will decrease relatively more in countries were firms are smaller. The same should be expected when taking into account differences in capital market efficiency. Small businesses are relatively more penalized during a recession in those countries where accessing capital is more difficult.[17] Indeed, SBs have a weaker financial structure than larger firms, have a lower or no credit rating, are heavily dependent on credit and have fewer financing options.[18]

Countries' ability to deal with the crisis depends to a large extent on the degrees of freedom available to them to effectively manage their fiscal and monetary policies. Our analysis shows that structural policies can also play a positive role. Among them, policies that facilitate firm entry and the increase of firms' size are important to exploit growth opportunities and to better overcome economic recessions.[19] By this we do not mean refusing to acknowledge that *small is still beautiful*, but... Most firms in all countries are and will be small-sized. However, we believe that the economic potential of countries goes along with sound and well-organized firms, which means more innovation, a better educated labor force, higher likelihood of access to financial resources and efficient investments. In turn, national governments and international institutions should adopt policies and incentives that encourage firm aggregation, more competitive financial markets, more R&D investments, less regulated labor markets and a reform of national education systems. The aforesaid, together with traditional students, also suggests the importance of post-secondary learning such as degree credit courses for non-traditional students, and non-degree career and workforce training through evening and online courses.

The purpose of the first two Urbino conferences was to highlight the importance of two of the issues related to small businesses: innovation and finance access. Therefore, we organized the book into two parts that contain analyses on, and policy recommendations in favor of, small-sized businesses.

---

[15] See Calcagnini et al. (2009) for an analysis of labor and market imperfections on investment decisions.
[16] See Dixit (1989).
[17] See Coluzzi et al. (2009).
[18] See O.E.C.D. (2009), p. 6.
[19] Davis and Lunati article reports that U.S. firm entrants are smaller than their European counterparts but, once over the initial start-up phase, they expand rapidly while European firms remain small.

Introduction

The first part of the book – Small Businesses and Innovation: Analyses and Policies – addresses the innovation issue. The first paper by Baumol, Litan, Schramm and Strom explores the policies that would promote the continuation and expansion of a community's innovative entrepreneurial activities and their contribution to stimulating economic growth in the most effective way. The authors identify the policies that are necessary to counter threats to such entrepreneurial activity, i.e. those existing now or looming on the horizon. Their paper focuses upon policies suitable for the United States, the country in which innovative entrepreneurship thus far has been most successful and evident. They explore how policies at multiple levels of government, but primarily policies at the national or federal level which have the broadest impact, can affect innovative entrepreneurship. The lesson we learn from the Baumol et al. contribution is simple, and has clear-cut policy implications for other countries as well. They point out that – together with (a) laws and systems that make it easy to start a new venture and facilitate the hiring of new workers and letting go of those who under-perform or whose skills do not match the constantly-evolving needs of innovative enterprises; (b) the removal of legal barriers to entry and price controls in a number of key industries, which has dramatically cut costs and made it easier for new firms to get started and grow; and (c) the existence of a large internal market that offers economies of scale and the openness to foreign goods, services, and capital – a key to success is that Americans have long perceived themselves as a nation of creative self-starters who welcome challenges and value individuality and self-reliance.

Ou's paper provides an overview of the U.S. State programs designed to promote innovation. The major justifications for government intervention in markets for new products are that (a) governments can best promote business growth by improving the working of the output and resource markets so that entrepreneurs can exploit market opportunities and (b) by investing in the resource markets to increase the supply of resources, innovative entrepreneurs can successfully develop new products at low costs. The author groups these interventions into four categories: (1) direct participation in the markets by State government(s) as the main supplier or as the main buyer; (2) State activities to improve the working of the markets by changing the culture/mindset of the participants in the markets; (3) investment in the market infrastructures to improve the supply and/or to reduce the transaction costs in the market; (4) direct State assistance to entrepreneurs as the buyers (for inputs) and the sellers (of products).

The Davis and Lunati article tries to fill the gap consisting in the lack of consistent and comparable information on small businesses and entrepreneurship across countries. Comparable data allow researchers to overcome the problem of examining any economy in isolation, and policy makers to design efficient and effective policies in favor of newly-created and existing small businesses and entrepreneurs, and economic growth. Davis and Lunati's contribution describes the genesis and underlying methodological and administrative framework for the OECD-Eurostat Entrepreneurship Programme. Further, it presents some early data results from the programme: internationally-comparable indicators to gauge the amount and type of entrepreneurship activity in twenty-three countries.

Gallo and Iezzi's paper brings to the fore how the loss in competitiveness experienced by several European countries, and especially Italy, is related to the lack of support for the creation of excellence as well as industry fragmentation. Both phenomena represent an obstacle to the generation of innovative technologies that drive economic growth. In the case of Italy, besides the lack of an adequate educational system, an encouraging business environment, and access to venture capital, the authors find that only 4.3% of Italian small- and medium-sized firms (SMEs) co-operate with other firms, Universities or innovation research centers. In addition the Italian SMEs prefer to co-operate with other firms, rather than with the public research system and, therefore, reduce the impact of technology transfer on the whole economy. Gallo and Iezzi describe the advantages of the Italian Network for Innovation and Technology Transfer for small- and medium-sized firms (RIDITT), as it aims at improving the competitiveness of SMEs by strengthening the supply of services for innovation and technology transfer. This is together with the creation of new hi-tech enterprises, while paying special attention to Italy's less developed areas.

Bruzzo's contribution is specifically focused on Italy. It contains a survey of the industrial policy measures addressed to SMEs adopted both by the central government and the regional and local administrations during the period considered. Further, it describes the state of the progress currently achieved by such measures. The author dwells in particular on the provision entitled "Industria 2015", regarding which he estimates the amount of the various financial incentives exclusively allocated to SMEs. The latter is a contribution of particular interest and originality to the current scientific debate. A few outcomes are worth noting here. First, the Italian incentive system is characterized by a large number of interventions, particularly at the regional level, even though this is mitigated by the fact that the majority of resources are concentrated on a limited number of incentive instruments. Furthermore, it emerges that generalized interventions outnumber targeted ones, as well as those of the evaluative and automatic type, just as those that involve capital contributions outnumber those involving other types of incentive. The main recommendation that emerges is logically that of reducing the number of, and the consequent overlaps among, the instruments used at the different levels of government, while continuing to preserve the specificities of the policies adopted. Second, Bruzzo notes that while European regulations introduced new types of aid closely focused on the needs of SMEs, which are usually those hardest hit by market failures, the Italian government's attention to SMEs has diminished in recent years. This is illustrated by the fact that, in the most recent Ministerial Report on interventions to support business, specification is no longer made of the proportion allocated to incentives for SMEs. Moreover, such interventions are no longer distinguished between those made by the Regions and those originating at the national level.

The second part of the book – The Financing of Small – and Medium – Sized Firms – contains six contributions on the SB financing issue.

Udell's paper examines new paradigms that have expanded the understanding of how SME loans are underwritten and how underwriting changes during a macro financial shock. Further, it discusses how the behavior of foreign-owned banks, particularly in developing economies, and the efficacy of government guarantee programs, have affected SME financing during the current financial crisis. It is well known that SMEs in general do not have access to the capital markets where they can issue publicly traded stock and corporate bonds. Thus, they tend to be dependent on financial institutions (particularly banks and finance companies) and mercantile trade (i.e., trade credit). Even in normal times, access to external finance can be problematic, particularly for those SMEs who are more opaque. This can become acute during a financial crisis that induces a credit crunch in the form of a contraction in the credit supply. To gain a better understanding of how SMEs might be affected by the current financial crisis, Udell emphasizes that there are a number of lending channels (or technologies) through which SMEs obtain financing and they vary across countries. The ultimate net effect of this credit crunch on SMEs will depend on how these lending channels behave. Indeed, some lending channels might shrink during a credit crunch, for example, while others do not. Some might even substitute for others during a credit crunch. That is, some might expand in order to offset those that contract. Notwithstanding the existence of many lending channels a funding gap caused by informational opacity may still occur. Directing government subsidies towards the SME sector has long been a popular public policy remedy for this problem. Particularly common among these programs have been government guarantee programs where the government guarantees (or partially guarantees) loans made by private banks. Since most programs place an upper limit on the size of loans that can be guaranteed they will be more suitable for smaller companies that, *ceteris paribus*, are likely more opaque and more financially constrained.

Chavis, Klapper and Love analyze the financial structure of a large sample of Eastern European firms, in both EU and non-EU member countries, to shed light on firm characteristics that are associated with greater access to financing, and the relationship between access to bank financing and investment decisions. The focus of their paper is on the relationship between firm age, the incidence of investment in fixed assets and the sources of funds used to finance this investment. The specificity of studying Eastern European countries is that their liberalization process has provided a major role for SMEs as a driving force behind the continuing transformation of the private sector. Indeed, the restructuring and downsizing of large firms, the privatization of public utilities and other large companies, the outsourcing of many support services, and the vertical fragmentation of production are all forces that promoted the creation and expansion of SMEs. Considering the importance of SMEs in promoting growth and dynamism in transition economies, the authors think that it is critical to analyze the willingness of the banking sector to lend money to SMEs and the degree to which financial intermediaries have facilitated their development. Indeed, it is only after the liberalization process that the banking sector has been able to choose its borrowers, and channel a larger share of its funding towards companies of different types. The findings of Chavis et al. show the importance of banks as a source of firm funding both in the EU and non-EU countries. However, in the latter case, and differently from what occurs in the EU, older firms are more likely to apply for loans and their applications are less likely to be rejected than those of younger firms. Further, they find that firms' ability to secure a loan is related to real behavior, measured by the incidence of investment and the amount invested; i.e., firms that were able to obtain a loan are more likely to make any investment than firms that were rejected for a loan. Chavis et al. also find that older firms are less likely to purchase fixed assets and when they do, they spend smaller amounts on fixed asset purchases. However, this impact is most pronounced in non-EU countries. This suggests that in those countries larger firms are not investing as much as their younger counterparts. In addition, firms in the EU are more likely to use retained earnings and less likely to use other sources of external finance. This suggests that, as firms in the EU mature, they are able to maintain the frequency and amount of their investments using their internal funds, while firms in non EU countries have to decrease their investment with age and rely relatively more on external funds.

Bentivogli, Cocozza, Foglia and Iannotti analyze the influence of the bank-firm relationship on growth plans of Italian SMEs after the revision of the standards governing bank capital adequacy carried out in 2006, known as Basel II. In order to verify if and how the relationships between banks and firms were evolving, in 2006 the Bank of Italy carried out a survey, adding a special section on Basel II to its yearly survey on a sample of private non-agricultural firms with 20 or more employees. Since the impact of Basel II was expected to differ according to firm size, the national survey was supplemented by a local survey on small and very small firms located in Emilia-Romagna (Northern Italy), Puglia, and Basilicata (Southern Italy). The local survey on small firms dealt with bank-firm relationships when the firm decides to expand its scale of operation: the type of financing involved, the non-financial support by the main bank, and the obstacles met by firms that decided to drop their growth projects. The national survey shows that not a small number of firms was aware of the effects of the new regulation on their relationships with lenders. The share is higher among the smaller sized respondents to the local survey. About one half of the firms which answered that they were aware of the new regulation thought it was necessary to carry out some organizational changes. This mainly consisted in enriching information about the firm, increasing the capital-to-debt ratio and strengthening the financial area. There was a wide range of answers on perceived changes in credit availability and terms, which could signal either differences in the way banks are adapting to the new regulation or their ability better evaluate borrowers' creditworthiness and better differentiate the credit supply. As for firm growth, the territorial survey shows that the perception of limitations connected to small size is more widespread among firms residing in Emilia-Romagna than among those located in the South of Italy. In Emilia-Romagna the finishing rate of growth projects is also higher, with important financial support by banks. However it seems that there is not wider backing by the intermediaries in terms of assistance and counseling; there are also obstacles to growth connected with problems in finding management as well as firm governance.

Calcagnini, Favaretto and Giombini's article focuses on the financing patterns of innovative SMEs in Italy. They use a sample of firms located in the Marche region, traditionally known as the region of small businesses, and compare the outcomes with those from a sample of non-innovative firms at the beginning of 2009. Their findings show that debt also plays an important role as a finance source for innovative firms. It contributes to financing almost 60% of investment. However, this share is significantly lower than that (83%) observed for non-innovative firms. Leasing, bank loans, and lines of credit are the main components of firms' financial debt. All three types of debt imply relationships with banks that, overall, continue to represent main sources of financing for firms. Indeed, even in the middle of the current economic and financial crisis, banks have refused to provide requested funds to only 9% of innovative firms. Further, innovative firms need to fund their investment by means of equity. On average, it represents 40% of all funds. However, most equity (80%) comes from owners and only one-fifth from external equity providers. This result is further confirmation of the propensity of Italian entrepreneurs to not dilute their ownership of companies which, in most cases, are family owned. Calcagnini et al. also show that external private equity providers are in most cases venture capital firms; that is, firms tend to mainly use formal channels of equity provision, while informal providers – such as business angels – are completely missing from the regional economic context. This is so even though entrepreneurs declared that the latter would be useful to overcome the procedural difficulties encountered with traditional fund providers. Further, in most cases private equity providers become firms' co-owners because, through their network, they allow original owners to enter into contact with other finance providers, and because private equity providers offer financial skills that are lacking within firms. Finally, one of the main reasons why external equity providers refused to supply funds is that firms had weak business plans.

The willingness of italian innovative firms to use external equity is confirmed by Coleman and Robb's article. They find that, differently from the Pecking Order theory, firm owners prefer to use inside equity and outside debt to avoid diluting their ownership position and giving up control. U.S. high tech firms – included in the Kauffman Firm Survey data – had a significantly higher probability of using both outside debt and outsider equity than medium-sized tech firms. Further, high tech firms use a significantly higher ratio of outsider equity than medium tech firms. These results suggest that the owners of high tech firms are more open to using a number of different sources of financing to ensure firm survival, development, and growth. Similarly, Coleman and Robb's results seem to refute the Life Cycle theory that states that newer firms are forced to rely on internal rather than external sources of capital. Their findings reveal that technology-based firms raised substantial amounts of both external debt and equity, even in their startup year: high tech firm owners who used outside equity raised over five times as much capital in their startup year as all firms together ($549,699 vs. $83,993). It would seem that external providers of capital are attracted by technology-based firms' prospects for growth and profits, even during the early stages of their existence. Coleman and Robb's results also reveal differences in the financing patterns of women and minority firm owners. Women were significantly less likely to use outside debt, bank loans, or insider financing than all firms. This finding is consistent with prior research indicating that women are more reliant on personal or owner-provided sources of financing than on external sources. Similarly, minority firm owners were less likely to use external sources of financing. However, Black-owned, Asian-owned, and Hispanic-owned firms did use a higher ratio of insider-provided financing, revealing that family and other insiders play a greater role in starting up minority-owned firms.

Finally, Bellucci, Borisov and Zazzaro analyze the influence of loan officers' personalities, dispositions and behavior during loan origination and in bank relationships with small businesses. Their review of the literature highlights that many of the factors that influence loan officers' behavior have proven to be gender-specific, or at least more pronounced for one gender than for the other. For instance, women (a) tend to be more risk-averse and less self-confident than men; (b) make slower career advancements than men and are less likely to accept jobs away from their family; (c) are typically less sensitive to competitive incentives than men; (d) might be less sensitive to incentive and display a greater sense of solidarity with borrowers. Further, men and women seem to respond differently to the sex of the other party involved in the transaction. For such reasons, female loan officers could be inclined to use stricter criteria when deciding upon loan applications in order to avoid defaults and maximize the probability of internal career progression. Since a critical part of the loan officer's job is relational – i.e., (s)he makes decisions through interpersonal interactions with specific borrowers, often on the basis of limited information and cognitive capacity – intuitional, emotional, behavioral and cultural factors drive loan officers' assessment of borrowers' creditworthiness. Finally, information is also obtained from financial statements: together the above mentioned factors lead loan officers to make a final decision of whether to grant or not grant a loan. Bellucci et al. conclude that the economic literature on the gender issue is still scarce, and most recent empirical studies only provide indirect insights into unobservable loan officer characteristics such as their degree of overconfidence or career concerns. Studies that try to directly measure loan officers' characteristics are either based on small samples or do not address all aspects of the lending process outcome. Moreover, the observed pattern in the data is often consistent with more than one explanation. Therefore, the gender issue of bank-loan officers remains an open question.

Small firms are and will remain at the core of most developed and developing economies, but size is not necessarily a sufficient condition to identifying them as economic players. We also need to understand how they are organized, which social and institutional environment they operate in, and who the other players they compete with are. This is a complex theme beyond the scope of this book, which has only focused on some of the issues such as innovation and access to financing. We hope, instead, that this book will provide fertile ground for the development of ideas for future research.

References

Barth JR, Li T, Lu W, Phumiwasana T, Yago G (2008) Capital access index 2007: best markets for business access to capital. Milken Institute. http://www.milkeninstitute.org/publications/publications.taf?function=detail&ID=38801036&cat=resrep
Calcagnini G, Favaretto I (eds) (2009) L'economia della piccola impresa. Rapporto 2009. Franco Angeli, Milano

Calcagnini G, Giombini G, Saltari E (2009) Financial and labor market imperfections and investment. Econ Lett 102:22–26

Caselli (1974) Replica al dibattito: Decentramento produttivo e teoria dell'impresa. Economia e politica industriale 7(8):79

Coluzzi C, Ferrando A, Martinez-Carrascal C (2009) Financing obstacles and growth. An analysis for Euro area non-financial corporations. ECB Working Paper Series, No. 997

Dixit A (1989) Entry and exit decisions under uncertainty. J Polit Econ 97:620–638

Duval R, Vogel L (2008) Economic resilience to shocks: the role of structural policies. OECD Econ Stud 44

Favaretto I (1995) Mercati imperfetti e decentramento produttivo. Genova: ASPI/INS-EDIT

IMD (2010) IMD World Competitiveness Yearbook. http://www.imd.ch/research/publications/wcy/wcy_book.cfm

O.E.C.D. (2009) The impact of the global crisis on SME and entrepreneurship financing and policy responses. O.E.C.D, Paris

O.E.C.D. (2004) Employment outlook. O.E.C.D, Paris

Schmiemann M (2009) SMEs were the main drivers of economic growth between 2004 and 2006. Eurostat, Statstics in focus, nr.71

Schumacher EF (1973) Small is beautiful: economics as if people mattered. Harper & Row, New York, NY

Contents

Part I Small Businesses and Innovation: Analyses and Policies

1. **Innovative Entrepreneurship and Policy: Toward Initiation and Preservation of Growth** 3
   William J. Baumol, Robert E. Litan, Carl J. Schramm, and Robert J. Strom

2. **State Programs to Promote the Growth of Innovative Firms in the United States – A Taxonomy** 25
   Charles Ou

3. **OECD-Eurostat Entrepreneurship Indicators Programme: Comparable International Measures of Entrepreneurship and the Factors that Enhance or Impede It** 49
   Tim C. Davis and Mariarosa Lunati

4. **The Peculiarities of SMEs in Europe and Italy: Technology Transfer Policies** 69
   Riccardo Gallo and Marco Iezzi

5. **Public Policies for Italian SMEs: Instruments, Results and Current Trends** 81
   Aurelio Bruzzo

Part II The Financing of Small – and Medium – Sized Firms

6. **SME Financing and the Financial Crisis: A Framework and Some Issues** 103
   Gregory F. Udell

7. **Access to Bank Financing and New Investment: Evidence from Europe** 115
   Larry W. Chavis, Leora F. Klapper, and Inessa Love

8	**Basel II and Changing Bank-Firm Relationship: A Survey** Chiara Bentivogli, Emidio Cocozza, Antonella Foglia, and Simonetta Iannotti	133
9	**Financial Models of Small Innovative Firms: An Empirical Investigation** Giorgio Calcagnini, Ilario Favaretto, and Germana Giombini	151
10	**Sources of Financing for New Technology Firms: Evidence from the Kauffman Firm Survey** Susan Coleman and Alicia Robb	173
11	**Do Male and Female Loan Officers Differ in Small Business Lending? A Review of the Literature** Andrea Bellucci, Alexander Borisov, and Alberto Zazzaro	195

Contributors

William J. Baumol Berkley Center for Entrepreneurial Studies, Henry Kaufman Management Center, New York, NY 10012, USA, william.baumol@nyu.edu

Andrea Bellucci Dipartimento di Economia e Metodi Quantitativi, Università di Urbino "Carlo Bo", 61029 Urbino, Italy, andrea.bellucci@uniurb.it

Chiara Bentivogli Banca d'Italia, Bologna Branch, Piazza Cavour 6, 40124 Bologna, chiara.bentivogli@bancaditalia.it

Alexander Borisov Kelly School of Business, Indiana University at Bloomington, Bloomington, IN 47405, USA, aborisov@indiana.edu

Aurelio Bruzzo Dipartimento di Economia, Università di Ferrara, 44121 Ferrara, Italy, bruzzo@economia.unife.it

Giorgio Calcagnini Dipartimento di Economia e Metodi Quantitativi, Università di Urbino "Carlo Bo", 61029 Urbino, Italy, giorgio.calcagnini@uniurb.it

Larry W. Chavis Kenan-Flagler Business School, University of North Carolina at Chapel Hill, Chapel Hill, NC 27599-3490, USA, larry_chavis@unc.edu

Emidio Cocozza Banca d'Italia, 00184 Roma, Italy, emidio.cocozza@bancaditalia.it

Susan Coleman The Barney School of Business, University of Hartford, West Hartford, CT 06117, USA, scoleman@hartford.edu

Tim C. Davis Organization for Economic Co-Operation and Development (OECD), 2 rue Andre Pascal, 75775 Paris Cedex 16, France, tim.davis@oecd.org

Ilario Favaretto Dipartimento di Economia e Metodi Quantitativi, Università di Urbino "Carlo Bo", 61029 Urbino, Italy, ilario.favaretto@uniurb.it

Antonella Foglia Banca d'Italia, 00184 Roma, Italy, antonella.foglia@bancaditalia.it

Riccardo Gallo Dipartimento Ingegneria Chimica Materiali Ambiente, Università di Roma "Sapienza", 00161 Roma, Italy, riccardo.gallo@uniroma1.it

Germana Giombini Dipartimento di Economia e Metodi Quantitativi, Università di Urbino "Carlo Bo", 61029 Urbino, Italy, germana.giombini@uniurb.it

Simonetta Iannotti Banca d'Italia, 00184 Roma, Italy, simonetta.iannotti@bancaditalia.it

Marco Iezzi Istituto per la Promozione Industriale, 00197 Roma, Italy, iezzi@ipi.it

Leora F. Klapper The World Bank, Development Research Group, Washington, DC 20433, USA, lklapper@worldbank.org

Robert E. Litan The Ewing Marian Kauffman Foundation, Kansas City, MO 64110, USA; Brookings, Washington, DC 20036, USA, rlitan@kauffman.org

Inessa Love The World Bank, Development Research Group, Washington, DC 20433, USA, ilove@worldbank.org

Mariarosa Lunati Organization for Economic Co-Operation and Development (OECD), 2 rue Andre Pascal, 75775 Paris Cedex 16, France, mariarosa.lunati@oecd.org

Charles Ou Small Business Administration, Office of Economic Research, Washington, DC 20416, USA, charles.ou@sba.gov

Alicia Robb Division of Social Sciences, University of California at Santa Cruz, Santa Cruz, CA 95064, USA, arobb@ucsc.edu

Carl J. Schramm The Ewing Marian Kauffman Foundation, Kansas City, MO 64110, USA, cschramm@kauffman.org

Robert J. Strom The Ewing Marian Kauffman Foundation, Kansas City, MO 64110, USA, rstrom@kauffman.org

Gregory F. Udell Chase Chair of Banking and Finance, Kelly School of Business, Indiana University at Bloomington, Bloomington, IN 47405, USA, gudell@indiana.edu

Alberto Zazzaro Dipartimento di Economia, Università Politecnica delle Marche, and Money and Finance Research Group (MoFiR), 60121 Ancona, Italy, a.zazzaro@univpm.it

Part I
Small Businesses and Innovation: Analyses and Policies

Chapter 1
Innovative Entrepreneurship and Policy: Toward Initiation and Preservation of Growth

William J. Baumol, Robert E. Litan, Carl J. Schramm, and Robert J. Strom

Abstract A wide range of United States political policies influence the level of innovative entrepreneurial activity in the country, that is the number of new businesses started each year that bring truly new products and ideas to the market. These policies begin with an educational system that fosters a creative, inventive, and educated population with the skills to start new businesses. Immigration policies, too, contribute to an entrepreneurial population by welcoming additional talent. The government also plays an important role in creating incentives for the utilization and commercialization of new products, from rights of property and contract that protect new businesses and patent laws that protect new ideas without creating roadblocks to further innovation, to tax policies that focus on consumption rather than income. Finally, the government can mitigate disincentives for starting new businesses, such as an employer-based health system that discourages potential entrepreneurs from leaving their employment, overly onerous regulations that create burdens for young and small businesses, and a litigious environment that creates more risk for new businesses than is necessary to protect consumers.

1.1 Introduction

Entrepreneurs – the missing actors in economic textbooks and much economic writing – are gaining attention and respect among mainstream economists. Growing numbers of articles on the subject are appearing in the major economic journals. The recent publication of an important biography of perhaps the leading expositor of the subject, the late Joseph Schumpeter, has also raised the public's awareness of the importance of entrepreneurs to the wider economy (McCraw, 2007).

R.J. Strom (✉)
Ewing Marion Kauffman Foundation, 4801 Rockhill Road, Kansas City, MO 64110, USA
e-mail: rstrom@kauffman.org

There is much debate and confusion, however, over the definition of the "entrepreneur." The outcome matters. Who is given the label frames the way the public and policymakers think about them, and more importantly, their contribution to economic performance.

We believe that management expert Peter Drucker was right when he noted that "not every new small business is entrepreneurial or represents entrepreneurship" (Drucker, 1985, p. 21). Some "entrepreneurs" innovate by commercializing new products or services or using new techniques to produce or deliver existing products and services. Other "replicative" entrepreneurs produce or sell goods and services already present in the marketplace, but in different locations.

By far the largest numbers of "entrepreneurs" are replicative. We do not mean to minimize their importance. Being able to launch and maintain such businesses offers many people a route out of poverty, or even a profitable living. But we submit that "innovative" entrepreneurs hold much more interest for economists and for policymakers, since the new products, services and techniques they bring to market generate beneficial externalities for the economy as a whole. Innovative entrepreneurship, in other words, is an important means by which technical change – the unexplained residual in standard growth equations – gets translated into economic growth.

Given the importance of understanding and encouraging growth, we concentrate in this essay on policies that promote innovative entrepreneurship. That is, we explore the policies that would promote the continuation and expansion of a community's innovative entrepreneurial activities and their contribution to economic growth most effectively. And we identify the policies that are necessary to counter the threats to such entrepreneurial activity, those existing now or looming on the horizon.

We focus in this paper upon policies suitable for the United States, the country whose economy we know best and the country where innovative entrepreneurship so far has been most successful and evident (although other countries are now also moving in this direction). In doing so, we note that policies at multiple levels of government can affect innovative entrepreneurship. We choose to focus here primarily on policies at the national or federal level, which have the broadest impact. However, there is also a limited but growing literature on appropriate local, state and regional policies for promoting new business formation, and indeed for fostering more localized economic growth.[1]

The notion that promoting entrepreneurship is a separate policy goal to be achieved by specific policy tools is a relatively recent one, and as such the subject has not yet clearly been defined. In particular, does "entrepreneurship policy" entail refining existing policy instruments – such as regulatory, tax or trade policies – that have broader objectives, or does it mean crafting entirely new, but targeted policies specifically to promote entrepreneurship? To date there are no

---

[1] See Acs (2008), Glaeser and Saiz (2003), Glaeser (2007a), Glaeser et al. (1992), and Glaeser (2007b).

bounds on "entrepreneurship policy." We make an effort to bring greater focus to this topic by concentrating on policies that affect incentives of individuals to form and grow innovative, for-profit enterprises.[2] In doing so, we draw on recent efforts by the Kauffman Foundation, the nation's largest foundation devoted to advancing understanding of entrepreneurship and an entity with which all of the authors are affiliated in one manner or another, to concentrate on the policy subjects that innovative entrepreneurs reportedly believe to be the most important to further such entrepreneurial activity. This effort began with formal and informal consultations with innovative entrepreneurs (Kauffman Foundation, 2007). We continued to refine these policy recommendations as we received ongoing feedback from entrepreneurs and the results of research on the subject conducted by Kauffman Foundation grantees and others. As we describe these policy subjects, we explain their relevance, offer our own views on some key implications, and identify the existing research that relates to them. At the same time, we also acknowledge that much further research is required on each of these topic areas, and we note some important areas for future work.[3]

1.2 Policies Relating to Education and Worker and Entrepreneurial Skills

At its most fundamental level, entrepreneurship is about the successful development and commercialization of novel ideas. This process requires highly educated individuals who will refine and improve the new products and processes provided to them by the nation's inventors and their entrepreneurial partners. A strong educational system – primary, secondary, college, and post-college – plays a vital role in the creation of the human capital necessary to ensure the availability of the requisite talent. There is good reason to conclude that the U.S. owes much of its economic success to its enviable record in providing universal primary and secondary education to its citizens and, perhaps even more important, to its university system and the postgraduate education that it offers not only to its own community but to the leaders in research throughout the world.

There are, however, attributes of American education – principally at the primary and secondary level – that have led to concern about the future prospects of the U.S.

---

[2] Much attention has been given in recent years by various scholars and universities to the teaching and practice of "social" entrepreneurship, a term we believe lacks clear definition, but which, according to the conventional wisdom, seems to involve mostly non-profit enterprises aimed at providing various public goods or addressing market failures. Our own view is more expansive: for-profit enterprises, too, generally advance "social interests" by serving the needs of consumers and society. In this survey, we restrict our attention to innovative entrepreneurship pursued by private, for-profit entities, without getting involved in the discussion over what constitutes social entrepreneurship, and how, if at all, policy should be designed to further it.
[3] For other entrepreneurship policy studies, see Hart (2003) and Holtz-Eakin and Rosen (2004).

economy and its continued leadership in innovation. As a number of recent reports have documented[4]:

- American pre-college students lag well behind students in other countries in international tests in mathematics and science.
- Nearly one-third of high school students in the U.S. do not finish within the standard 4 years or drop out altogether.
- There are wide and, by some accounts widening, disparities in educational achievement among students of different racial, ethnic, and socioeconomic backgrounds in the U.S.

These trends have raised doubts in the United States about the continued ability of the U.S. economy to prepare a creative and skilled workforce that will generate future innovation and growth. But, at the same time, there is also reason for concern that educational systems in the rest of the world – where students may be outperforming U.S. students on standardized tests – may be ineffective in fostering the imagination and creativity that are indispensable for invention and innovative entrepreneurship. Indeed, there are reasons to suspect (but with little systematic evidence) that the more rigid educational approaches that characterize teaching in a number of countries provide good technicians but a paucity of entrepreneurs and inventors with radical breakthrough contributions. The fact is that there is no systematic information that tells us how these abilities can be imparted effectively by the educational process. Indeed, there is evidence suggesting that many current educational practices in the United States also inhibit the heterodox thinking that such progress requires.[5]

This important issue – exactly how education should be structured to maximize creativity, skills and knowledge of students all at the same time – has not been adequately explored and is characterized by divergent conclusions. On the one hand, there are studies suggesting that before being able to contribute a significant insight to a field, an individual must first have substantial preparation in that field, and have built huge reservoirs of discipline-relevant information (Simonton, 1999a, b). Simon and Chase even quantified the required expertise by studying chess grand masters and other experts, concluding that individuals need approximately 50,000 "chunks" of richly connected information before making a fruitful discovery (Simon and Chase, 1973). Other researchers have observed that individuals typically require at least a decade of intense study in a particular domain of knowledge before they can provide any significant contribution in that domain (Gardner, 1993; Hayes, 1989; Simonton, 1999a, 1999b). The more knowledge individuals possess in a particular domain, the more likely they are to understand the nature of the relationships among

---

[4]See, e.g., National Center on Education and the Economy (2006) and National Academy of Sciences (2007).
[5]We are grateful to Professor Melissa Schilling of NYU for the material in the following paragraphs.

different ideas. As associations within the domain are challenged or reinforced over time, recognition of the pattern of associations should become more accurate, and the individual should become more efficient in searching for relationships among them (Dosi, 1988).

On the other hand, there are studies suggesting that an individual's substantial previous experience in a domain can also inhibit creative problem solving (Wertheimer, 1945/1959). Individuals who acquire highly specialized knowledge within a particular domain are prone to "einstellung," whereby learners who have earlier learned to solve a problem in a particular way will adopt a pattern that mechanizes their problem solving, inhibiting them from arriving at creative solutions (Luchins, 1942; Mayer, 1995). Many forms of learning can become routinized to an extent that, when faced with a variant issue, individuals automatically recall and tend to use a conventional approach; it is difficult for them not to do so (Gick and Lockhart, 1995). When individuals have well-reinforced expectations about the direction a search path should take, this constrains their ability to explore different possibilities, and may prevent them from generating "pre-inventive forms" with a more natural or universal structure (Finke, 1995: 262). Similarly, individuals who are deeply immersed in the established orthodoxy of a field of study may find their creativity stifled by extant paradigms and institutional pressures to conform (McLaughlin, 2001).[6]

Extensive training in a particular field can thus impede cognitive insight. Here it is notable that both Einstein and Piaget claimed that formal schooling detracted from their intellectual development (Feldman, 1999). Sociologically inspired work on the "marginal man" provides support for that contention. This work argues that marginal intellectuals (those who may participate in multiple intellectual domains but are central to none) are more likely to introduce creative breakthroughs than well-established experts in those fields (Ben-David and Collins, 1966; Dogan and Pahre, 1990; Edge and Mulkay, 1976; Martindale, 1995:252; McLaughlin, 2001). The two primary theoretical explanations for this relationship between marginality and innovation are that marginal scientists use different assumptions or skills than specialists in the field, permitting more novel outcomes, and marginal scientists are motivated to undertake riskier areas of research as a faster route to recognition and resources (Gieryn and Hirsh, 1983).

Consistent with this line of reasoning, an early study by Channon (1979) observed that entrepreneurs were likely to come from relatively humble origins, and receive an education through secondary school only. Similarly, a study by Collins and Moore (1970) concluded that it was common for entrepreneurs from relatively disadvantaged backgrounds to pursue aggressive, often flamboyant strategies, presumably in order to achieve recognition and esteem. Earlier writings, some of them also rather dated, also support the idea that individuals who are "self-made" are

---

[6]This is also argued by Simonton, who pointed out that excessive specialization can inhibit cognitive insight: "Too often, persons fail to make significant insights because they exclude whole domains of elements from entering into the combinative hopper. Yet what appears logically irrelevant may actually provide the missing piece of the puzzle" (1995:473).

more risk prone and more likely to pursue innovation than people who receive a professional education in management (such as an MBA) (Collins and Moore, 1970; Hambrick and Mason, 1984).

In any event, the U.S. educational system is a long way from embracing entrepreneurship and innovative thinking as central organizing principles.[7] There is an abundance of evidence that the quality of public education is highly uneven, and state laws inhibit the formation and equitable funding of charter schools that could introduce innovative educational methods and healthy competition. At best, it seems generally agreed that a central task for educators and policymakers is to give students the key skills to thrive in any work environment – reading, math, science, technology and history – and, where possible, also to nurture whatever creative and entrepreneurial skills each of us has by birth. Programs that teach basic entrepreneurial skills to middle and high school students may be especially valuable for children from disadvantaged backgrounds, and may be one way to encourage their interest in academic achievement more generally. At the college level, more universities have been attempting to infuse entrepreneurship and creativity more deeply into their curricula, for both students majoring in business and those in other subjects. And a number of universities have added an "entrepreneurship door" to their career counseling centers. These programs legitimate entrepreneurship as a worthy career path and offer mentoring and networking opportunities for students seeking to develop their interest.

But the conclusion suggested by the preceding review of the evidence is that we do not yet have adequate information on the best ways to organize a comprehensive educational system that optimally prepares future inventors and innovative entrepreneurs. This, surely, is an arena in which the gathering of evidence and rigorous research is a priority. Arguably, the U.S. government has the resources and is in the best position to fund this research and take steps necessary to help reverse the disappointing national trends in math and science achievement by students in primary and secondary schools.

1.3 Entrepreneurship-Friendly Immigration Policy

Immigration represents an opportunity to bring additional talent into the country. Foreign-born scientists and engineers historically have contributed significantly to the growth of U.S. high-tech industries. The U.S. nuclear and space programs, for example, benefited enormously from the immigration of foreign scientists both before and after World War II.

The United States continues to attract foreign-born scientists today, often through the science programs in American universities. In the last several decades, in

---

[7] For an excellent set of papers on how to enhance entrepreneurship in K–12 education, see Hess (2006) and Gordon et al. (2006).

fact, roughly half of all those who earned an undergraduate or graduate degree from American universities in science, engineering, computer science, and other technology-related fields were foreign students (Freeman, 2006). But with Asia and Europe now wooing highly-qualified students (and even senior-level researchers) from other countries to their universities and easing restrictions on the entry of skilled workers, the United States faces increased competition in drawing the world's best and brightest to study, work, and start businesses here ("The Battle for Brainpower," 2006; Freeman, 2005).

Immigrants, especially those who have or seek technical skills in the United States, already play a key entrepreneurial role in the U.S. economy:

- Census data indicate that immigrants as a group have had consistently higher rates of business formation than native-born individuals for many years (Fairlie, 2008).
- Immigrants from China and India helped to create 24% of technology companies launched in Silicon Valley between 1980 and 1998 (Saxenian, 1999).
- According to the National Venture Capital Association (NVCA), since 1990, one in four venture-backed firms in the entire country has been started by immigrants. The NVCA estimates that these firms have created more than 400,000 jobs and collectively represent a market capitalization of roughly $500 billion (Anderson and Platzer, 2006).
- A team of researchers at Duke University and the University of California at Berkeley found that between 1995 and 2005, immigrants founded or co-founded 25% of all the high-tech firms in the United States, and accounted for 24% of international patent applications from the United States in 2006 (Wadwha, et al., 2007).

Despite the clear importance of skilled immigrants for technical progress and the generation of new firms in this country, the U.S. has tightened legal immigration in the name of national security and on other grounds, even before the terrorist attacks of September 11, 2001. In 1990, for example, Congress imposed an annual ceiling of 65,000 skilled foreign workers for temporary periods (up to 6 years) under the H1-B visa program. *Any* such ceiling imposes a self-inflicted wound on our economy. Already there is evidence that entrepreneurial firms have put more of their personnel abroad because of an inability to obtain H1-B visas for foreign workers (Anderson and Platzer, 2006). Further, because the H1-B visa is of limited duration, it makes it practically impossible for workers who come into the United States to work to start their own companies.

One measure that would address this difficulty, without costing the federal government much in the way of additional resources, would be to grant permanent residency and work status, and perhaps even automatic citizenship, to those immigrants who come here to study mathematics, engineering, or the sciences, upon receipt of their degrees from qualified institutions of higher learning.[8] The promise of a permanent work permit and perhaps citizenship upon satisfactory completion of their studies may prove to be a powerful incentive for many to come. Even if some decide to return to their home countries – as increasing numbers appear to be doing, and which is beneficial for these economies – the United States would have the benefit of their skills and entrepreneurial energy for as long as they remain here.[9] The provisions of the EB-5 visa, the "entrepreneur's visa," could also be relaxed, requiring prospective immigrants to bring much less cash into the country. Or a renewable "job creator's visa" could be created for graduates or foreign residents already in the U.S. on a temporary (H1-B) visa who have founded a company that employs at least one other individual.

In short, in a world where brainpower and skills lead to economic power, it is difficult to defend a policy that discourages talented, skilled workers from coming to the United States, to study, work, or launch new companies.

1.4 Policies Directly Promoting Innovation and Entrepreneurship

Even when invention is abundant, innovative entrepreneurship is at its most effective when there are strong incentives for the effective utilization and commercialization of new products, new productive techniques and new forms of organization. This requires institutions, such as the patent system, which ensure that inventors and their entrepreneur partners are not precluded from appropriate compensation by unrestricted and rapid imitation. But, at the same time, it is important that dissemination and widespread utilization of significant novelties not be handicapped and delayed. Unimpeded entry is particularly critical to advancing innovation, given such evidence that firms with fewer than 500 employees produce 13 times more patents per employee than larger firms, and that these patents are twice as likely as patents taken out by large firms to be among the 1% most cited (citations being a good measure of the commercial importance of a patent) (U.S. Small Business Administration, 2008).

At the same time, it is essential that *only truly non-obvious innovations* receive patent protection and that the length of the period of exclusive property protection is not too long. Otherwise, the legal system will enable patent-holding firms to impose legal roadblocks in the way of new entrants, effectively handing out monopolies

---

[8]This idea would constitute one "national strategic plan" for recruiting international students, a central conclusion of a recent report by the Government Accountability Office on consensus recommendations by a panel of national education experts. See Government Accountability Office (2007).

[9]The McKinsey report commissioned by the Mayor of New York on the financial services industry in that city also highlighted among its recommendations the need to attract and retain highly-skilled immigrants to work in that industry in particular. See McKinsey & Co. (2007).

in exchange for little public benefit and making the economy less competitive and less innovative.

There is mounting, though not yet irrefutable evidence, that intellectual property protection, particularly patents, may have tilted too far in the monopoly direction – that is, toward creating inappropriate roadblocks that impede the competition that entrepreneurs and other entrants into a field can provide (Jaffe and Lerner, 2004; U.S. Federal Trade Commission, 2003; National Academy of Sciences, 2007). A significant problem here is the enormous pressure on an overburdened and overworked patent examiner staff at the United States Patent and Trademark Office (USPTO) to review the increasing number of patent applications that are filed each year. In fiscal year 2007, in fact, these applications reached an all-time high of 362,777 (U.S. Patent and Trademark Office, 2007). With limited resources, patent reviewers have little time to do a thorough search of "prior art" to make well-informed decisions in every case as to whether a patent application represents something that is truly novel. As a result, the office may be granting an increasing number of undeserving applications, a problem exacerbated by the fact that patent examiners' decisions have a legal presumption of validity if later challenged in court, an expensive and time-consuming process. Indeed, the profusion of patent applications in the U.S. is perhaps at least in part ascribable to the ease with which the low invention standard enables them to be obtained.

Various proposals for improved effectiveness of patent systems in promoting innovation have been under discussion. These include increased funding for the Patent Office; allowing third-party challenges to applications at some point *before* the patents are actually awarded (on the assumption that such challenges will be less costly and time consuming than post-award lawsuits); adoption in the U.S. of the "first to file" system for awarding patents that is prevalent in most countries rather than the "first to invent" standard applicable in the United States; limiting successful lawsuits by "patent trolls" (firms that acquire patents solely for the purpose of licensing them rather than commercially developing patented technologies) to offering compensation for damages, but not injunctions for infringement; and changing the measure of damages for infringement from lost profits to loss of reasonable royalties.

The implications of these reforms for innovation, especially innovation by entrepreneurs, are unclear at this point. For while strong patent protection can help entrepreneurs, it also can deter them from entering fields where incumbents have patent protection that may be of dubious merit but deep pockets to prosecute any litigation for infringement. Given the uncertainties, such ideas require further scrutiny before policymakers embrace them.

Moreover, these proposals do not seem to address the fundamental dilemma – provision of protection incentives to the innovator while not at the same time inappropriately impeding dissemination and rapid replacement of the obsolete. The remarkably rapid rate of expansion of voluntary (and compensatory) licensing in practice suggests that this merits encouragement as a means to overcome the basic conflict between invention incentives and facilitation of dissemination. One heterodox proposal may be worth considering here: differential taxation of the earnings of intellectual property, favoring the earning of license fees, particularly if they are set to cover no more than the opportunity cost of the grant of a license fee by the IP holder.[10]

Another potentially promising reform may be greater reliance by the PTO on the opinions of informed third parties to judge whether a patent application is truly novel. The Peer-to-Patent pilot program, for example, allowed many individuals to view patent applications online and to comment on their "obviousness." This small-scale experiment, devised by professors at New York Law School enjoyed success during its first year, starting in June 2007, and it was extended the following year until June 2009. While the program was recognized nationally and internationally, and was identified by the White House Open Government Initiative as one of the innovations in Open Government, the PTO chose not to extend the program further. We believe that innovative programs like this one that harness technology to address a central problem in patent administration today may, in the long run, be even more important than legal reforms (Schramm and Litan, 2008).

1.5 The Availability and Cost of Health Insurance and Entrepreneurship

The employer-based health insurance system in the United States is coming under increasing strain as health care costs continue to mount. Established U.S. enterprises find it increasingly difficult to compete against firms in other advanced countries where the government shoulders the cost of health care, let alone firms in developing countries where health insurance is not widespread and, in any event, is not supplied by employers. Workers who have insurance through their employers appear increasingly anxious about the prospect of losing their jobs and being forced to accept less generous health care coverage at their new places of employment. One issue on which further research is needed is whether and to what extent workers who are currently employed are reluctant to leave to start entrepreneurial ventures because they will lose access to their employers' health care coverage; anecdotal evidence from media reports suggests that this indeed is a problem. At a minimum, individuals with preexisting conditions can find it difficult to find insurance on their own – and if they do, it may be difficult to afford. As for the entrepreneurial firms themselves, they suffer a disadvantage relative to their large firm counterparts by virtue of the entrepreneurs' smaller employee risk pools. As a result, it can be more difficult for entrepreneurs to attract the skilled workforce they need to grow as rapidly as the demand for their products or services would permit.

As pressing as these problems may be, it is important that they be considered in their proper perspective. The fact that health care costs have been rising rapidly and are widely projected to continue increasing is simply a manifestation of the "cost disease" that drives up the relative prices of products and services that can only

---

[10]On this, see Swanson and Baumol (2005).

be produced or delivered by "handicraft" – services whose labor content cannot be materially changed (see, e.g., Baumol, 1993). Examples abound in government-provided services such as education and trash collection; in live entertainment; and throughout much of the health care sector.

But the cost disease does not condemn society to a future in which it will be unable to afford those things that are important for quality of life, as long as productivity improvements continue throughout the economy, particularly where capital and technology can most readily economize on the use of labor. Thus, for example, health care costs go up, *not* because health care providers become less efficient but because labor in computer manufacturing constantly grows *still more* efficient, driving up wages.

Accordingly, it is the *unevenness* of growth that can save an economy from the cost disease. Increasing productivity that pervades most of an economy, even if unevenly distributed among industries, must make that economy wealthier, not poorer. It does *not* make it unable to afford things that could be afforded in the past. Increasing productivity means that a society can afford ever more of *all* things – televisions, electric toothbrushes, cell phones, *and* medical care, education, and other services (Bradford, 1969). These observations led the late Senator Daniel Patrick Moynihan to characterize the future predicted by the cost disease as "profoundly hopeful" (Moynihan, 1993). It was also he who drew attention to the fact that the services provided by government tend to be precisely those most heavily affected by the cost disease, helping to explain the pattern of rising public sector outlays over time. The same reasoning applies to health care.

Nonetheless, the resulting problems for employer-based health care – for small and large firms alike, as well as for employees anxious about job loss – are very real. It is useful to recall how this system arose, for knowledge of the answer provides some guidance toward a solution. Employer-based health care grew significantly because of one simple accident in American history: that employers began offering health insurance during World War II as a way of circumventing wage controls then in place, and employees were not required to recognize the health care benefit as part of their taxable income.[11] Once the tax treatment of health care insurance was clear, more firms began offering health care coverage, ultimately leading to the current employer-based system of health insurance, and the attendant problems just cited – which should grow in magnitude as health care costs continue to climb.

At the time of this writing, the United States is engaged in a national debate on health care reform. While the debate on this issue is much larger than the impact of healthcare on entrepreneurship, we articulate here the overarching principle that is most important from the perspective of encouraging more entrepreneurial activity in this country: untether health care insurance from employment, likely by phasing out the tax policy that led to the current employer-based health insurance system. However the decoupling of health insurance from employment is accomplished,

---

[11] Initially this was a ruling of the Internal Revenue Service, but it was later codified in the Internal Revenue Code by Congress in 1954. See Gratzer (2006).

any such reform must also address the problem of insurers denying coverage for pre-existing conditions. This could be done simply by prohibiting the practice (requiring what is called "guaranteed issue") or requiring health insurers to use "community rating" so that their rates are based on broad pools of insureds. These, or possible other reforms, are necessary to reduce workers' legitimate anxieties about health care coverage if they lose their jobs, while reducing any "job lock" – the fear of leaving a company to start a new enterprise because of the difficulty of finding adequate health insurance – that may now exist.

1.6 Regulation, Litigation and Entrepreneurship

All economies and the actors within them need rules of the road to guide behavior. In market economies, legal protections of property and contract are critical, especially to entrepreneurs, who could not and would not undertake the risks of launching their enterprises without such protections.

At the same time, even with secure rights of property and contract, markets can fail to deliver efficient outcomes. Information about product or workplace risks may not be voluntarily disclosed. Firms can pollute, safe in the knowledge that it is generally too expensive and time-consuming for those harmed to negotiate a better outcome collectively. These are among the reasons governments regulate the activities of private firms and why the legal system permits victims of negligence, whether committed by individuals or companies, to seek compensation for their harm.

Entrepreneurship and business activity generally can suffer, however, if regulation and litigation are carried too far or pursued in ways where costs outweigh benefits. For example, earlier in this paper it was argued that not all entrepreneurial activity is productive, and that inappropriate institutional arrangements can lead to the allocation of entrepreneurial effort into activities that do not contribute to the efficiency and output of the economy and may even serve to undercut it. Rent-seeking was cited as a prime example, with misuse of the courts for such purposes evidently not a negligible problem. An oft-cited illustration is provided by the liability rules, resulting in verdicts that set norms for behavior by firms and individuals throughout the economy. An inherent difficulty besetting such "regulation-by-litigation" is that the rules that emerge from individual, fact-specific litigated cases are decided by randomly-chosen juries, in cases that are randomly filed across the country. In a national economy, it is thus somewhat anomalous that a jury in one particular location can effectively set national norms, with the most restrictive venue thereby effectively setting the national standard.

Enterprising plaintiffs can take advantage of this decentralized legal system and find hospitable locales for bringing suit against companies doing business nationwide, thereby engaging in a process of "forum shopping." It serves to encourage the activities of enterprising law firms whose rent-seeking takes the form of launching litigation with financially-promising prospects.

Steps have been taken in recent years to reduce uncertainties about firms' exposures to liability awards, thus improving the climate for entrepreneurial endeavors.

1 Innovative Entrepreneurship and Policy

In 2005, Congress enacted legislation to limit forum shopping in class actions filed in state courts, though it is possible that some degree of forum shopping may persist in federal courts. Various states have enacted caps on damage awards and other liability-related reforms that have taken some of the uncertainty out of liability litigation.

In our view, one additional constructive measure, aimed at deterring rent-seeking "sham" litigation, would be adoption of the English rule on payment of attorneys' fees – the loser pays – but presumably only for commercial litigation where there are commercial interests on both sides. A "loser pays" rule for all tort litigation could chill individuals or classes representing them from seeking redress for wrongs committed against them.[12] Another useful reform would bring greater clarity to punitive damage awards by immunizing defendants from liability for punitive damages where they can prove that their actions complied with prevailing regulatory standards. In combination, these measures would reduce some of the risks over which entrepreneurs have no control while preserving the rights of injured parties to recover compensation to which they are entitled.

As for regulation, many, if not most, economists advocate benefit-cost analysis as the chief policy reform, or where benefits cannot be quantified or denominated in a currency, cost-effectiveness analysis.[13]

1.7 Tax Policy and Entrepreneurship

Given the importance of incentives in encouraging entrepreneurial behavior, an obvious question is how tax policy influences entrepreneurial activity. On first thought, one would surmise that as marginal income tax rates increase on entrepreneurial income – whether realized as personal income to the entrepreneur or as income to a corporation – the after-tax rewards from engaging in entrepreneurial activity decline, and therefore so should the activity itself.[14] But the empirical and theoretical work that has been done so far on this subject yields some insights on this question that are not so obvious.

For example, one early (and now classic) article on this subject suggested that while higher marginal income tax rates may discourage economic activity in general, they may *encourage* risk-taking of the kind displayed by entrepreneurs (Domar and Musgrave, 1944). The reasoning is that as tax rates increase, the government bears more of the risk from entrepreneurial endeavors. With more risk-sharing by another party, the entrepreneurs' own risk premiums will be lower, encouraging them to take more risk.

---

[12] There are different views on the incentive effects of the English rule for attorneys fees. See Johnston (2006) and Olson and Bernstein (1996).
[13] See Arrow et al. (1996).
[14] There is some evidence that this is true of corporate taxation. See Garrett and Wall (2006).

A much more recent analysis suggests that it is the *shape of the tax schedule* that is more important for entrepreneurs than the actual *level of the marginal tax rate*. In particular, as the tax schedule grows steeper – or more progressive – then the reward for entrepreneurial activity, at the margin, declines (Gentry and Hubbard, 2000). Other analyses find that the level of the marginal tax rate does in fact make a difference, but in a counter-intuitive way: higher marginal tax rates *encourage* self-employment or entrepreneurship (Bruce, 2000; Schuetze, 2000). One possible reason is that small business owners can more easily underreport their income, or find ways to deduct some personal expenses, than employees earning wages and salaries.

A further complication is the interaction of personal and corporate income tax rates with incentives to engage in entrepreneurial activity. Generally, individuals launch their enterprises as non-corporate endeavors, and have tax incentives to do so as long as the personal tax rate exceeds the corporate rate. If so, and if they experience losses in the beginning (as many, if not most, entrepreneurs do), then the tax savings are greater if the enterprise is not incorporated (so that the losses can offset the entrepreneur's personal income). When the enterprise begins to be profitable, if the corporate rate is lower than the personal rate, entrepreneurs will want to switch to the corporate form to take advantage of lower taxes (and also because the corporate form is more suitable for an enterprise with employees). Thus, somewhat paradoxically, as the personal income tax rate increases relative to the corporate tax rate, entrepreneurship may be encouraged. Conversely, cuts in the personal income tax rate relative to the corporate rate may discourage entrepreneurship.

But all this does not get us to the heart of the long-run tax issue: the ever-rising tax burden that seems to be in prospect. For the apparently inescapable role of government in matters such as health care, education, research, care of the indigent, and a variety of other activities evidently beset by the cost disease, together presage an ever-rising share of public sector revenues in GDP. Even if our analysis is correct in concluding that we will be able to afford it, it is by no means a matter to be ignored, because of the well-recognized incentive effects of such a scenario. If this argument is correct, then the realistic issue is not one of constraining taxation, which would eventually lead to a future beset by deterioration in all these arenas, as well as collapsing infrastructure and ever-poorer public services, such as garbage collection. The reader's imagination can easily show why such a future will be considered unacceptable. The available alternative is not a substantial decline in taxation, but curtailment of the undesirable incentive effects.

Economists have long argued that these effects are *not* all damaging to the general welfare. Indeed, some of the resulting incentives, most notably the "sin taxes," can be socially beneficial. The arena in which this has perhaps been emphasized longest is in the field of environmental protection, where, at least since the writings of A.C. Pigou (1912), it has been recognized that taxation of emissions is a prospective source of revenues to the government whose incentive effects are to be welcomed. It would then be a good thing to increase reliance on such sources, offsetting the resulting gains with cuts in those taxes whose incentive effects are less palatable.

But can such taxes with beneficial effects make more than a dent in the problem? This is by no means impossible, though it must entail some radical departures from current fiscal practice.[15] To be sure, groups that are asked to bear part of the growing tax burden argue, not altogether without justification, that rising imposts (and, of course, that part of the cost that falls on themselves) is unfair, counterproductive or an impediment to growth. Equally predictably, those who will escape the resulting increase in tax burden support proposed increases in business taxes enthusiastically on the ground that it is only fair for the cost to be shouldered by the wealthy firms.

But neither side's argument is of more than limited validity. Various careful studies appear to have found little correlation between the level of business taxes in general and the level of investment.[16] On the other side, it is generally not recognized by consumer groups that a substantial proportion of any increase in taxes on business activity will actually be shifted to consumers via higher prices of the products of the firms that bear the taxes.

The moral, however, is not that business taxes should be left as they are. Rather, what is called for is a program carefully tailored to recognize and take advantage of the incentive effects. For example, consider the advantages of a *regressive* business tax in which the firm is subjected to *a lower tax rate the faster the percentage rate of growth of its output and sales*. The average tax rate can be adjusted to yield as large a revenue total to the government from the business sector as seems appropriate. This arrangement clearly would not be unfair to small firms, for which a given percentage increase in sales may be easier to achieve than it is for a firm that already has a large share of the market. Yet such a tax also would provide an incentive for enhanced investment, and lead to a shift in investment from markets and industries with low growth prospects into others where the opportunities for growth are greater.[17]

Let us be clear: we are discussing additional taxes only as a last resort way to address the growing costs of entitlements. Policy measures should place their primary attention, in our view, on harnessing market forces to reduce the escalation of health care costs, which are driving the projected increases in the costs of Medicare and Medicaid (the public health insurance program in the United States for the indigent). Secondarily, policy makers should look to modifying the benefit structures of these programs (and Social Security) for future beneficiaries, or those young enough not to have had the expectations of the benefits that now exist.

---

[15] See Baumol and Knorr (1961).

[16] Certainly, there is good ground for questioning whether reduction of taxes is an effective and reliable tax stimulus. If taxes were a significant barrier to more rapid growth, then how does one explain the severe and persistent slowdown in productivity growth in Japan, where taxes are among the lowest (relative to GDP) of any of the rich OECD countries?

[17] If it is felt that the program is unfair to activities such as food retailing, which provide services necessary for the community, but offer little opportunity for growth, one can remedy the problem by adopting a two-avenue tax arrangement. Each firm would be given a choice between the current tax arrangement and the growth-incentive tax program. Once its selection is made, the firm would not be permitted to switch. Then, firms with low-growth opportunities could be expected to select the current tax arrangement, while the others would elect the growth-incentive tax.

Only if reforms in these first two categories prove insufficient to meet the costs of the entitlement programs do we then suggest that policy makers explore ways to raise additional revenues. In the end, the least distorting way to enhance revenues, to the extent this is necessary, is to rely, at the margin, on taxes on consumption rather than on income. It is better, in our view, to tax consumption than to tax income and thus to penalize hard work and entrepreneurial activity.

1.8 Capital Markets Regulation and Finance

It is well-accepted that access to finance is critical for most, if not all, entrepreneurial ventures. This is the rationale for the creation for the Small Business Administration, which guarantees loans for smaller enterprises. Over the years, however, financial markets and credit in particular have been "democratized" by the increased availability of financing through mortgages and credit cards, which provide many start-ups with their initial financing (U.S. Census Bureau, 2002). In addition, the business lending market, too, has been the subject of much innovation. In light of these developments, the continued role for the SBA is a subject of some debate (See De Rugy, 2007 and Craig et al., 2007).

Focusing on innovative entrepreneurs, policy-related financing issues are not so much related to launch – there has been explosive growth in the amounts of venture and angel capital over the past several decades – but to the cost of public financing versus other sources. During the Internet boom of the 1990s, the favored course of financing for successful entrepreneurs, and the venture capitalists who often backed them, was "going public" through an initial public offering (IPO). The "bust" of this boom, reflected in the peaking of stock prices for technology companies in particular in the spring of 2000, has changed both the venture capital market as a source for early stage financing, as well as the preferred means of "exit" for initial equity funding sources of innovative start-ups. And here, there are ample public policy issues that remain to be explored.

The main issues relate to the policy reforms that were enacted in the wake of the various corporate financial reporting scandals that surfaced shortly after the Internet bust: the Sarbanes-Oxley Act of 2002 enacted by the Congress, as well as related changes in listing requirements by the various public company exchanges. Among the reforms were new corporate governance rules (such as requiring majorities of boards of directors to be "independent"); new certifications required of chief executive officers relating to the reliability of their companies' financial statements, and substantial criminal penalties in the event those financial statements are in error; new obligations for auditors to review companies' internal controls; and a new system for overseeing auditors, as well as restrictions on the activities of auditing firms designed to ensure their independence.

Space does not permit a full review of the extensive and growing literature on the wisdom and effects of these reforms. Three of the most widely publicized and debated assessments, released in late 2006 and early 2007, separately addressed the question whether the combination of the recent reforms, coupled with trends in shareholder litigation and SEC enforcement were driving U.S. and foreign companies to list their shares on exchanges outside the United States, to the detriment of the securities and related industries in New York in particular.[18] Whatever one may believe about the appropriateness of this particular goal, these reports raise several important questions about the impact of these recent reforms on innovative entrepreneurship.

In particular, the founders and initial investors in highly innovative and successful entrepreneurial endeavors in the 1990s often liquefied their initial investments through initial public offerings, or IPOs. Since the bursting of the "Internet bubble" in stock prices in April 2000, other forms of "exit" – sales to other large companies or to private equity firms – have become increasingly popular. To what extent have the recent corporate governance and accounting reforms contributed to this trend? And regardless of the cause, what has been and is likely to be the effect of this shift in exit patterns for entrepreneurial companies? Specifically, does the sale of a young innovative company to a more established company dull its entrepreneurial spirit, or does it provide the talent and capital that the enterprise requires to grow and more rapidly reach its potential? Similar questions can be asked of the impact of sales of companies to private equity firms. Although it is likely that several more years of market experience will be required to yield the data to permit definitive answers to these questions, it is not too early to begin tackling them.

1.9 Conclusion

The policies we suggest here build on a long history of institutions and laws that have successfully promoted entrepreneurship since the beginnings of the United States. We have laws and systems that make it easy to start a new venture and facilitate the hiring of new workers and letting go of those who under-perform or whose skills do not match the constantly-evolving needs of innovative enterprises. We have removed legal barriers to entry and price controls in a number of key industries – in particular transportation and telecommunications – which has dramatically cut costs and made it easier for new firms to get started and grow.

Entrepreneurs and larger businesses alike have also benefited from our large internal market that offers economies of scale. We are open to foreign goods, services, and capital. For the most part, we welcome immigrants and the innovative ideas they bring with them. At a more fundamental level, Americans have long perceived themselves as a nation of creative self-starters who welcome challenges and value individuality and self-reliance. Our challenge now is to maintain and strengthen the entrepreneurial economy in the U.S. and the growth it brings, in order to make it easier to meet the multiple economic challenges we now face and to meet them effectively.

---

[18] See Committee on Capital Markets Regulation (2006), U.S. Chamber of Commerce (2007), and McKinsey & Co. (2007).

Acknowledgment The authors gratefully acknowledge the editorial and research assistance of Alyse Freilich and Jared Konczal.

References

Acs Z et al (2008) Entrepreneurship and urban success: toward a policy consensus. Ewing Marion Kauffman Foundation, Kansas City, MO

Alberto, AF, Edward LG (August 1999) Evidence on growth, increasing returns, and the extent of the market. Q J Econ 114:3. The MIT Press, pp 1025–1045. http://www.jstor.org/stable/2586890

Anderson S, Platzer M (2006) American made: the impact of immigrants and professionals on US competitiveness. http://www.nvca.org/index.php?option=com_content&view=article&id=254&Itemid=103

Arrow KJ et al (1996) Benefit-cost analysis in environmental, health, and safety regulation: a statement of principles. AEI Press, Washington, DC

Baumol WJ (1993) Social wants and dismal science: the curious case of the climbing costs of health and teaching. Proc Am Philos Soc 137(4):612–637

Baumol WJ, Knorr K (1961) What price economic growth? Prentice-Hall, Englewood Cliffs, NJ

Baumol WJ, Litan RE, Schramm CJ (2007) Good capitalism, bad capitalism, and the economics of growth and prosperity. Yale University Press, New Haven, CT

Ben-David J, Collins R (1966) social factors in the origins of a new science: the case of psychology. Am Soc Rev 31:451–465

Bradford D (1969) Balance on unbalanced growth. Zeitschrift ffir NationalSkonomie 29:291–304

Bruce D (2000) Effects of the United States tax system on transitions into self-employment. Labor Econ7:545–574

Channon D (1979) Leadership and corporate performance in service industries. J Manage Stud 16:185–201

Cullen JB, Gordon RH (2002) Taxes and entrepreneurial activity: theory and evidence for the U.S., NBER Working Paper no. 9015, June. Accessible at http://www.nber.org/papers/w9015

Collins OF, Moore DG (1970) The organization makers. New York: Appleton Century Crofts Committee on Capital Markets Regulation (2006) Interim report of the commission on capital markets regulation. November 30 http://www.capmktsreg.org/pdfs/11.30 Committee_Interim_ReportREV2.pdf

Craig BR, Jackson WE, Thomson JB (2007) Does government intervention in the small-firm credit market help economic performance? FRB of Cleveland policy discussion paper No. 22, August Available at SSRN: http://ssrn.com/abstract=1003298

De Rugy V (2007) The SBA's Justification IOU. Regulation, 30:1, pp 26–34, Spring Available at SSRN. http://ssrn.com/abstract=978532

Dogan M, Pahre R (1990) Creative marginality. innovation at the intersections of social sciences. Westview Press, Boulder, MA

Domar ED, Musgrave RA (1944) Proportional income taxation and risk-taking. Q J Econ 58:388–422

Dosi G (1988) Sources, procedures, and microeconomic effects of innovation. J Econ Lit 26(3):1120–1171

Drucker PF (1985) Innovation and entrepreneurship: practice and principles. Harper & Row, New York, NY

Edge D, Mulkay M (1976) Astronomy transformed. Wiley, New York, NY

Fairlie RW (2008) Kauffman index of entrepreneurial activity, 1996–2007. Ewing Marion Kauffman Foundation, Kansas City, MO

Feldman DH (1999) The development of creativity. In: Sternberg RJ (ed) Handbook of creativity. Cambridge University Press, Cambridge, pp 169–186

1 Innovative Entrepreneurship and Policy

Finke RA (1995) Creative insight and preinventive forms. In: Sternberg, RJ, Davidson JE (eds) The nature of insight. MIT Press, Cambridge, MA, pp 255–280

Freeman RB (2005) Does globalization of the scientific/engineering workforce threaten U.S. economic leadership? NBER Working Paper 11457. http:/www.nber.org/papers/w11457

Freeman RB (2006) Investing in the best and brightest: increased fellowship support for american scientists and engineers, Hamilton project discussion paper, The Brookings Institution, Washington, DC

Gardner H (1993) Multiple intelligences: the theory in practice. BasicBooks, New York, NY

Garrett TA, Wall HJ (2006) Creating a policy environment for entrepreneurs. Cato J Fall 26(3): 525–552

Gentry WM, Hubbard RG (2000) Tax policy and entry into entrepreneurship. Am Econ Rev 90(2):283–287

Gick ML, Lockhart RS (1995) Cognitive and affective components of insight. In: Sternberg RJ, Davidson JE (eds) The nature of insight. MIT Press, Cambridge, MA, pp 197–228

Gieryn TF, Hirsh RF (1983) Marginality and innovation in science. Soc Stud Sci 13: 87–106

Glaeser EL, Saiz A (2003) The rise of the skilled city. NBER working paper No. 10191. http://www.nber.org/papers/w10191.pdf

Glaeser EL, Kallal HD, Scheinkman JA, Shleifer A (1992) Growth in cities. J Pol Econ 100:6, Centennial Issue. The University of Chicago Press, pp 1126–1152. http://www.jstor.org/stable/2138829

Glaeser EL (2007a) Entrepreneurship and the city. National Bureau of Economic Research (NBER) working paper

Glaeser EL (2007b) The economics approach to cities. NBER working paper No. 13696, Dec. http://www.nber.org/papers/w13696.pdf

Gordon R, Staiger DO, Kane TJ (2006) Identifying effective teachers using performance on the job, Hamilton project white paper, April. The Brookings Institution http://www.brookings.edu/views/papers/200604hamilton_1.pdf

Government Accountability Office (2007) Global competitiveness: implications for the Nation's higher education system, highlights of a GAO forum, January www.gao.gov/new.items/d07135sp.pdf

Gratzer D (2006) The cure: how capitalism can save American health care. Encounter Books, New York, NY

Hambrick DC, Mason PA (1984) upper echelons: the organization as a reflection of its top managers. Acad Manage Rev 9:193–206

Hart DM (ed) (2003) The emergence of entrepreneurship policy: governance, start-ups, and growth in the U.S. knowledge economy. Cambridge University Press, Cambridge

Hayes JR (1989) The complete problem solver, 2nd edn. Erlbaum, Hillsdale, NJ

Hess F (ed) (2006) Educational entrepreneurship: realities, challenges, possibilities. Harvard Education Press, Cambridge, MA

Holtz-Eakin D, Rosen HS (eds) (2004) Public policy and the economics of entrepreneurship. MIT Press, Cambridge, MA

Jaffe A, Lerner J (2004) Innovation and its discontents: how our broken patent system is endangering innovation and progress, and what to do about it. Princeton University Press, Princeton, NJ

Johnston MD (2006) The litigation explosion, proposed reforms, and their consequences BYU. J Public Law Fall 21(1):179–207 www.law2.byu.edu/jpl/papers/v21n1_Michael_Johnston.pdf

Kauffman Foundation (2007) On the road to an entrepreneurial economy. A research and policy guide. Available at http://www.kauffman.org/uploadedFiles/entrepreneurial_roadmap_2.pdf

Luchins A (1942) Mechanization in problem solving: the effect of Einstellung. American Psychological Association 54:6, Washington DC

Martindale C (1995) Creativity and connectionism. In: Smith SM, Ward TB, Finke RA (eds) The creative cognition approach. MIT Press, Cambridge, MA, pp 249–268

Mayer RE (1995) The search for insight: grappling with gestalt psychology's unanswered questions. In: Sternberg RJ, Davidson JE (eds) The Nature of Insight. MIT Press, Cambridge, MA, pp 3–32

McCraw TK (2007) Prophet of innovation: Joseph Schumpeter and creative destruction. Harvard University Press, Cambridge, MA

McKinsey & Co. (January 2007) Sustaining New York's and the US' global financial services leadership. http://www.nyc.gov/html/om/pdf/ny_report_final.pdf

McLaughlin N (2001) Optimal marginality: innovation and orthodoxy in Fromm's revision of psychoanalysis. Soc Q 42:271–288

Moynihan DP (1993) Don't blame democracy: the socialization of slow-growth jobs. Editorial Page. The Washington Post (June 6):C7

National Academy of Sciences (2006) Rising above the gathering storm: energizing and employing America for a brighter economic future. The National Academy of Sciences, The National Academy of Engineering and The Institute of Medicine Washington, DC

National Center on Education and the Economy (2006) Tough choices for tough times: the report of the new commission on the skills of the American workforce. National Center on Education and the Economy, Washington, DC

Olson, W, Bernstein D (1996) Loser-pays: where next? Maryland Law Rev 1996 55:1161, pp 1161–1163. http://www.pointoflaw.com/articles/Loser-Pays.pdf

Pigou AC (1912) Wealth and welfare. Macmillan, London

President's Advisory Panel on Federal Tax Reform (2005) Simple, fair, and pro-growth: proposals to fix America's tax system. November. http://govinfo.library.unt.edu/taxreformpanel/final-report/index.html

Saxenian A (1999) Silicon valley's new immigrant entrepreneurs. Public Policy Institute of California, San Francisco, CA

Schramm C (2006) The entrepreneurial imperative: how America's economic miracle will reshape the world. HaperCollins Publishers, New York

Schramm C, Litan RE (2008) The growth solution. The American, July/August

Schuetze H (2000) Taxes, economic conditions and recent trends in male self-employment: a Canada-US comparison. Labor Econ 7:507–544

Simon HA, Chase WG (1973) Skill in chess. Am Sci 61:393–403

Simonton DK (1995) Foresight in insight? A Darwinian answer. In: Sternberg RJ, Davidson JE (eds) The nature of insight. MIT Press, Cambridge, MA, pp 465–494

Simonton DK (1999a) Creativity as blind variation and selective retention: is the creative process Darwinian? Psychol Inq 10:309–328

Simonton DK (1999b) Origins of genius. Oxford University Press, New York, NY

Swanson D, Baumol WJ (2005) Reasonable and nondiscriminatory (RAND) Royalties, standards selection, and control of market power. Antitrust Law J 73 (1):1–58.

The Battle for Brainpower: a survey of talent, 2006. The Economist, 7 October 7, pp 12–14

U.S. Chamber of Commerce (2007) Commission on the regulation of U.S. Capital markets in the 21st Century: Report and Recommendations. http://www.uschamber.com/sites/default/files/reports/0703capmarkets_full.pdf

U.S. Small Business Administration (2010) Frequently asked questions. http://www.sba.gov/advo/stats/sbfaq.pdf

U.S. Federal Trade Commission (2003) To promote innovation: The proper balance of competition and patent law and policy. U.S. Federal Trade Commission, Washington, DC

U.S. National Research Council (2004) A patent system for the 21st century. National Academies Press, Washington, DC

U.S. Patent and Trademark Office (2007) USPTO 2007 Fiscal year-end results demonstrate trend of improved patent and trademark quality: production at all-time record levels. November 15. http://www.uspto.gov/news/pr/2007/07-46.jsp

U.S. Census Bureau (2006) Characteristics of Business: 2002. http://www2.census.gov/econ/sbo/02/sb0200cscb.pdf

Wadwha V, Saxenian A, Rissing B, Gereffi G (2007) America's new immigrant entrepreneurs. Master of Engineering Management Program, Duke University and School of Information, University of California at Berkeley

Wertheimer Max (1945/1959) Productive thinking. University of Chicago Press, Chicago

Chapter 2
State Programs to Promote the Growth of Innovative Firms in the United States – A Taxonomy

Charles Ou

Abstract This article provides an overview of state programs designed to promote innovation– especially to those targeted at growing innovative firms throughout the United States. It argues that governments can best promote business growth by improving the working of the output and resource markets so that entrepreneurs can exploit the market opportunities and that by investing in the resource markets to increase the supply of resources, innovative entrepreneurs can successfully develop new products at low costs.

2.1 Introduction

This article provides an overview of state programs designed to promote innovation– especially to those targeted at growing innovative firms throughout the United States. Since poor performance of the markets is one of the major justifications for government actions in the marketplaces for new products, these programs will be reviewed from the standpoint of whether and how much they enhance the working of the markets – i.e., by reducing the transaction costs and in increasing the supply of resources for new product developments. The arguments are that governments can best promote business growth by improving the working of the output and resource markets so that entrepreneurs can exploit the market opportunities and that by investing in the resource markets to increase the supply of resources, innovative entrepreneurs can successfully develop new products at low costs.

A framework depicting a system of interconnected markets (for production resources) in developing new products is introduced. This provides a framework for

---

C. Ou (✉)
Small Business Administration, Office of Economic Research, 409 Third Street, SW, Washington, DC 20416, USA
e-mail: charles.ou@sba.gov

Opinions expressed here are those of the author, not of the U.S. Small Business Administration. Editorial assistance from his colleagues in the Office of Advocacy is most appreciated. However, all errors found in the presentation are mine.

analyzing factors affecting the operation and growth of new product markets. This framework also suggests ways government actions can influence these factors by improving efficient operation of these markets leading to new product development. State programs in each of these markets were reviewed and summarized in Exhibits A through D (with discussions of some individual programs in Appendix 1). These programs are grouped into four categories – (1) direct participation in the markets by state government(s) state participation as the supplier or as the buyer, (2) state activities to improve the working of the markets by changing the culture/mindset of the participants in the markets, (3) investment in the market infrastructures to improve the supply and/or to reduce the transaction costs in the market, and (4) direct state assistance to entrepreneurs as the buyers (for inputs) and the sellers (of products). Finally, the paper concludes with a brief discussion on the effectiveness of state programs in promoting innovation and the formation and the growth of innovative firms.

2.2 A Multiple Market Ecosystem for Developing New Products in a Market Economy

I. Chart 2.1 depicts a framework for a complex system of marketplaces usually accessed by entrepreneurs in developing new products. This framework include:

- A system of interlinked marketplaces for products and production resources (of workers, talents, research activities, capital, etc). These markets differ in their level of market development (i.e., in the breath and efficiency in promoting exchanges) and many smaller segmented markets are characterized by high information and transaction costs.
- The important role of entrepreneurs in this ecosystem – in developing new products by participating in the output and resource markets. They are the *catalysts* in organizing economic resources to produce new products, the *creators* of production capacity, the *risk-taking investors* who develop new products and/or find better solutions in uncertain markets, and the *enterprise builders*.
- Moreover, there are sub-markets within each major resource markets. For example, the markets for skilled workers are found in widely dispersed geographic locations linked by state and local employment networks and affected by skilled worker mobility. Chart. 2.2 provides a simplified description the market for credit and capital in the U.S.[1] The breath and the efficiency of each submarket differs significantly: submarkets range from a very limited and segmented ones for individual investors/lenders and the entrepreneurs,

---

[1] While money is known to be very fluid, savers, lenders', and borrowers' access to different capital markets may be hindered by various factors affecting the working of the markets.

to a nation-wide or even world-wide market for public securities. Public securities markets characterized by myriad rules, regulations, and business practices affecting the conduct and decision making for all players – e.g. the borrowers, brokers and dealers, the lenders such as businesses, individual lender/investors, and institutional lenders/investors.
- Key participants in the capital and credit market include:

  – *Suppliers/lenders/investors*: households as savers, businesses as savers and investors, governments as savers and investors, the rest of the world (ROW); financial institutions as intermediaries gathering savings from savers for lending/investing
  – *Buyers/borrowers*: households, businesses, and governments as the borrowers; financial institutions as the intermediaries in the borrowing and lending markets; and the ROW as the borrowers.
  – *Providers of support services*: brokers, dealers, financial intermediaries, service providers, etc.
  – *Government(s)* as the regulator of market activities as well as the contract enforcer

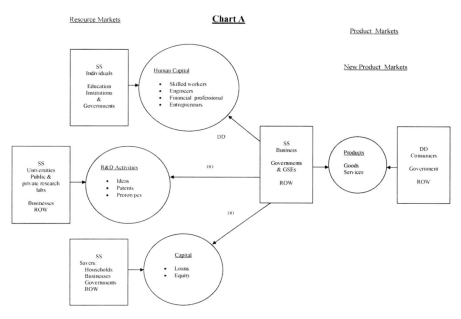

Chart 2.1 A multiple market ecosystem for developing new products

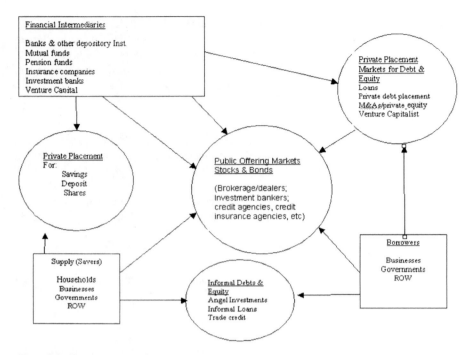

Chart 2.2 Credit and capital markets

2.3 Factors/Forces Affecting the Operation of a Marketplace and Thus the Formation and the Growth of Innovative Businesses (Businesses that Develop New Products)

In market economy, a market is an arrangement/mechanism that facilitates the exchange of resources between the owners and the users.[2] An efficient market allows the buyers and the sellers to complete the exchange transactions a market-clearing price– a price high enough to encourage continued business investments overtime to produce more and better products. Many structural, institutional, and behavioral factors influence the efficient operation of a market. These factors include:

- *Culture/mindset/social networks*: Values, preferences, and attitudes toward business activities, profits or other monetary gains, risk taking of the market participants (the buyers, the sellers, the service providers, including governments).

---

[2] The so-called "enabling environments" versus "barriers to entry" and "market impediments", etc.

2 State Programs to Promote the Growth of Innovative Firms 29

Importance of their mindsets in affecting their behaviors and decision making of the market place;
- *Market infrastructures-hardware*: Transportation facilities; physical capital structures/buildings, communication facilities; public utilities; research labs, etc;
- *Market infrastructures-software*: Laws, rules, and regulations; institutions and business organizations; customs and practices/administrative practices affect the transaction costs in the markets.[3]

These factors affect the decision making of the market participants (the buyers, the suppliers, and exchange facilitators) and thus the costs of exchange in the product and the resource markets, which, in turn, affect the costs of developing new products and the success of firm formation and the growth.

2.4 Poor Performance of New Product Markets – One Major Justification for State Governments' Actions in New Product Markets

Special characteristics/elements of the market for new product development, Some of these special characteristics include:

- The product markets– the market is not well defined and constantly changing, (the demand and supply are vague; with high startup costs and a long investment-to-profit cycle;) and the successful introduction of new products is characterized by high failure rates and huge returns on investment (ROI) but only for a small number of successful ventures;
- The resource markets – small and/or not developed because of small demand and non-market-oriented – e.g. nonprofit oriented research & development (R&D) in universities and government labs; small capital markets to fund and commercialize R&D products; undeveloped support service sectors-deal facilitators, other professional services.

These market imperfections resulted in the poor market performance in developing new products. Complaints about slow growth and/or inadequate supply at high production costs in the forms of financing gap, innovation gap (or the R&D gap),

---

[3] Examples – programs and networks to facilitate R&D collaboration between business and R&D institutions such as government and universities; programs and centers providing training and advice to entrepreneurs, venture investors, engineers and researchers; Laws, regulations and administrative practices that affect market exchanges, business startups and growth; court and legal framework that affect enforcement of contracts and settlement of business disputes, etc. See also, the World Bank, "DoingBusiness 2008", Heritage Foundation, "2008 Index of Economic Freedom", 2008

and of skilled worker gap are aired constantly in the presses in the United States.[4]
Examples:

- Gaps in the market for qualified workers, engineers, researchers, innovative -entrepreneurs, and business development professionals;
- Gaps in the markets for R&D activities – market-focused concepts, prototypes, solutions, products;
- Gaps in capital/credit markets for entrepreneurs, especially for equity capital to innovative startups.

2.5 State Programs to Promote Innovation and the Growth of Innovative Firms in the United States

State governments in the United States have been actively involved in promoting state and regional development since late 1970s when a stagnant national economy was hampered by high energy costs and rapidly rising inflation. Since late 1980s, promoting entrepreneurships and innovation became a development priority since late 1980s as state development officers switched promotion strategies from attracting big-box companies to promoting development and the growth of local entrepreneurs.[5]

Actions taken range from direct participation by state governments in the market place, e.g. as the direct suppliers, to investment in market infrastructures to improve market operation. Approaches to promote innovation and innovative entrepreneurship can be categorized as follows:

- *Direct participation in the markets by the government(s) as the buyer(s) or supplier(s)*:
  - Supplement and/or replace the market operation, such as: buying R&D products from businesses; generating R&D outputs from government labs (for use by entrepreneurs); creating national universities or technical schools for more engineer graduates; etc.

- *Improve the working of the markets*:
  - Change/transform the culture and mindset of the market participants including community leaders and policy makers to change the altitudes, behaviors, decision making and national priority
  - Change/reform the software infrastructure of the market – rules and regulation, business and administrative practices, and taxations of business transactions

---

[4] See, for example, ASTRA (2007).
[5] The debate continued. See "Southern States to Ply the Art of the Deal" Federal Reserve Bank of Atlanta, EconSouth 10(1):QI, 2008.

and/or business income, etc. Reduce the costs of transactions in the relevant markets through better regulations, better incentive/motivation programs, effective networks, etc.
- Promote investment in market infrastructure directly or indirectly: Examples;
    - invest in physical facilities in the markets
    - invest in technology, networks, programs, information collection to facilitate the efficient operation of the markets
    - invest to increase the availability and the quality of resources (skills, talent, knowledge, capital, etc.)
    - collect and disseminate information to market participants at low costs;
    - Increase/improve skills/knowledge of market participants (the buyers, the sellers, and support service providers.)

- *Direct assistance* to businesses to promote development of market-focused outputs

    - Public funding/subsidies to businesses to lower the costs of products;
    - Assistance to access the markets (for resources as the buyers) and in output markets (as the sellers).

Exhibits A through D provide a summary of major actions by the state governments in the three major resource markets and in new product market participated by entrepreneurs.[6] Discussion of individual programs in some states are provided in the Appendix 1. Summary tables for state programs in promoting bioscience from the report on "Technology, Talent and Capital: State Bioscience Initiatives 2008" appeared in Appendix 2.[7]

Exhibit A: Policy action to improve the markets for human capital: A summary

Outputs

- Workers/talents with skills demanded in the markets. Graduates with specialized skills or professional training – skilled workers, engineers, researchers/scientists. Entrepreneurs, and venture investment professionals, including angel investors;

Problems: "Public good" nature of the output; supply not market focused
Goals: Ample supply at "reasonable" costs to the entrepreneurs
Policy actions: Improve the working of the markets through public and private investment and other public initiatives to facilitate education of workers/talents demanded in the markets

---

[6] See reports by National Governors Association (NGA), Council on Competitiveness, Kauffman foundation, Office of Advocacy (of SBA), World Bank, etc. as listed in the References.
[7] Battelle Technology Partnership Practice (June 2008)

Examples:

- Transform culture/mindset of the market participants
  - Create an education compact of government officials, community leaders, and business leaders;
  - Change public and student mindsets about SMET (science, math, engineering, and technology);
  - Formulate an education strategy to grow the supply of skills/talents demanded by entrepreneurs;
  - Formulate priorities, initiate, coordinate and promote market focused education programs;
  - Create market/demand sensitive public and private school systems;
  - Introduce incentive/motivations into the education system;
- Improve and invest in education infrastructure – hardware and software:
  - Colleges and universities, programs in SMET, programs for entrepreneurs or scientist/entrepreneurs, etc;
  - Networks, education exchanges, job centers;
  - Financial assistance/incentives to schools and to students in SMET areas;
  - Invest in educational & training programs-increase the supply of educators, SMET programs, scientist-entrepreneur programs, entrepreneurship programs, programs for venture investors;
- Other measures affecting the working of the labor markets:
  - Reducing the employment–related costs – payroll taxes, health insurance costs, pension benefit costs;
  - Immigration system conducive to international flows of knowledge/talent;
- Direct assistance to entrepreneurs as employers in the market:
  - Tax credit to lower the costs of employment;
  - Employee training credits;

Exhibit B: Policy actions to improve the markets for R&D activities: a summary

Outputs: knowledge, ideas, solutions, patents, and prototypes.
Problems: Again, public good nature of the output supplied mostly by not-for-profit institutions. Supply not market focused.
Goals: Ample supply of R&D outputs at "reasonable" costs to the entrepreneurs.
Policy actions: To improve the working of the markets to facilitate market-oriented/focused R&D outputs.

Example:

- Direct participation as the providers of R&D
- Transform the mindset/culture in the R&D activity markets – public research labs, educational and non-profit research centers, private researchers, etc. – A public compact on R&D activities – to create a mindset in community leaders/public officers; public private collaboration
- Improve and invest in the market infrastructure:
  - Introduce incentives/motivation for R&D institutions to encourage market focused R&D in research institutions;
  - An environment that facilitates the exchanges of intellectual property – protection of property rights (patent, royalty, etc); technology transfer mechanisms from public institutions to private users;
  - Effective networks and collaboration arrangements for all market participants to create and exchange market-oriented R&D activities;
  - Invest in R&D infrastructure; research labs in federal and state government and universities;
  - Promote public-private research collaboration;
  - Establish innovation centers, manufacturing technology centers, incubators, etc.;
  - Invest in education and training programs for professional service providers to facilitate commercialization of R&Ds by public institutions. Invest in infrastructure.
- Direct assistance to entrepreneurs as the buyers of R&D outputs from Federal labs:
  - R&D tax credits;
  - Provide funding to entrepreneurs to commercialize government R&D products.

Exhibit C: Policy actions to improve the markets for equity capital for innovative firms: A summary

Outputs: Equity capital from external sources invested in innovative firms.
Problems: Inadequate supply of seed capital because of small segmented private-placement markets participated by risk averse investors.
Goals: Adequate supply capital at "reasonable" costs to the entrepreneurs.
Policy actions:

Example:

- Government(s) as the provider(s) of funds directly or indirectly to businesses with or without subsidies. See also below for arrangements involving leveraging of public money for private funds.

- Change/transform the culture, mindset, etc., about investing in innovative businesses – risk taking behaviors of institutional investors and individual investors;
- Improve the working of equity capital markets (through public investment and other initiatives);
- *Regulation and deregulation in the equity capital markets*
    - Regulation of investors;
    - Regulation of business firms;
    - Regulation of Intermediaries, e.g., brokers, dealers, agents, etc.
- *Regulation and deregulation of financial institutions, especially the depository institutions*: Promote competition in small business loan markets;
- *Investment in development of intermediaries and networks*: Brokers/dealers/agents and other professionals; institutional investors versus individual investors; "angel investment networks"; other physical and virtual networks for entrepreneurs and angels;
- *Investment in infrastructure*: Physical and virtual networks; telecommunication centers; educational/training facilities for entrepreneurs/investors/deal facilitators; IT technology; credit information collection and dissemination, financial modeling;
- *Maintain and increase competition in the markets*: Promote low cost access to the markets by all participants and lower information costs;
- *Reduce taxes on business income, investment gains, and other business taxes*: Tax credits (investment tax credits, R&D tax credits, etc.); taxes on capital gains;
- *Information infrastructure*: Collecting and disseminating credit information about market participants and information on market transactions to reduce the costs of information and due diligence;
- *Other public actions to facilitate commercialization of R&D*:
    - Examples: state-wide business plan contests, government and media promotion of innovation activities, programs to promote tech transfers, etc.
- Public funding to increase the availability of equity capital;
- *Direct public investment*: Direct funding to innovative firms (SBIR, R&D grants/contracts, direct investment by a public investment board/fund);
- *Public/private partnership*: Leveraging of private resources (money, expertise, and experience): public investment funds managed by private venture capital companies (VC firms); public-private development fund, etc.; Funding to promote collaboration in public-private R&D organizations; Tech transfer promotion – facilitate commercialization of public R&D by entrepreneurs;
- *Tax expenditures to encourage private investments in innovative firms and/or to increase business profits*:
    - Tax credits to investors and/or innovative firms: Investment Tax Credits (ITC), angel investment tax credit; R&D tax credit; CAPCOs, etc.;
    - Tax abatement to investors and/or firms-for business income, investment gains, sales tax, and business properties.

- *Direct assistance to business as a borrower in the capital markets*: education of informed borrowers; assistance in locating financial resources; cut corporate income taxes;

Note: Improving the working of all resource markets will help reduce the financing needs for seed capital by reducing overall costs of innovation. Actions in the capital market will reduce the transaction costs of obtaining financing by reducing the financing related costs such as costs of due diligence, search costs, costs of information, costs of intermediation, and costs of contract enforcement.

Exhibit D: Policy action to improve the product markets: A summary

Outputs: New products introduced to the markets by entrepreneurs.
Problems: uncertain markets; market entry barriers; product liability, intellectual property protection against unfair and illegal competition; etc.
Goals: to successfully introduce new products to markets at home and abroad.
Policy actions: Improve the working of the markets through public and private investment and other public initiatives to facilitate successful introduction of new products.

Examples:

- *Government as the buyer(s)* –as the buyer(s) of the new products;
- *Transform culture/mindset of the market participants*:
  - Promote risk taking in new product innovation;
  - Change government and public mindsets about free trade, etc. the economic role of entrepreneurship, business profits, open and free markets in promoting economic growth;
  - Formulate priorities, initiate, coordinate, and promote market focused education programs;
- *Improve and invest in market infrastructure* (hardware and software):
  - Promote competition and free/open exchange/trade in the markets;
  - Eliminate barrier to entry to the markets;
    Export zone – cutting the costs of exporting;
  - Reduce regulation on new product introduction;
  - Promote new forms of business organizations, e.g. limited liability corporation (LLC), etc.;
  - Reduce the costs of product liability litigation; etc;
  - Provide networks to facilitate exchange of information and business advices;
  - Invest in educational & training programs to improve management efficiency of new entrepreneurial firms;
  - Reduce the costs of doing business – e.g. costs of litigation, contract enforcements, product liability;
  - Reduce taxes on business assets and on profits;

- *Direct assistance to innovative entrepreneurs*
    - Marketing assistance – promoting products abroad (foreign market exhibition);
    - Assistance to promote access to resource markets.

2.6 On the Effectiveness of State Programs in Providing Assistance to Innovative Firms: Brief Remarks

A perennial issue in the discussion and evaluation of government programs is related to the relative efficiency or inefficiency of a government program in allocating limited public resources to different projects, localities, industries, and firms.

A. A state–guided investment program has been subjected to several criticisms – namely, they are usually misguided by past success; characterized by excessive investment; picking the wrong winners and losers; difficulties in evaluating program performance because of multiple and sometimes conflicting objectives; and the difficulty in changing directions (i.e. difficulty to cut losses because of built-up vested interest groups, saving face.) Moreover, the moral hazard issue is always present when the program manager(s) manages other people's money.[8]
B. An allocation mechanism that relies on the market process – the price mechanism and profit motivation, is usually brought up as an alternative model in the discussion. Philip Cooke of England emphasized the efficiency of the private investment dictated model in financing successful innovations in the U.S., especially the success in Silicon Valley, when he compared the ineffectiveness of Europe's regional innovation system (RIS) with new economy innovation system (NEIS).[9] He concluded that "Europe's innovation gap with the United States rested on excessive reliance on public innovation..."
C. The relative role of government in innovation in a market economy depends on the relative development of the output and the resource markets – the efficient operation of these markets in facilitating the exchanges of resources at low transaction costs. The highly developed resources and output markets for new electronic products in Silicon Valley enable efficient investment by private venture investors – allocating limited investment funds to successful innovation. However, the costs of inefficiency from wrong investments during a cyclical peak, 2000, should remind us of the volatility of investing in new product markets. In many R&D markets where the markets are less developed and information and transaction costs are very high, the important role of

---

[8] Baumol et al. (2008)
[9] Philip Cooke, "Regional Innovations, Clusters, and the Knowledge Economy", University of Wales, UK

government – as the demonstrator for pilot projects in the early stage of learning cycle; as the risk takers intended to capture external benefit of new discoveries, etc., cannot be denied. By working to improve the functioning of the markets and by relying more on the market process to administer government assistance programs, government programs can contribute significantly to the success of innovation

D. It is therefore inevitable that there are as many proponents of government programs as there are opponents. In many occasions, programs enacted with enthusiastic support from both executive office and the state legislators, were abandoned after critical evaluation by State's auditors.[10]

2.7 Conclusion

Performance of many state programs to promote the growth of innovative firms has improved overtime as state development officers continued to learn from their owned experience and from their fellow development officers in other states. A review of state programs to promote the growth of innovative entrepreneurs during the past decade identified the following emphasis that contributed to the improved performance in these programs.

- *Public-private partnerships*
  - Collaboration between research organizations and businesses/entrepreneurs – to promote market-oriented R&D;
- *Networks (of information, participants, expertise)*
  - To facilitate the exchange of R&D knowledge, market information, services, etc., (lowering transaction costs);
- *Incubators as one effective instrument*
  - Providing coordinated assistance (both financial and technical);
- *Emphasize building the capacity to supply in the markets* – capacity to conduct R&D activities, to educate and train talent (in innovation, entrepreneurship, etc.), and to invest, etc.;

---

[10] A typical example of the criticism of the business support programs in the U.K. is provided in the " The Richard Report on Small business and Government." The report concluded .. the programs .."A system which is overly complex, ineffective and undirected. Some 3000 business support schemes are being run by over 2000 public bodies and their direct contractors at a direct costs of at least 2.5 billion pounds... for example, at least a third of the money spent on regional schemes is lost in administrative costs" "Equally, little is known about the effectiveness of existing programs." –lack of evidence about the effectiveness of the programs and interventions. Not analytical measurements of effectiveness

- *Cluster* as a regional economic development strategy;
- *Reliance on market process* in the allocation of resources to selected firms;
- *Importance of information collection* for program design as well as in monitoring, auditing, and evaluating program performance.

The importance of a comprehensive database on market activities cannot be overemphasized. Information about the market operation and the market outcome – i.e. the demand, the supply, and the costs and the price of the products and resources are the basis to formulate effective assistance programs. It also provides the only assurance for effective monitoring of the performance of government programs.

Appendix 1

Case studies of state programs to promote innovation and the growth innovative firms in the United States.

Example: Higher Education Compact for STEM Graduates (CA)

- A public-private compact of stakeholders of private sector, postsecondary education institutions, and government and community leaders;
- Goals/targets – to double the number of credentialed math and science teachers (750 to 1,500), etc.;
- The process –
    Identify the business needs – the specific needs in the economy for postsecondary graduates;
    Periodic policy audits to understand how state rules and regulations effect postsecondary performance;
    Agree on the mission, priorities, and key outputs of the overall postsecondary system, including production of STEM teachers and critical occupations, and acceleration of innovation;
    Share the responsibility for the success – outlining state government commitment to provide clear direction to postsecondary education; align and stabilize budgets and adequately fund compact efforts over the long term; and reduce the bureaucratic and regulatory burden to allow postsecondary education to be more flexible;
    Establish mutual accountability systems to enforce the compact that includes tools such as: transparency; reward-linked funding, and deregulation; and sanctions for noncompliance;
    Underpin accountability system with robust longitudinal data systems with performance tied to the above enforcement tools.

Source: National Innovation Initiatives' "National Innovative Agenda" for Federal and state programs.

Example: "Creating an education system for an entrepreneurial economy in Kentucky"

New objectives of the system:

- *Changing culture*:
  - From one that develops employment skills to one that develops necessary skills to build new businesses,
- *Creating entrepreneurship atmosphere;*
  - Throughout education system for k-12 through post-secondary institutions, and
- *Developing students' knowledge/skills*:
  - deploy technology resources in high-growth businesses.

Investment to promote innovation by State governments – a sample of cases

Michigan – Michigan's 21st Century Jobs Fund, (funded in 2006 with $400 million; $75 million per year) Situated within Michigan's Economic Development Corp., the Fund has an applied research focus in five areas – life sciences; alternative energy; advanced automotive; manufacturing and materials; and homeland security and defense.

Minnesota – In 2003 – the Initiative on Renewable Energy and the Environment at the University of Minnesota. The goal – by 2025, that the state should get 25 percent of its power from renewable sources. The initiative invested nearly $19 million in more than 110 research and demonstration projects; leveraged some $12 million in matching funds, including some from business and industry; and collaborated on research with upwards of 40 business and industry partners.

Georgia – Putting all the pieces together includes building expertise in appropriate technologies and orchestrating collaboration among key partners. The Georgia Research Alliance (GRA) provides funding to recruit "eminent scholars" to Georgia universities. To date, 54 scholars have been recruited. The GRA also funds "Venture Lab" fellows – experienced entrepreneurs who work with faculty members and others to evaluate research and build companies that meet a demonstrated commercial need.

Ohio – The state in 2003 launched its 10-year, $1.6 billion "Third Frontier" initiative establishing the Wright Centers of Innovation in biosciences and engineering. Run through the Third Frontier Commission, the state has also spent more than $50 million to develop a fuel-cell industry and more than $100 million for the Biomedical

Research and Commercialization program, and awarded $60 million to create a Global Cardiovascular Innovation Center at the world-renowned Cleveland Clinic Foundation.

Maryland – The Maryland Industrial Partnerships (MIPS) Program is a project of the Maryland Technology Enterprise Institute to jointly fund technology-based research and development between Maryland industries and University of Maryland researchers. Since 1987, the state has contributed $27.8 million and industry $115.6 million.

Source: NGA Center for Best Practices, "Innovation America: A Final Report – Enhancing Competitiveness: A Review of Recent State Economic Development Initiatives" National Governors Association (NGA)

Example: establishment of State Development Board/Corporation

Mission: to develop programs to promote innovation, entrepreneurship, and economic development in the states

Program components an investment fund; funding authority to increase R&D capacity in the state and to establish/support incubators, etc.

Investment fund(s)

Investment through venture and/or seed venture funds for innovative startups in the state

Incubators/innovation centers at state's research universities

Example: The Biotechnology Investment Incentive Tax Credit (Maryland)

Goals: to help fund seed and early-stage biotech and bioscience companies by providing an incentive for investors- a refundable tax credit equal to one-half of initial investment.

Qualified company: biotechnology company based in Maryland with fewer than 50 full-time employees, in business no longer than 10 years, and certified by the Department of Business and Economic Development (DBED).

Qualified investor: an investor who invests at least $25,000 or a corporation that invests at least $250,000 in a qualified company."

The credit available to investors: 50 percent of an eligible investment made during the taxable year. There is a cap ($50,000 for individual investors or $250,000 for corporations and venture capital firms.) The amount of credits granted during the tax year also cannot exceed the amount funded.

Investment period: hold on to the investment for at least two years after getting the credit approved.

Other Examples:

- 2008 Kansas Angel Investor Tax Credit Program
- Ohio TechAngel Fund LLC – Fund I and Fund-II,

Example: ATDC: Helping Georgia Entrepreneurs Build Great Technology Companies

Advanced Technology Development Center: a tech incubator based at Georgia Technology University

- *Missions*: Stimulate economic growth through technology sector
- *Services offered*: Strategic business advices, networks of people and resources, entrepreneurial learning community, and turnkey facilities and services
- *Programs include*: Entrepreneur Resource Center, Venture@Lab, ATDC Seed Capital Fund, and Innovation Centers;
- *Technology emphasis* – Internet technology, telecommunications, and bioscience;

Source: Office of Advocacy, "Putting It Together: the role of entrepreneurship in economic Development", conference Proceedings, March 2005.

Example: Maryland's TEDCO (Technology Development Corporation): An evaluation

- *Objective*: business incubation to encourage, promote, stimulate, and support research and development (R&D) activity through the use of different investments leading to commercialization of new products and services by small businesses.
- 18 centers in existence; 4 new proposed centers
- Most helpful in providing inexpensive work space – office and lab space;
- Other helps from the centers–
- Reason for the success: Industry clusters – Academic R&D; over $2.4 billion; over 40 research centers (some nationally known Federal labs and major universities; over 5000 high-tech establishment employing almost 200,000
- Need for business accelerators to help the graduates to grow

Source: RTA International

Appendix 2

Sample tables on State programs summary to promote Bioscience in the United States– Tables 2.1, 2.2, 2.3, and 2.4 reprinted from: Battelle Technology Partnership Practice, "Technology, Talent and Capital: State Bioscience Initiatives 2008"

Table 2.1 Pre-commercialization/proof of concept funding in FY 2007 and FY 2008

State	Commercialization funds*	Maximum award	One-time funding	Annual funding	
AZ	Arizona Technology Enterprises (ASU), Univ. of Arizona Tech Transfer Office, Catapult Bio	$50,000		$250.000–$300,000	$2.5–3 million
CA	Entrepreneurial Joint Venture Matching Grant Program (CSUPERB)	$25,000–$30,000			
CO	Colorado Bioscience Discovery Evaluation Grant Program	$150,000	$2.5 million	$2 million	
	Colorado Bioscience and Life Science Fund	$250,000 for companies, $15,000 for research institutions	$26.5 million over 5 years		
CT	BioSeed Program	$500,000	$5 million		
DE	Technology Based Seed Funds	$100,000		$1 million	$1 million
FL	State University Research Commercialization Assistance Grant Program		$2 million		
GA	VentureLab	$50,000 for Phase I; $100,000 for Phase II; $250,000 for Phase III		$4 million	$4 million
IL	Entrepreneur in Residence Program, PROPEL and iBIO Entrepreneurship Center; other Entrepreneurship Centers (12); Innovation Challenge Technical Assistance and Matching Grant Programs	Entrepreneur in Residence $80,000 Entrepreneurship Centers: $10,000 Innovation Challenge Grant Program: $50,000		$3.8 million	$1.65 million
IA	Demonstration Fund	$150,000		$2.5 million	$2.5 million
KS	Bioscience Innovation and Matching Fund	$2 million		$5.5 million	$8 million

Table 2.1 (continued)

State	Commercialization funds*	Maximum award	One-time funding	Annual funding	
KY	KTEC Proof of Concept Fund ICC Concept Pool	$25,000		$2.7 million	$2.5 million
ME	Maine Technology institute Development Awards, Seed Grants, SBIR Phase 0, Cluster Enhancement Grants	$500,000		$6.3 million	$8.5 million
MD	University Technology Development Fund	$50,000		$450,000	$400,000
MA	MTC/JAII Centers of Excellence Program, Matching Fund Programs, Innovation Fund Programs, Mass Tech Transfer Center Technology Commercialization Programs	Varies by program	$50 million		
MI	21st Century Jobs Fund Michigan Pre-Seed Capital Fund			$15 million	$9 million
MS	Mississippi Seed Fund	$15,000	$4 million		
MO	Missouri Life Sciences Trust Fund,	No maximum			$2.6 million
	Missouri Technology Incentive Program	Phase I–$5,000 Phase II–$50,000			$1.25 million
MT	Montana Board of Research and Commercialization Technology	$500,000		$3.5 million	$3.5 million
NJ	Edison Innovation R&D Fund	$600,000		$5 million	$5 million
NY	NYSTAR Technology Transfer Incentive Program	$500,000		$4 million	$3.9 million
NC	North Carolina Economic Development Investment Fund (BIO only)	$250,000		$1 million	$1 million

Table 2.1 (continued)

State	Commercialization funds*	Maximum award	One-time funding	Annual funding	
OH	Entrepreneurial Signature Program	$100,000	$84.4 million		
OK	Oklahoma Applied Research Support Program	$45.000/year for up to three years		$1.6 million	$1.14 million
OR	University Venture Development Fund	NA		$7 million	$7 million
PA	Life Sciences Greenhouse		$100 million	$12 million	$15 million
PR	PRIDCO-SBTR-Tied Grants	$375,000		$400,000	$400,000
RI	Slater Technology Fund			$3 million	$3 million
SD	Part of 2010 Initiative	$1 million		$3.8 million	$5.7 million
TX	Texas Emerging Technology Fund	$3 million	$25 million	$12.5 million	$12.5 million
VA	Commonwealth Technology Research Fund (CTRF)	No maximum		$2 million	$1 million
WA	UW Technology Gap Investment Fund and WSU Cougar Gap Fund	$50,000		<$1 million	<$1 million
WV	Small Business Innovation Research (SBIR) Program			$100,000	$100,000
WI	Innovation and Economic Development Research Program	$50,000		$600,000	$600,000

Reprinted from: Battelle Technology Partnership Practice, "Technology, talent and capital: State Bioscience Initiatives 2008"

2 State Programs to Promote the Growth of Innovative Firms

Table 2.2 State-supported pre-seed Fund

State	Pre-seed funds	Total size of fund	Typical size of investment
CO	Colorado Fund I	$40 million	$500,000–$1 million
CT	Eli Whitney Fund	$45 million (approximately)	$500–$1 million
DE	Tech-Bbased Seed Fund I, Tech Based Seed Fund II, Pre-Venture Funding, Delaware Strategic Fund	$32.5 total all funds 2006–2008	$50,000–$100,000
FL	Florida Opportunity Fund	$30 million	
GA	ATDC Fund	$8 million	$200,000–$500,000
HI	Investment in multiple funds	$50 million	$200,000–$500,000
IL	Illinois Department of Commerce and Economic Opportunity Indirect Equity Fund (Angel & Seed Fund);	$3.44 million	$500,000–$1 million
	Illinois State Treasurer's Technology Development Bridge;	$75 million	
	IllinoisVENTURES and LLC	$40 million	
IN	Indiana Seed Fund	$6 million	$100,000–$200,000
KS	KTEC Equity Fund	$1.5 million plus additional funding for proof of concept	$200,000–$500,000
KY	Commonwealth Seed Capital	$21 million	$200,000–$500,000
LA	Investments in several funds	$65 million	$500,000–$1 million
ME	Maine Technology Institute Accelerated Commercialization Fund; Small Enterprise Growth Fund	$8 million	$200,000–$500,000
MD	Maryland Venture Fund; Challenge Investment Program/ TEDCO's MTTF Program	$6 million $5.5 million	$50,000–$100,000
MA	Massachusetts Technology Development Corp	NA	$200,000–$500,000
MI	21st Century Investment Fund and Venture Michigan Fund	$109 million $95 million	More than $1 million
MS	Mississippi Seed Fund	$4 million	$50,000–$100,000
MO	Missouri Venture Partners	$15 million	Up to $50,000
NM	Flywheel Gap Fund	$2 million	$50,000–$100,000
	LANL Venture Acceleration Fund	$600,000	
NY	NYSTAR's Small Business Technology Investment Fund	NA	NA
OH	Third Frontier Pre-Seed Fund Initiative	$263 million	$10,000–$200,000
OK	OCAST Technology Business Finance Program, managed by i2E	$1.15 million annually	$100,000–$200,000
PA	Life Sciences Greenhouses	$100 million	$200,000–$500,000
PR	Bio Science Investment Fund	$250 million	NA
RI	Slater Technology Fund	$3million	$50,000–$100,000
TX	Emerging Technology Fund	$200 million	$500,000–$1 million
VA	CIT GAP BioLife Fund	$500,000	$50,000–$100,000

Reprinted from: Battelle Technology Partnership Practice, "Technology, talent and capital: State Bioscience Initiatives 2008"

Table 2.3 State seed capital tax credits

State	Angel investors	Bioscience angel investors	Investors in early-stage venture funds	Investors in bioscience early-stage venture funds
AZ	•	•		
HI	•			
IN	•			
IA	•		•	
KS	•	•		
KY	•		•	
LA	•			
ME	•		•	
MD	•	•		
MI	•			
MT	•		•	
NM	•			
NY	•			
NC	•	•	•	•
ND	•		•	
OH	•		•	
OK	•		•	
OR			•	
VA	•			
WI	•	•	•	•

Reprinted from: Battelle Technology Partnership Practice, "Technology, talent and capital: State Bioscience Initiatives 2008"

Table 2.4 State investments to increase the availability of locally managed, later-stage venture capital, 2006–2008

State	Invested in fund of funds	Invested in private VC firms	Invested in bioscience companies	Other
DE	•	•	•	
HI				Appropriated funds for contract with private nonprofit to provide funding for companies
IL	•	•	•	•
KS			•	
KY	•	•	•	
MA			•	Through Massachusetts Technology Development Corporation
MI	•			
MT	•			
NJ	•	•	•	

Table 2.4 (continued)

State	Invested in fund of funds	Invested in private VC firms	Invested in bioscience companies	Other
NM		•	•	
NC		•		
OH	•	•	•	
OK	•		•	
OR	•			
PA		•		
RI			•	
SD			•	Provides financing for feasibility studies in the form of a forgivable loan
VA			•	
WI		•	•	

Reprinted from: Battelle Technology Partnership Practice, "Technology, talent and capital: State Bioscience Initiatives 2008"

References

Alliance for Science & Technology Research in America (ASTRA) (2007) Riding the rising tide: a 21st century strategy for U.S. competitiveness and prosperity

Battelle Technology Partnership Practice (June 2008) Technology, talent and capital: state bioscience initiatives 2008. Prepared for: BIO – Biotechnology Industry Organization

Baumol W, Litan R, Schramm C (2007) Good capitalism, bad capitalism, and the economics of growth and prosperity, chap. 4. Yale University Press, New Haven

Council on Competitiveness (December 2004) National innovation initiative report

Kauffman Foundation (1999) State programs to grow entrepreneurs. Kauffman

NASVF NetNews Archives. www.nasvf.org. Accessed 8 November 2010

NGA Center for Best Practices (September 2004) Innovation America: a final report – enhancing competitiveness: a review of recent state economic development initiatives. National Governors Association (NGA) www.nga.org/Center. Accessed 8 November 2010

NGA Center for Best Practices (February 2005) Enhancing competitiveness: a review of recent state economic development initiatives. NGA Center for Best Practices Issue Brief

NGA Center for Best Practices (2000) Growing new businesses with seed and venture capital: state experiences and options 2000. A report prepared by Heard, Robert & John Sibert for the NGA Center for Best Practices

NGA Center for Best Practices (May 2006) Seed and venture capital: state experiences and options. A report prepared by National Association of Seed and Venture Funds (NASVF) for NGA

Pages ER, Kenneth P (January 2003) Understanding entrepreneurship promotion as an economic development strategy: a three-state survey. A Joint Project of the National Commission on Entrepreneurship and the Center for Regional Economic Competitiveness

PolicyOne Research Inc. Maine innovation index 2008. for Maine Department of Economic and Community Development

Research Triangle International (RTI) (January 2008) Economic assessment of Maryland technology incubators, for TEDCO of Maryland

U.S. Small Business Administration (March 2005) Office of advocacy, Putting it together: the role of entrepreneurship in economic development. A conference report

World Bank (2007) "DoingBusiness 2008"

Chapter 3
OECD-Eurostat Entrepreneurship Indicators Programme: Comparable International Measures of Entrepreneurship and the Factors that Enhance or Impede It

Tim C. Davis and Mariarosa Lunati

Abstract Entrepreneurship has been identified as a high priority and emerging policy area for governments throughout the world, especially during the current crisis. The rapid pace of economic restructuring and change means that business statistics must do a better job of describing the dynamics of business creation, development and growth. What are the factors that encourage or impede the desired outcomes? And how do the situations in different countries compare? It is not sufficient to examine any economy in isolation; data must be consistent and comparable across countries. This chapter describes the work by the OECD and Eurostat to develop comparable enterprise-based data sets to assist researchers, policy analysts and policymakers in understanding the entrepreneurial performance of countries and how such performance can be transformed through policy tools. Governments have embraced fact-based policymaking and have appealed to National Statistics Offices for the information they need. The OECD-Eurostat Entrepreneurship Indicators Programme (EIP) is an attempt by national and international statisticians to respond to the challenge. In cooperation with statistical experts in NSOs and the policy analysts who will use the data, the EIP identified data requirements and set out to satisfy them, primarily using data from existing sources. A number of countries were part of the pioneering effort to develop core concepts and prove that the data could be produced. Eurostat and the OECD are moving ahead with the programme and invite all others to join.

3.1 Introduction

Entrepreneurship has long been discussed within the research community but serious attention from policy analysts and policymakers has been more recent. The global economic crisis has heightened interest in the topic as entrepreneurial

M. Lunati (✉)
Organization for Economic Co-Operation and Development (OECD), 2 rue Andre Pascal, 75775 Paris Cedex 16, France
e-mail: mariarosa.lunati@oecd.org

activity is seen as an essential element of revitalisation plans throughout the world.

But sound economic policies must be based on relevant and consistent data. Most entrepreneurship research relied on ad hoc data compilations developed to support a single project and virtually no "official" statistics on the subject existed. Furthermore, the growing demand for information about the activities and experiences of young, and often small, firms came at a time when governments were making serious efforts to reduce the burden on businesses, especially small ones.

In OECD and EU countries, officials working in the Business Statistics field are facing some particularly difficult challenges. Governments have embraced fact-based policymaking and have appealed to National Statistics Offices for the information they need. Yet governments are also attentive to the demands from business to reduce administrative burdens, including those occasioned by statistical queries.

The OECD-Eurostat Entrepreneurship Indicators Programme (EIP) is the first attempt to compile and publish international data on entrepreneurship and its determinants from official government statistics sources. To meet the challenge of providing new Entrepreneurship Indicators, while minimising burden on business, the OECD and Eurostat focussed attention on exploiting existing sources of data.

This paper describes the genesis and underlying methodological and administrative framework for the OECD-Eurostat Entrepreneurship Programme. It also presents some early data results from the programme: internationally-comparable indicators to gauge the amount and type of entrepreneurship activity in some twenty-three countries.

The objectives and methodology of the programme are discussed, in response to governments' needs for empirical evidence to guide the formulation and evaluation of entrepreneurship policies.

3.2 The Importance of Entrepreneurship

For many years, economists and policymakers have identified "entrepreneurs" as important drivers for employment, innovation and economic growth. Indeed, the recognition of the role of entrepreneurship dates back centuries if one considers the work of Cantillon, the first academic to explicitly attempt to define, and describe the role of, entrepreneurs. It was not until the 1990s, however, that the term "entrepreneurship" became a buzzword both in the media and in political debate. Newspapers were full of success stories about self-made billionaires and politicians wanted to support and encourage their endeavours more widely.

Entrepreneurship is viewed as an essential activity to regenerate and sustain economic growth in strong economies and also as a means of boosting employment and productivity in depressed regions or in developing countries. The dynamic process of new firm creation introduces and disperses innovative products, processes and organisational structures throughout the economy. As firms enter and exit the market, theory suggests that the new arrivals will be more efficient than those they displace. Furthermore, existing firms that are not driven out are forced to innovate and become more productive to compete. Empirical support for this process of "creative destruction", first described by Schumpeter, has been provided by numerous studies by the OECD and others.

3.3 The Relevance and Role of Entrepreneurship in Government Policy

As is discussed further below, the goal of the EIP was to create practical entrepreneurship indicators that would be relevant and useful for government policy makers. Thus, an important early step was to consider how governments viewed entrepreneurship. A number of observations that emerged from this research are summarised below.

What are the policy goals of governments in the area of entrepreneurship? If increasing levels of entrepreneurship are sought in all countries, do countries have common goals? Is the goal simply to maximise the number of new entrants? Since some have offered evidence that the churning effect of entry and exit is beneficial, should policy facilitate exit as well? Once established, is it better for a firm to prosper and grow for a long period of time? Or, do new dynamic firms quickly become old less productive firms that should, in turn, exit to make way for another more dynamic entrant?

Clearly, a government's policy objectives related to entrepreneurship will depend on the state of economic development as well as on other higher-level economic goals. Thus, some countries want to encourage any kind of firm creation, even very small firms that replicate existing activities, have no or few employees and littler prospects for growth. In most OECD and EU economies, however, entrepreneurship is not only about firm creation; it is also associated with innovation, competitiveness and high growth.

While academic studies have long recognised the importance of entrepreneurship, policy makers have only recently explicitly discovered it. Indeed, entrepreneurship was long considered an exogenous factor in government policies, and policy efforts were often directed simply towards the large population of very small firms rather than aimed at stimulating entrepreneurs to introduce new products, processes or organisational forms in order to exploit new markets and grow.

However, many OECD and non-OECD countries have now made entrepreneurship an explicit priority and are exploring policy options that would alter the rate and type of entrepreneurship, rather than simply create or sustain SMEs. As globalisation reshapes the international economic landscape and technological change creates both uncertainty and opportunity in the world economy, governments are turning to entrepreneurial dynamism to help to meet the new economic, social and environmental challenges and kick-start a prolonged recovery.

The interest of both developed and developing countries in how government policies and other national "business environment" factors influence the rates and types of entrepreneurship has increased considerably in recent years. Nurturing entrepreneurship is an explicit policy priority for many OECD countries, whether they already have significant levels of entrepreneurship or they are seen to be trailing the leaders in this domain.

Entrepreneurship is of considerable interest to policy-makers everywhere, whether they are convinced that entrepreneurs are the dominant force in economic development or just significant contributors. But there are many different perspectives on entrepreneurship, even within the same country. Entrepreneurship objectives and policies differ considerably, owing to different policy priorities and diverse perspectives on what is meant by entrepreneurship. In some countries, entrepreneurship is linked to regional development and firm creation and growth are stimulated in order to boost employment and output in depressed regions. In others, entrepreneurship is an element of strategies designed to facilitate the economic participation of certain target groups, such as women or minorities.

For most OECD countries, though, governments increasingly consider promotion of entrepreneurship to be an important element of their strategy to develop an internationally-competitive economy. In most developed economies, entrepreneurship policies are in fact closely connected to innovation policies, with which they share many characteristics and challenges. Both are associated with "doing something new" and, designed correctly, they can be mutually reinforcing. The dynamic process of new firm creation introduces and disperses innovative products, processes and organisational structures throughout the economy.

The United States is often viewed as the epitome of entrepreneurship with high rates of new dynamic, firm creation than other countries. But as better, internationally-comparable data becomes available it is clear that US start-up rates are often lower than those of European countries, while growth performance after start-up is indeed higher in the US. Furthermore, an OECD study (Bartelsman et al., 2002) found that US firm entrants were smaller than their European counterparts but, once over the initial start-up phase, they expanded rapidly while European firms remained small.

There are still debates about the contribution of new firm entrants to net employment growth but there is little disagreement about the fact that a relatively small proportion of firms that are growing rapidly account for the majority of new jobs. The Canadian Growth Firms Project, for example, showed that 2.7% of firms met the criteria for "leading growth firms" and they accounted for 60% of job growth between 1997 and 2000.[1] Naturally, governments are particularly interested in this category of firms and want to understand determinants of and obstacles to high growth. But while there are numerous examinations of high growth firms throughout OECD countries, there is no agreement whatsoever on just what high growth means. What are the appropriate metrics and thresholds to measure growth? Many studies

---

[1] Growth Firm Workshop Synopsis, Industry Canada, September 29, 2004.

focus solely on growth in employment, often because it is more readily available on business dynamics databases than other suggested measures such as payroll, sales, revenue, profit or productivity.

Furthermore, some governments do not want to limit entrepreneurship policy only to newly-created firms. Some policy analysts have noted the importance of also measuring the contributions of existing firms and entrepreneurs. If government policy interests relate to job and productivity growth, then established entrepreneurs are just as valuable as new ones.

This brief summary of the role and relevance of entrepreneurship for government policy confirmed the importance of entrepreneurship. But it also demonstrated that entrepreneurship is a multi-faceted concept that is viewed differently in different countries and contexts. Clearly, no single, simple indicator of "entrepreneurship" would satisfy the varied interests. Recognition of the widely-varied policy interests influenced the OECD-Eurostat approach to defining entrepreneurship and to determining relevant indicators.

3.4 The Need for Entrepreneurship Data

Despite the increasing importance of entrepreneurship and associated policies, measurement of the phenomenon, particularly at the international level, has long been deficient. There had been numerous ad hoc initiatives at local, regional or national levels, and even a few at the international level, but consistent, comparable data were scarce. Moreover few, if any, National Statistics Offices recognised the concept of entrepreneurship and no international forums existed to permit agreement on definitions or measures.

The OECD itself had addressed entrepreneurship through various analytical studies and reports, but no systematic effort had been made to establish an ongoing database devoted to comparing entrepreneurship across OECD countries. In 2004, an OECD Ministerial Conference on SMEs and Entrepreneurship concluded that the statistical base for entrepreneurship research was weak. In their conclusions, the Ministers urged the OECD to develop "a robust and comparable statistical base on which policy can be developed".

The rationale for developing entrepreneurship indicators is to help policy makers to understand how the policies they create or adjust will affect entrepreneurship and, eventually, higher-level objectives for the economy and society. In order for countries to benefit from the experience of others, it is also essential that the indicators allow for comparisons across countries and over time.

But it is not sufficient to measure how much entrepreneurship takes place. Countries need to understand the determinants of and obstacles to entrepreneurship, and they need to analyse the effectiveness of different policy approaches. The lack of internationally-comparable empirical evidence has constrained serious research and many questions remain unanswered. Ultimately, policy making must be guided, as far as possible, by evidence and facts.

3.5 The Entrepreneurship Indicators Programme (EIP)

Over a period of more than 10 years, beginning in the mid-1990s, the OECD had addressed the impact and importance of entrepreneurship through various analytical studies and reports. While these studies compiled some relevant data to support the specific research or policy tasks, no effort was made to establish an ongoing database specifically related to comparisons and studies of entrepreneurship across OECD countries.

In 2004, events conspired to move the OECD to examine the feasibility and utility of developing an ongoing programme of statistics on entrepreneurship. One key event was the 2nd OECD Ministerial Conference on SMEs in Istanbul, entitled "Promoting Entrepreneurship and Innovative SMEs in a Global Economy". The Ministerial declaration urging development of an internationally-comparable statistical base was cited above.

However, while the Ministerial recommendations served as a strong incentive for the OECD to work on improving entrepreneurship statistics, no additional funds were provided to support such work. It was fortunate that other stakeholders also became involved and offered resources to make the work possible. In late 2004, the Kauffman Foundation of the USA offered the OECD financial support for a study to explore what could be done to improve entrepreneurship data. At the same time, a Danish-led Consortium of OECD countries, known as ICE (International Consortium for Entrepreneurship), funded several special projects related to entrepreneurship data development. The initiative and support of the Kauffman Foundation and the ICE countries were also instrumental in convincing the OECD of the requirement and feasibility of such an international programme of indicators.

After a feasibility study, the OECD launched the Entrepreneurship Indicators Programme (EIP) to build internationally-comparable statistics on entrepreneurship and its determinants in late 2006. In 2007, Eurostat joined forces with the OECD to create the joint OECD-Eurostat EIP whose aim was to create a durable, long-term, programme of policy-relevant entrepreneurship statistics, in cooperation with official government statistics agencies. Importantly, the early work involved development of standard definitions and concepts, establishment of a framework for understanding entrepreneurship, selection and prioritisation of indicators themselves and cooperative work to engage National Statistics Offices in the collection of data.

3.6 Defining Entrepreneurship

The goal of the Entrepreneurship Indicators Programme (EIP) was to establish a framework of indicators relevant for the study of entrepreneurship and encourage countries to produce as much of the data in the framework as possible, using the same definitions, methodologies and classifications. The development of such a framework was a challenging task since there was no agreement even on the definition of entrepreneurship itself. Although the function of the entrepreneur is probably as old as the notion of economics itself, numerous authors have noted that there is no widely-accepted definition of the term "entrepreneurship" (Hornaday, 1992; Ucbasaran et al. 2001; Watson, 2001).

Thus, the first challenge for the EIP was to reach agreement on a definition of entrepreneurial activity that would provide the basis for collection and comparison of valid indicators across countries. Clearly, entrepreneurship is a multifaceted concept that manifests itself in many different ways. Nevertheless some fundamental concepts had to be agreed to so that statisticians could be guided to collect the relevant indicators that would allow analysts and policy-makers to better understand the factors that influence the rate and type of entrepreneurial activity, as well as the outcomes or impacts of entrepreneurship.

The challenge of developing fundamental definitions for entrepreneurial activity was made all the more difficult because of the considerable confusion that exists in the way that people use the term entrepreneurship, both in casual conversation and serious academic discussion too.

Indeed, even the OECD itself has contributed to the confusion since virtually every study that has focussed on entrepreneurship has presented a different definition of the term. For example, in an OECD Economic Survey in 1997, it was defined as "the dynamic process of identifying economic opportunities and acting upon them by developing, producing and selling goods and services". In "Fostering Entrepreneurship", it was defined as "...the ability to marshal resources to seize new business opportunities...". In a 2001 publication on Youth Entrepreneurship, the term was equated with self-employment: "... an entrepreneur is anyone who works for himself or herself but not for someone else...". Finally, another 2001 publication entitled Drivers of Growth, stated that "The concept of entrepreneurship generally refers to enterprising individuals who display the readiness to take risks with new or innovative ideas to generate new products or services."

Many definitions have evolved from a theoretical or philosophical perspective, without any concern for measurement. In the EIP, this is referred to as the "top-down approach". This approach continues today, even in policy-oriented papers that discuss a concept of entrepreneurship without attempting to represent or measure it using concretely defined statistics or indicators. Other papers bypass the discussion of entrepreneurship definitions altogether and simply state that entrepreneurship is "defined" by a specific empirical measure (bottom-up approach). Not surprisingly, the measures used are those that are readily available and only rarely do authors justify or explain how the measures represent "entrepreneurship". This approach, in which authors simply state, for example, that they "...define entrepreneurship as the self-employed", confuses the empirical measure of the concept defined as entrepreneurship.

The OECD-Eurostat approach is different in that the programme founders determined conceptual entrepreneurship definitions both from the top-down perspective of theoreticians and policy-makers, to ensure relevance, and from a bottom-up perspective, with an eye to feasible measurement. This approach is detailed in an EIP

Working Paper (Ahmad and Seymour, 2008). In this paper, we provide only a brief historical review of the theoreticians' contributions to explain the foundation of our chosen definitions.

3.6.1 The Top-Down Approach

The French economist Richard Cantillon is generally accredited with being the first to coin the term entrepreneurship in about 1730.[2] Loosely, he defined entrepreneurship as self-employment of any sort, and entrepreneurs as risk-takers, in the sense that they purchased goods at certain prices in the present to sell at uncertain prices in the future. Many eminent economists and scholars have elaborated on Cantillon's contribution, including Adam Smith, Jean Baptiste Say, Alfred Marshall, Joseph Schumpeter, Israel Kirzner and Frank Knight.

Schumpeter's discussion of entrepreneurship in 1934, introduced a more modern interpretation of the concept. Schumpeter saw entrepreneurs as innovators who take advantage of change, broadly interpreted as the introduction of a new (or improved) good or method of production; the opening of a new market; the exploitation of a new source of supply; or the re-engineering or re-organization of business management processes. Schumpeter's definition therefore equates entrepreneurship with innovation in the business sense.

A very wide variety of definitions were identified and examined in the EIP Working Paper, revealing that theoreticians have explored the entrepreneur's characteristics, resources, activities and impacts or results, just to name a few of the aspects covered. Though varied, some common themes were identified in the historical works. Summarising these points and the top-down approach in general, the definitions generally used in the literature broadly converge on the following points: Entrepreneurship is about *enterprising human activity* or identifying and acting upon opportunities that *create value,* be that economic, cultural or social value. Typically, entrepreneurial activities require the leveraging of resources and capabilities through innovation, but the opportunities themselves always relate to the identification of new products, new processes or new markets.

3.6.2 The Bottom-Up Approach

With an eye to the theoretical concepts of entrepreneurship, the EIP then added the practical considerations of what matters to policy-makers and what could be measured that is relevant to policy makers' needs.

The themes summarised above suggested the key elements of a set of definitions. But it was critical that the entrepreneurship definitions would provide the basis for relevant indicators to support evidenced-based policy making and reviews

---

[2]The word *entrepreneur* itself derives from the French verb *entreprendre*, meaning "to undertake".

3   OECD-Eurostat Entrepreneurship Indicators Programme   57

of progress against measurable goals. Thus, before finalising definitions, the programme's founders elaborated a general framework for addressing and measuring entrepreneurship. The first step was to formulate a model for how the entrepreneurship process takes place and how its impacts are generated. Then they identified relevant indicator topics that linked to policy interests and to the themes derived from the top down approach. When it was clear that there were indeed good linkages between the conceptual themes derived from the top-down approach, the policy interests and the feasible indicator topics, the definitions were confirmed.

The bottom-up approach is reflected through the Framework for Measuring and Addressing Entrepreneurship. OECD-Eurostat researchers confirmed that suitable measures were available or could be developed in the short or medium term either from existing sources or from new surveys. The entrepreneurship framework, indicator topics and core indicators are set out in the next section. At this point it is sufficient to note that the themes of enterprising human activity that creates value through leveraging of resources and capabilities in some new way were matched with indicator topics such as firm creation and destruction, and a variety of measures of survival, growth and innovation and performance.

3.6.3 The EIP Entrepreneurship Definitions

The concurrent development of a definition with the development of the framework reflects pragmatism and a need to meet policy-makers needs. Drawing on the above analysis and arguments, the following definitions of the entrepreneur, entrepreneurship and entrepreneurial activity were struck:

> *Entrepreneurs* are those persons (business owners) who seek to generate value, through the creation or expansion of economic activity, by identifying and exploiting new products, processes or markets.
> *Entrepreneurial activity* is the enterprising human action in pursuit of the generation of value, through the creation or expansion of economic activity, by identifying and exploiting new products, processes or markets.
> *Entrepreneurship* is the phenomena associated with entrepreneurial activity.

3.7 The Entrepreneurship Framework

Given the multifaceted nature of entrepreneurship, and the myriad factors that might influence it, establishing a realistic yet relevant set of measures to be produced as core Entrepreneurship Indicators was a challenge. To simplify the task, a first step was to describe a simplistic entrepreneurship model that provides a framework within which one can list indicators that are both potentially relevant and available.

The rationale for developing entrepreneurship indicators is to help policy makers to understand how the policies they put in place or adjust will impact on

Fig. 3.1 Framework for measuring entrepreneurship

entrepreneurship and, eventually, on some higher-level objectives for the economy and society. Figure 3.1 portrays a simple, three-stage entrepreneurship model, which was inspired by a number of previous scholarly and policy-oriented studies, most notably by the FORA research group in Denmark. The Framework is described in more detail in an OECD Working Paper.[3] The framework consists of three stages in the entrepreneurship process. The first stage of this model comprises various *determinants* which policy can affect and which in turn influence entrepreneurial *performance,* or the amount and type of entrepreneurship that take place. The final stage is the *impact* of entrepreneurship on higher-level goals such as economic growth, job creation or poverty reduction.

This entrepreneurship model or framework is presented in a linear fashion for simplicity. It is recognized that there are numerous inter-relationships that exist between the three main components of the conceptual model and, indeed, between the subcomponents as well. For example, while the model postulates that Determinants can alter the amount and type of Entrepreneurial Performance, which in turn leads to changes in an Impact category, such as economic growth, it is also recognised that economic growth itself will have an impact on Determinants. The general health of the economy may affect ease of access to finance, for example. Furthermore, a buoyant economy might encourage more entrepreneurs to take the steps to implement a business idea even if other Determinants are unchanged.

As illustrated in Fig. 3.2, within each of the three main stages of the process, the EIP has identified several sub-categories to guide the selection of indicators. For example, under *Determinants*, indicators in areas such as access to finance; market conditions and the entrepreneurial culture will be relevant for study. Under *Impact*, sub-categories of Job Creation, Economic Growth and Poverty Reduction are offered as examples. The focus for data collection in the short to medium term

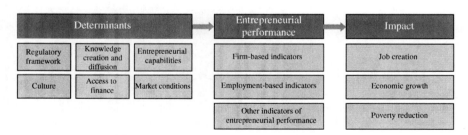

Fig. 3.2 Topic categories for entrepreneurship indicators

---

[3]This Framework is developed and explained to a greater extent in an OECD Working Paper prepared by members of the EISG. See "A Framework for Addressing and Measuring Entrepreneurship", OECD Statistics Directorate Working Paper, STD/DOC(2008)2.

Firms	Employment	Other
Employer enterprise birth rates	Share of high-growth firms (by employment)	Share of high-growth firms (by turnover)
Employer enterprise death rates	Share of gazelles (employment)	Share of gazelles (by turnover)
Business churn	Ownership rate start-ups	Value added, young or small firms
Net business population growth	Ownership rates business population	Productivity contribution, young or small firms
Survival rates at 3 and 5 years	Employment in 3 and 5 year old firms	Innovation performance, Young or small firms
Proportion of 3 and 5 year old firms	Average firm size after 3 and 5 years	Export performance, young or small firms

Fig. 3.3 Core indicators of entrepreneurial performance

has been the indicators on Entrepreneurial Performance, though some expansion beyond the core list is already evident in the second round results discussed in Sect. 3.8, below. Figure 3.3 sets out the core indicators of entrepreneurial performance.

The EIP does not propose any single measure. While the definition of entrepreneurship is broad, encompassing virtually all new firm creation activity for example, it is also very important for policy analysts to be able to understand and distinguish different types of entrepreneurial performance. Entrepreneurs are engaged in many different types of entrepreneurial activities and only some of those will be of interest to a given country's policy-makers. Furthermore, while some policies may enhance or restrain overall entrepreneurship, most policy instruments target particular types of entrepreneurship. Thus, it is critical that analysts and policy-makers are able to measure the specific categories of entrepreneurship they are trying to affect. In order for countries to benefit from the experience of others, it is also essential that the Entrepreneurship Indicators support comparisons across countries by type of entrepreneurship.

The list of core indicators reveals an important concept that is a fundamental part of the EIP, namely, the "employer firm" or, more correctly, the "employer enterprise". Conceptually, an employer enterprise is one with at least one employee, beyond the owner or founder. This employer enterprise population excludes a large number of self employed or zero employee firms that make up a very large part of the enterprise population in all countries. The employer enterprise sub-population is of particular interest since such firms are more likely to pursue growth objectives that involve innovation and employment creation. Firms with employees and growth objectives are often the target of entrepreneurship policies.

The employer enterprise data are also more comparable internationally since some of the differences due to business register thresholds and coverage are eliminated. The concept is not without comparability problems though. While efforts are made to ensure the employer enterprises actually have an employee, some countries may encourage a legal structure that results in the owner being an employee for the firm.

Thus, the list of Core Indicators of Entrepreneurial Performance includes a number of measures that each target, to varying degrees, different aspects of entrepreneurship and different types of entrepreneurs. So for example, whilst the list includes the rate of business ownership in an economy, including the self-employed, high priority is also placed on measuring the creation of firms with employees, the number of high-growth firms and the number of young, high-growth firms (gazelles). Indeed one might view these indicators as reflecting some evolution of entrepreneurship on a scale of economic importance. High-growth firms require the creation of a firm, typically with employees, and many firms with employees, started out initially as sole traders.

Finally, it should be noted that the total population of all enterprises, and their distribution by size class and industry are still relevant and interesting for entrepreneurship studies. Data on all enterprises are found within the Structural Indicators of the EIP.

The goal of the EIP was to establish a framework of relevant indicators as well as a core list of indicators with standard definitions, methodologies and classifications. The Steering Group that developed the metadata comprised policy analysts and, importantly, the responsible data experts from NSOs. This approach assured relevance and also feasibility. The core entrepreneurship indicators selected were either available or potentially available, from existing data sources.

3.8 Results from the EIP

In November 2008, the EIP released the first set of indicators, just less than 2 years after the official launch of the program. In the first round, 18 countries contributed data corresponding to the new "entrepreneurship" concepts. A second publication in late 2009 saw the participation of 23 OECD and non-OECD countries or regions.

In the first round, data collection focused mainly on indicators of entrepreneurial performance. The EIP works closely with national statistical offices that calculate these indicators, which are typically sourced from data in business registers. However, while business registers allow for the development of high-quality, internationally-comparable indicators, they are not very timely.

Given the growing demand for more timely indicators, in part due to the worldwide economic crisis, the second EIP publication of indicators added more recent empirical evidence relating to entrepreneurship. The 2009 edition presented initial results based on different data sources, often administrative databases. This work built on research undertaken by Eurostat aimed at estimating, by country, more recent business demography data based on different sorts of national sources.[4]

---

[4]"Estimation of recent business demography data", report prepared by Gemma Asero for the Eurostat Working Group on Business Demography, Luxembourg, 2–3 March 2009.

In future years, the EIP will devote more effort to such timely indicators, though not at the expense of the regular production of high-quality, business register-based data that was the original foundation of the programme.

The 2009 edition also saw an expansion of the number of indicators presented, particularly those measuring *Determinants of Entrepreneurship*. Here, too, the EIP had to move beyond the official business register data sources that were the foundation of the core Entrepreneurial Performance indicators and develop data based on various sources, from official government surveys and other sources as well. For this initial release of determinant indicators, only four indicators were presented for each of the six themes set out in Fig. 3.3, above. Many more entrepreneurship determinant indicators are available, though, and this will be a focus of future EIP work. Many sources of data for entrepreneurship determinants will be reviewed to determine availability, relevance, quality and international comparability.

Finally, as noted above, the 2009 edition offered increased geographic coverage with indicators now available for twenty three geographical units, including one emerging country (Brazil) and one region (Andalucía, Spain).

This chapter presents a selection of the EIP indicators. The reader is referred to the publications, available through the EIP website,[5] for all indicators, underlying data tables and additional metadata. The following two sections present the structural indicators and entrepreneurial performance indicators respectively.

3.8.1 Structural Indicators

Unlike the entrepreneurial performance indicators, which focus on employer enterprises, the structural indicators are based on the entire enterprise population. Given differing thresholds and measurement conditions in countries, comparability of data across countries is less strictly observed. All countries present information using the enterprise as the statistical unit except Japan, Korea and Mexico, which use establishments. This may create some lack of comparability but, because most establishments are also enterprises, especially those in smaller size classes, this difference is not felt to be significant. More significant non-comparability may be due to differing thresholds or size-class cut-off depending, often, on tax legislation and efforts to minimise reporting burdens on the smallest businesses.

Nevertheless, this structural information provides a useful general picture of the enterprise population in countries. The charts below illustrate the importance of different size classes in terms of numbers of enterprises, employment, value added and exports. In a sense, these stock indicators can be considered to reflect the results of past entrepreneurship.

As Fig. 3.4 shows, the large majority of enterprises are so-called micro-firms. Firms with fewer than ten employees represent three-quarters or more of the firm population in most countries. Their importance is somewhat less in a number of

---

[5] www.oecd.org/statistics/measuringentrepreneurship

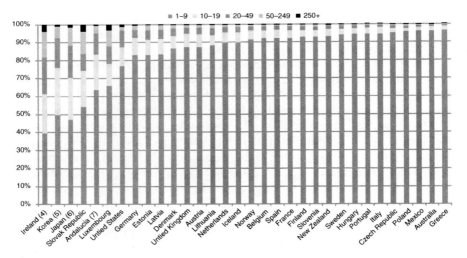

Fig. 3.4 Number of enterprises.[1,2] By size class, 2006[3]
Notes: 1. Market economy, excluding financial intermediation. Manufacturing sectors only for Ireland, Japan, Korea, Luxembourg and the Slovak Republic. 2. Number of establishments for Korea, Japan and Mexico. 3. 2005 for Iceland, 2003 for Mexico. 4. Enterprises with 3 or more persons engaged. 5. Establishments with 5 or more persons engaged. 6. Establishments with 4 or more persons engaged. 7. The data refer to active enterprises, with 4 or more persons engaged and with headquarters in Andalucia.
Source: OECD Structural and Demographic Business Statistics (SDBS) Database.

countries, including Ireland, Korea, Japan, Luxembourg and the Slovak Republic. These differences warrant further study, to ensure that they are not simply due to coverage differences, but the higher proportion of large firms in countries such as Korea and Japan is consistent with other observations on both cultural and administrative impediments to entrepreneurship in these countries. Also, notably, in the United States micro-firms are relatively less prominent than in most other OECD countries. It has been observed that while the United States exhibits rates of churn (entry and exit) similar to other countries, surviving firms grow to larger sizes.

Not surprisingly, Fig. 3.5 shows that the importance of micro-firms is much smaller in terms of employment with a share below 40% in most countries. Indeed, in most countries micro-firms are responsible for between 20 and 30% of total employment in the economy while the share of large firms (over 250 employees) averages between 30 and 40% across countries. The patterns vary considerably, though, and the large firms have a significantly smaller share of employment in countries such as Greece, Italy, Portugal and Spain than in most other countries.

The importance of large firms is even more pronounced in terms of value added and exports, as Figs. 3.6 and 3.7 show. In the majority of countries large firms (more than 250 employees) account for close to 50% of value added. Italy and Greece are

3 OECD-Eurostat Entrepreneurship Indicators Programme

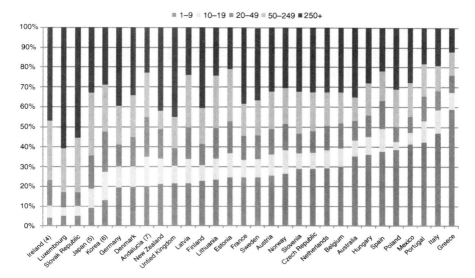

Fig. 3.5 Employment by size class.[1,2] Number of persons engaged, by size class, 2006[3]
Notes: 1. Market economy, excluding financial intermediation. Manufacturing sectors only for Ireland, Japan, Korea, Luxembourg and the Slovak Republic. 2. Number of employees for New Zealand. 3. 2003 for Mexico. 4. Enterprises with 3 or more persons engaged. 5. Establishments with 4 or more persons engaged. 6. Establishments with 5 or more persons engaged. 7. The data refer to active enterprises, with 4 or more persons engaged and with headquarters in Andalucia.
Source: OECD Structural and Demographic Business Statistics (SDBS) Database.

exceptions, though. In these countries, micro-firms account for a larger portion of value added than those with more than 250 employees. Because of the importance of scale economies and fixed costs in exporting, micro (1–9 employees) and small (10–49 employees) firms account for only a small share of total exports. Large firms are responsible for the majority of exports in most countries.

3.8.2 Entrepreneurial Performance Indicators

As mentioned, the core set of indicators developed by the EIP aims to describe the amount and type of entrepreneurship that take place, in particular as concerns birth, death, survival and high-growth of enterprises. Figures 3.8a and 3.8b shows the rate of birth and death in the manufacturing and services sector respectively. For most of the OECD countries, the rate of birth of employer enterprises in manufacturing ranges between 4 and 8%, while rates are slightly higher in East-European countries (including some OECD members). Birth rates are on average higher in the services sector, where they are between 8 and 12%. Also the death rates are higher in services than in manufacturing, but in the majority of countries net entry is positive in both the manufacturing and services sector.

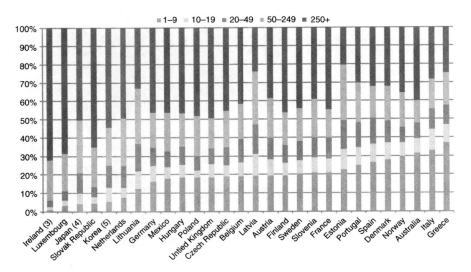

Fig. 3.6 Value added.[1] By size class, 2006[2]
Notes: 1. Market economy, excluding financial intermediation. Manufacturing sectors only for Ireland, Japan, Korea, Luxembourg, Netherlands and the Slovak Republic. 2. 2003 for Mexico. 3. Enterprises with 3 or more persons engaged. 4. Establishments with 4 or more persons engaged. 5. Establishments with 5 or more persons engaged.
Source: OECD Structural and Demographic Business Statistics (SDBS) Database.

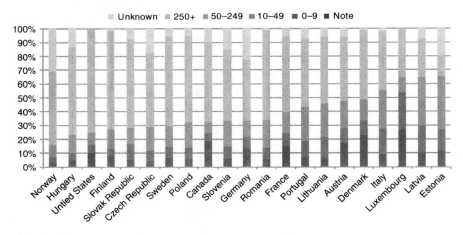

Fig. 3.7 Export by size class 2006, as a percentage of total value. Source: OECD Trade by Enterprise Characteristics (TEC) Database

If the birth and death rates are relatively similar across countries, the survival rates after the first and second year of a new enterprise's life vary more widely and are overall higher in manufacturing than in the services sector (see Figs. 3.9a and 3.9b).

3 OECD-Eurostat Entrepreneurship Indicators Programme

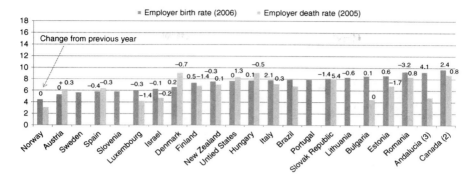

Fig. 3.8a Employer enterprise birth and death rates in manufacturing.[1] As a percentage of the population of active enterprises with at least one employee (figures above the bar indicate change from previous year)
Notes: 1. Mining and quarrying; Manufacturing; Electricity, gas and water. 2. Employer enterprises with fewer than 250 employees. 3. The data refer to establishments and enterprises with 4 or more persons engaged in an economic activity in Andalucía.
Source: OECD Structural and Demographic Business Statistics (SDBS) Database.

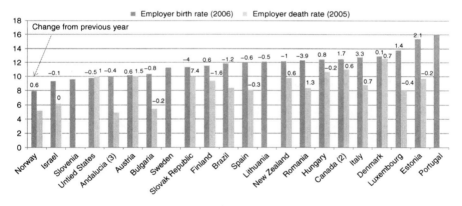

Fig. 3.8b Employer enterprise birth and death rates in services.[1] As a percentage of the population of active enterprises with at least one employee (figures above the bar indicate change from previous year)
Notes: 1. Wholesale and retail trade; Hotels and restaurants; Transport, storage and communications; Financial intermediation; Real estate, renting and business activities. 2. Employer enterprises with fewer than 250 employees. 3. The data refer to establishments and enterprises with 4 more persons engaged in an economic activity in Andalucía.
Source: OECD Structural and Demographic Business Statistics (SDBS) Database.

The indicators presented above, together with the data on high-growth enterprises and gazelles collected by the EIP, constitute an original set of internationally-comparable measures of entrepreneurial performance. For the research community and policy makers, it represents a step forward toward sound comparable analysis and well-designed policy in the area of entrepreneurship.

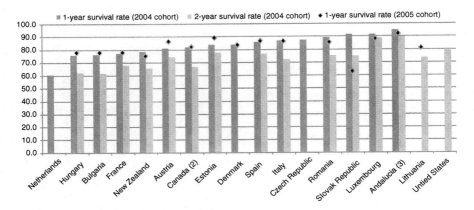

Fig. 3.9a One- and two-year survival rates in manufacturing[1], 2006. As a percentage of the respective 2004 and 2005 population of employer enterprise births in manufacturing
Notes: 1. Mining and quarrying; Manufacturing; Electricity, gas and water. 2. Employer enterprises with less than 250 employees. 3. The data refer to establishments and enterprises with 4 or more persons engaged in an economic activity Andalucia;.
Source: OECD Structural and Demographic Business Statistics (SDBS) Database

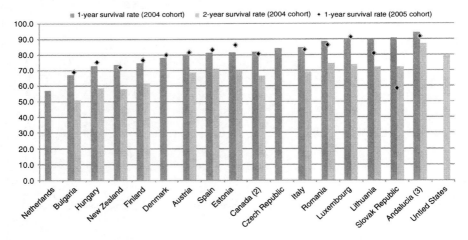

Fig. 3.9b One- and two-year survival rates in services[1], 2006. As a percentage of the respective 2004 and 2005 population of employer enterprise births in services
Notes: 1. Wholesale and retail trade; Hotels and restaurants; Transport, storage and communications; Financial intermediation; Real estate, renting and business activities. 2. Employer enterprises with fewer than 250 employees. 3. The data refer to establishments and enterprises with 4 or more persons engaged in an economic activity in Andalucia.
Source: OECD Structural and Demographic Business Statistics (SDBS) Database.

Finally, it is worth underlying that the EIP draws the indicators of determinants from various existing data sources, including OECD databases (such as the database on Indicators of Product Market Regulation and the Tax Database), the World Bank, GEM, the European Commission and the World Economic Forum. This is to avoid any duplication with other work done within the OECD or by other international organisations. Instead, the EIP concentrates efforts in those determinant areas where data gaps exist or clarification of concepts and definitions is needed; one example of such a gap is "access to finance", as explained below.

It is expected that a deeper understanding of entrepreneurship will result from analytical work investigating the correlation between various determinants and the data on entrepreneurial performance developed by the EIP. The OECD strongly encourages the research community to make use of the EIP data, which are available on the OECD website.

3.8.3 *Future Directions of Work for the Entrepreneurship Indicators Programme*

The current work on the Entrepreneurship Indicators Programme is aimed at achieving greater country coverage and extending the range of performance and determinant indicators. The main objectives include:

Country coverage: The countries/regions currently covered include: Austria, Brazil, Bulgaria, Canada, Denmark, Estonia, Finland, Hungary, Israel, Italy, Lithuania, Luxembourg, New Zealand, Norway, Portugal, Romania, Slovak Republic, Slovenia, Spain, Sweden, United States, and Andalucia (Spain). It is important to extend the coverage of the performance indicators to more OECD members, in particular to large countries not yet participating in the programme, and G20 countries.

The EIP comprehensive framework of indicators is currently being studied as a reference model by UNCTAD for the development of entrepreneurship measures in emerging and developing countries. UNCTAD might start the collection of a reduced set of the EIP performance indicators in emerging and developing countries, adapted to the challenges of data collection in these countries.

New indicators of entrepreneurial performance: The Programme has launched work to develop a number of specific indicators in response to policy makers' interest in deeping understanding in the following areas:

Indicators	Contributing to OECD activities on:
Women entrepreneurship	Horizontal Project "Gender Equality in the Economy: Education, Employment and Entrepreneurship"
Green entrepreneurship	Green Growth Strategy
Migrant entrepreneurs	International Migration Division work on "Entrepreneurship and Employment creation of immigrants in OECD countries"
Ownership rate of start-ups and business population	Studies on globalisation
Value added, productivity contribution, innovation and job creation by young firms	Follow-up to the OECD Innovation Strategy OECD Employment Analysis
(improving measures of) High-growth firm rates	At the request of several members, sensitivity analysis to test different ways of calculating the share of gazelles

Timely indicators of entrepreneurship: This module of the EIP consists in developing more "timely indicators" of entry and exit rates by using alternative national data series (e.g. chambers of commerce, business associations, bankruptcies). While the performance indicators produced by the EIP have a high degree of comparability as they are based on internationally harmonised definitions, their downside is that they typically are 2- or 3-years old. The collection of more timely indicators will complement the EIP indicators by using data based on national definitions only. When possible, adjustments will be made to get as close as possible to the EIP standard definitions (for example by removing agriculture and public companies, excluding inactive companies, etc.). The project involves an in-depth analysis of available data sources to understand the concepts underpinning the data and the differences with the EIP harmonised definitions.

Entrepreneurial determinants: The EIP will continue to improve the selection of indicators for each of the six determinant areas by identifying additional or alternative indicators from existing sources and developing new indicators when needed. In particular, work has been undertaken to enhance comparability of measures of access to finance, specifically equity capital. The work will review the OECD definition of venture capital currently used for harmonising venture capital data across countries; investigate the possibility of constructing indicators from information collected from invested firms as opposed to data collected from venture capital or business angels associations; and develop concepts and methodologies for the collection of data on business angels.

References

Ahmad N, Seymour R (2008) Defining entrepreneurial activity: definitions supporting frameworks for data collection. OECD Statistics Directorate Working Paper, STD/DOC(2008)1

Bartelsman EJ, Scarpetta S, Schivardi F (2002) Comparative analysis of firm demographics and survival: micro-level evidence for the OECD countries. OECD Economics Dept Working Paper, 2002

European Commission (2003) Green paper entrepreneurship in Europe. Brussels, 21.01.2003, COM(2003) 27 final

Eurostat/OECD (2007) Eurostat-OECD manual on business demography statistics. OECD, Paris

Hoffmann A (2007) A rough guide to entrepreneurship policy. In: Thurik R, Audretsch D, Grilo I (eds) Handbook of research on entrepreneurship policy. Edward Elgar Press, Northampton, MA, pp. 140–152

Hornaday RW (1992) Thinking about entrepreneurship: a fuzzy set approach. J Small Bus Manage 30(4):12–23

OECD (2006) Structural and Demographic Business Statistics 1996–2003, 2006 Edition. OECD, Paris

OECD (2008) Measuring entrepreneurship, a digest of indicators. OECD, Paris

OECD Structural and Demographic Business Statistics (SDBS), OECD Database

OECD Productivity Database

Schumpeter JA (1934) The theory of economic development: an inquiry into profits, capital, credit, interest and the business cycle. Harvard University Press, Cambridge, MA

Ucbasaran D, Westhead PH, Wright M (2001) The focus of entrepreneurial research: contextual and process issues. Entrepreneurship Theory Pract (Summer): 57–80

Watson CH (2001) Small business versus entrepreneurship revisited. In: Brockhaus RH, Gerald EH, Heinz K, Harold PW, (eds) Entrepreneurship education: a global view. Ashgate, Aldershot

Chapter 4
The Peculiarities of SMEs in Europe and Italy: Technology Transfer Policies

Riccardo Gallo and Marco Iezzi

Abstract This paper aims to review and summarize the theme of technology transfer. Introducing the topic, first of all, the Authors will focus on the peculiarities of Italian small- and medium-sized enterprises. They will begin comparing the productive structure of Italian economy with other countries'; then they will focus on small-sized enterprises and their low innovation and co-operation capabilities. A relevant part of this work will be on the strategic relevance of the technology transfer; finally the authors will describe the role of RIDITT: this acronym stands for Italian Network for Innovation and technology transfer to SMEs.

4.1 Introduction

In the last decades competitiveness has become a key parameter in the economic policy of several states: it includes innovation, flexibility and research & development (R&D). It is essential to support the creation of excellence and to reduce fragmentation in order to generate innovative technology to drive economic growth. The regional dimension has become more and more important in improving European competition at a global level.

The Italian economic system has peculiarities that set it apart from the main international players. As we know, the Italian industrial system is characterized by a predominance of small- and medium-sized enterprises (SMEs). SMEs are about 90% of Italian companies (four million SMEs, representing 20% of all the SMEs in Europe, to give a general impression) mainly traditional industries, where innovation only means modernization in machinery and not a long term strategy. There is a lack of large technology-based companies in industries such as microelectronics,

R. Gallo (✉)
Dipartimento Ingegneria Chimica Materiali Ambiente, Università di Roma "Sapienza",
Via del Castro Laurenziano 7, 00161 Roma, Italy
e-mail: riccardo.gallo@uniroma1.it

This paper is the result of a common work, however paragraphs 1, 2 and 3 have to be attributed to Marco Iezzi and paragraphs 4, 5 and 6 to Riccardo Gallo.

robotics, chemicals and biomedical technologies, a limited vocation to patent applications or to efficient exploitation of existing patents in high-tech commercial activities. Then, in Italy there is a low percentage of students undertaking scientific and technical degrees compared to other European countries and to the US, and a shortage of financial support for R&D due to insufficient participation of private investors.

Moreover, a venture capital market still needs to be developed, especially in the high technology fields and public administration has introduced significant activities, but a long-term vision (pluri-annual planning) is frequently lacking, resulting in uncoordinated measures.

In this scenario, we will describe the strategic relevance of technology transfer, showing how technological progress is undertaken in a limited number of developed countries: with seven OECD countries that account for 90% of all expenditures on R&D, the United States alone accounting for as much as 40%. The inventions are transferred to other countries through various channels. Most countries make thus an insignificant contribution to the development of new technology. Adoption of foreign invented technology has proved to be a condition for industrial development.

At the end of our work, we will focus on the role of the Italian network for innovation and technology transfer to SMEs and we will try to explain how this network can improve the competitiveness of the productive system reinforcing the supply of technologies services developed by Italian universities and research centres.

4.2 The Productive Structure of Italian Economy Vs Other Countries'

In the last 2 years, the Italian economy has been characterized by a low growth rate that has kept it well below its potential production frontier, also entailing a sharply lower public deficit. The main driver has been strong foreign demand and an evident adjustment process among Italian exporters that has allowed them to benefit from the favourable external conditions. Even so, Italy's export structure remains heavily biased toward low-skill production, highly exposed to cost competition by emerging economies in the present era of globalisation. The process of deindustrialisation has also not triggered a take off in services sectors, as in some of the more successful OECD countries. This macro-structural weakness can be attributed to a lack of total factor productivity growth, reflecting the shortcomings in efficiency, process and product innovation. A main policy challenge is to raise human capital and market competition to spur both the supply and demand for innovation and skills and to dynamize to the economy.

Employment creation has been a main bright spot in the economy, but there is the need to go further by rebalancing employment protections to reduce labour market duality. As we can see from the OECD *Economic survey of Italy 2009*, a large regional gap and a still too low formal labour market participation may be part of the current problem, but they are also the source of significant unrealised growth potential. Gross public debt was around 106% of GDP in 2008. Substantial progress had been made in cutting the ratio of debt to GDP since the mid-1990s, but partly based on one-off tax and revenue measures that were not sustained.[1]

In addition, economic and political troubles had a negative effect on the development of industrial sectors, although agents hope that new programmes and increased marketing will bring in new business over the next 12 months. Bank of Italy, in a recent economic forecast, assumed that economy has slowed along with many other countries worldwide as a result of the downturn in the US property market in 2007. Regarding the Italian public deficit, OECD projections suggest that the public deficit will reach 6% of GDP in 2010, with debt over 115% of GDP and rising, even with some effort at fiscal consolidation.

For the Institute for Studies and Economic Analyses (ISAE) it is expected that Italy's GDP will decrease at an annual rate of around 4.7% in 2009 and 0.6% in 2010. Consumer inflation is expected to average just over 0.8% in 2009, dropping to around 1% at the end of the year. This reflects the price decrease in crude oil. Exports are likely to expand at a slower pace than international trade, reflecting the loss of price competitiveness of Italian goods, which is forecasted to continue in 2010.[2]

As Table 4.1 shows, we can appreciate the relevant role of SMEs in the main industrialized economies. The chart is divided in two different parts. Analysing the dataset, we can see that both periods show a great number of small enterprises in Italy.

Table 4.1 The Role of SMEs in the main industrialized economies

	2000				2006			
	1–9	10–49	50–249	+250	1–9	10–49	50–249	+250
France	82.0%	13.7%	3.4%	0.9%	83.4%	12.9%	3.0%	0.8%
Germany	67.3%	23.7%	7.2%	1.9%	60.2%	29.3%	8.4%	2.1%
ITALY	83.6%	14.4%	1.8%	0.3%	82.9%	14.8%	2.0%	0.3%
Spain	78.6%	18.5%	2.4%	0.4%	78.6%	18.2%	2.8%	0.5%
United Kingdom	70.7%	21.7%	6.1%	1.5%	74.5%	18.9%	5.3%	1.2%
Eu-14	78.2%	17.3%	3.7%	0.9%	79.4%	16.4%	3.5%	0.7%
United States	59.7%	32.0%	4.8%	3.4%	62.6%	30.2%	4.3%	2.9%

Source: OECD
Note: Eu14 and UK 2005 dataset; USA 2004 dataset. Eu 14 excluding Luxemburg

---

[1] OECD (2009).
[2] Bank of Italy (2009).

4.3 Enterprises' Small Size and Their Low Innovation and Co-operation Capabilities

As European Commission wrote *innovation can be both a simple and difficult concept to grasp*, at its most basic it refers to new products and procedures, a different organization or a novel marketing strategy, and these do not necessarily have to be high tech. There are no easy solutions to innovation growth. To have a real impact, the policy requires support for risk taking and a holistic approach that encompasses a range of balanced and complementary measures.[3]

Research is one component, but other ingredients are also important. The right kind of education to produce the necessary skills, the existence of an encouraging business environment and support services, access to venture capital, technology transfer, and the development of clusters are just some of the factors that encourage entrepreneurs to push forward the boundaries of knowledge.

International collaboration in R&D is becoming a crucial way of developing knowledge. This has a decisive importance in the competitiveness of research and business. As both the business environment and knowledge creation become more and more global, small- and medium-sized enterprises act in a global environment and their activities, including R&D, are increasingly crossing national boundaries.

Despite the increasing importance of global business and international R&D, innovation and technology policy largely remain within the responsibility of national governments. Although much data on innovation is collected within the borders of nation states, knowledge creation and transfer does not respect such boundaries. There is no evidence for assuming that corporate knowledge creation would be tied to the nation, nor that future developments will depend on national systems. However, an examination of the dynamics of knowledge creation suggests that knowledge networking and creation is increasingly taking place at the global level. As both business environment and knowledge creation become more and more global, even SMEs are acting in a global environment and activities, including R&D, are increasingly perceived as truly global, not national or cross-border activities.

Figure 4.1 illustrates the size and sector breakdowns; in particular it shows the proportion of enterprises with innovation activities (sometimes referred to as the proportion of innovation active firms). *Innovation activity* indicates, here, that the firm reported the introduction of a new product or process and had innovation activities that were incomplete or leaved in the period 2002–2004. In all countries, we have considered only large enterprises investments in innovation technology.

In the period 1990–2005, (Fig. 4.2) the labour market showed a substantial change, with structural unemployment becoming increasingly severe from one recession to another. At the same time, the skill profile changed too, with knowledge workers assuming a dominant position in terms of growth despite its small share.

That was also the period during which computerization recorded the most rapid growth as technology advanced. The employment effects of technology, in general, and of computers, in particular, have been a topic of controversy. Some criticize

---

[3] European Commission (2006).

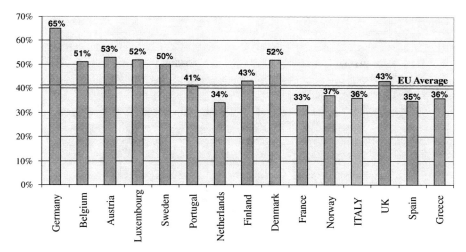

Fig. 4.1 Enterprises with innovation activity, % of all enterprises 2002–2004
Source: Fourth Comminity Innovation Survey

the intrinsic labour-saving bias, which leads to income inequality and marginalizes a large category of workers, especially the low-skilled, forcing them to join the increasing ranks of the unemployed.

For those who share this pessimistic vision, the end result is structural unemployment, where displaced workers have considerable problems becoming reemployed, since they may not have the skills needed to work in a context in which technology is key. In those decades, electronics and microelectronics have given impetus to the development of new and powerful technological trajectories which will eventually have a much greater impact than any effect computerization may have.

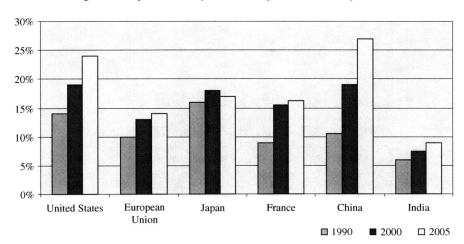

Fig. 4.2 High-tech share of all manufactureing industry value-added revenue for selected regions/countries: 1990, 2000, and 2005
Source: Science and Engineering Indicators, 2008

In other words, the computer has been very successful in replacing modifiable knowledge but quite inadequate in replacing tacit knowledge. The new generations of technology, created through the fusion of electronics, biology and other technologies, will quite probably directly target the replacement of tacit knowledge which, up to now, has been fundamentally a human preserve. We can see, also, the extreme growth of China in last years.

Next bar-chart (Fig. 4.3) gives a measure of firms' propensity to engage in innovation activity, through the introduction of a new product to the market or the performance of a new means of production or supply of goods and services.

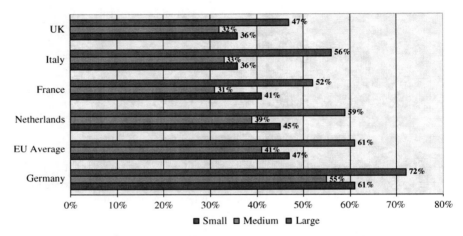

Fig. 4.3 Proportion of enterprises with innovation activity (by size of enterprise)
Source: International Comparisons of the Third Community Innovation Survery, 2004

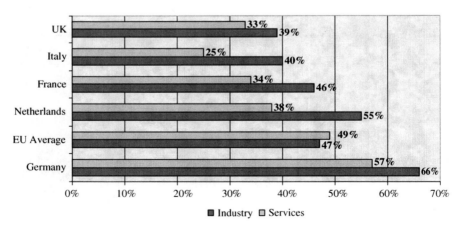

Fig. 4.4 Proportion of enterprises with innovation activity (by sector of enterprise)
Source: International Comparisons of the Third Community Innovation Survery, 2004

Otherwise in this work, we analyse innovation activity by sector of enterprise. It is remarkable that in all countries considered (Fig. 4.4) the industrial sectors invest more in technologies than the service sector.

Germany has the highest proportion of enterprises with innovation activities in the industrial sector, with 66% and is a long way ahead of its main competitors, although this may in part be a reflection of the different sample structure used in Germany.

Analysing the European Innovation Scoreboard of 2006 (EIS), the instrument developed at the initiative of the European Commission, under the Lisbon Strategy, to evaluate and compare the innovation performance of the EU Member States, we can see that only 4.3% of Italian SMEs co-operate with other firms, Universities or Research Centres on innovation projects. In addition the Italian SMEs prefer to co-operate with other firms, rather than working with the public research system (Fig. 4.5).

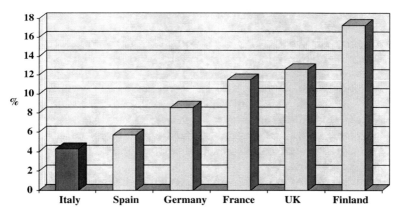

Fig. 4.5 The industrial network (European Innovation Scoreboard 2006)
Source: Gallo R, Mallone M, and Zenna V (2008), Trasferimento tecnologico: l'intervento Riditt

From the European Innovation Scoreboard of 2007, we see that Sweden, Finland, Denmark, Germany and UK are the most innovative EU countries and ahead of US. Italy is included in the *moderate innovators* with Australia, Cyprus, Czech Republic, Estonia, Italy, Norway, Slovenia and Spain. The *moderate innovators* are close to or below average across the dimensions. However, Norway is performing relatively well in Innovation drivers, performance is relatively worse for Italy in Innovation drivers and Innovation & entrepreneurship. The relative gap between the moderate innovators and innovation leaders tends to be greatest in Intellectual Property.[4]

---

[4] European Innovation Scoreboard (2007).

4.4 The Strategic Relevance of the "Technology Transfer"

Technology Transfer (TT) has become a major issue for research institutions. It is used, not only for generating business by licensing out inventions made by the researchers but, also, to demonstrate the relevance of the research projects for the general society. New and better products create new jobs, spin-off companies contribute to the modernizing of the industry and are a source for co-operation projects in new and innovative fields of technology.

In other words, technology transfer refers to the dissemination of new knowledge from a source, such as a research laboratory, to recipients, such as commercial firms, or the public, who benefit in some way from the knowledge.

As a capital good, new knowledge is employed as an input to an economic production process: new knowledge contributes to the production of goods and services in much the same way that raw materials, machinery, and workers do. More specifically, new knowledge can affect the mix of inputs in a way that increases the net benefits that can be realized from a productive process.

The trouble of technology transfer is to identify efficient means for new knowledge dissemination. The licensing of commercially valuable research results is one form of technology transfer. As we appreciate, technology to be new knowledge created through research and development, scientific publication is another form of technology transfer, although it is not widely recognized as such. Technology transfer is linked to the process of knowledge creation; for example, policies that encourage technology licensing may result in a shift from basic to applied research efforts and possibly a reduction in scientific publication. Therefore technology transfer policy must be analyzed as a component of more general policies to encourage new knowledge creation.

The main purpose of technology transfer is to aid different economies by making their products more competitive in world markets. The concept of technology transfer is to get the ideas, inventions and technologies developed into the hands of the private sector as quickly as possible in a form useful to that community. The idea is to get the private sector involved in the development of technology products at an early stage so that the end result is a useful new product or service offered on world markets. There are a multitude of benefits for all players in the technology transfer challenge. Industry benefits with new and better products, processes, and services that lead to increased efficiency and effectiveness, greater market share and increased profits. By benefiting industries, the economy is strengthened which, in turn, benefits all citizens. Different laboratories benefit by becoming more responsive to the needs of the constituents that they serve, demonstrating their viability and worth to the diverse sector, and generating non-appropriated funds to aid them in performing their important research and development missions. About the employees, they can benefit by earning rewards above and beyond their regular salary through patents, licenses, and other technology transfer awards. They also can benefit intellectually and professionally working collaboratively with their peers in the industrial sector.

4.5 The Role of RIDITT in Italy

Launched in January 2003, RIDITT (the Italian Network for Innovation and Technology Transfer to SMEs) aims at improving the competitiveness of SMEs by strengthening the supply of services for innovation and technology transfer as well as the creation of new hi-tech enterprises, with special attention to Italian less developed areas. RIDITT acts as the Italian focal point of the International Network for SMEs (INSME).

RIDITT aims at being an information hub and a reference point in Italy for innovation centres in order to:

- promote the exchange of information, experiences, methodologies and good practices at national level;
- encourage the integration, specialisation and marketing of services for SMEs' innovation, also through the use of ICT;
- stimulate the creation of partnerships and projects on a sectoral and geographical basis;
- facilitate access to financial resources by creating, extending and developing networks for innovation;
- support the internationalisation of innovation centres, even by means of the INSME international network.

RIDITT offers free-of-charge services to public and private operators. The services are mainly provided via the internet, at the web site www.riditt.it, and includes first of all *Information Services* as catalogues of services and technologies provided by innovation centres, as well as an observatory on good practices, public financing sources and national and regional programmes and initiatives; and also *Technical Assistance and Training* in partner search; ideation and development of pilot projects; assistance in the acquisition of public and private funds; benchmarking on policies, programmes and the performance of innovation centres.

Innovation centres for innovation and technology transfer to SMEs are the main beneficiaries of RIDITT's services. These centres include Science and Technology Parks, Incubators, Universities' and Research Bodies' industrial liaison offices, Local development agencies, etc. SMEs will also benefit from the RIDITT Network, which will enable them to be connected to a hub for the search of know-how and competences across the country. Public bodies operating in the planning and management of research and innovation programmes targeting SMEs can also access the network services.[5]

RIDITT is promoted by the Italian Ministry of Economic Development and managed by the Italian Institute for Industrial Promotion (IPI). It is an initiative aimed at improving the competitiveness of the productive system by strengthening and

---

[5] Cf. RIDITT brochure.

integrating the available supply of services for innovation. It offers a database on technologies developed by Italian universities and research centres. Information is organised by industrial sector and technological area of interest.

Regarding the amount of financing technology transfer projects, we can declare that, up to now, 2.72 million of Euro are available for the Program and the measures of the distinctive elements regards:

- technology transfer;
- pre-defined technological areas (automation, materials, biotechnologies);
- co-operation university & entrepreneurial associations.
- In replaying to *2005 call* we have counted 42 calls for industrial innovation projects submitted for 40 million of Euro, with 203 organizations involved (66 Entrepreneurs' Associations, 50 Universities, 24 Research Centres). Reading these data we can assume that the relevance of technology transfer will increase in the future, due to enhanced complexity and need of explanation of new technologies.

4.6 Concluding Remarks

Innovation, and especially technological innovation, has become the *touchstone* in the last decades. Furthermore, Italy and Europe are not the only countries seeking it. Innovation has been the focal point both of enterprises as well as of governments at an international level. It is what the biggest internationalized companies are seeking for their development but, also, a condition for the survival of the small- and medium-sized enterprises in all fields and economies at a global level.

Innovations improve the way works are applied and may automate a considerable part of them achieving thus lower costs, higher quality of products and fast results. The core of innovation is twofold. We mean business innovation which concerns new, more efficient procedures of the enterprise, new ways of work, new markets and new ideas and approaches as regards co-operation with the suppliers, customers and executives. From the other side, we mean technological innovation, new innovative technologies of every kind which strengthen the capabilities of enterprises. These two dimensions are clear and complement each other. According to the definition of OECD[6]: *competitiveness at a national level is the degree to which a country can, under free and fair market conditions, produce goods which meet the test of international markets, while simultaneously maintaining and expanding the real incomes of its people over the long-term, national competitiveness, therefore, depends on the competitiveness of the individual branches of the economy.*

After almost 50 years, the investments on infrastructures and the macroeconomic targeting did not manage to amazingly promote the growth rates of the

---

[6]OECD (2007).

less rich countries. These countries benefited, of course, getting away from poverty in many cases, but did not manage to compete on equal terms with the advanced countries. Competitive economies have faster growth rates, that is, the economies which liberalized their markets and in which enterprises are competitive in the international environment, having dynamically adopted innovations.

It is important to remember that the competitiveness of a country depends on the productivity of the fields of its economy, even if they are fields of the *old economy*; but macro-economic stability is a main prerequisite. Than restrictions which encumber the productivity of enterprises (such as setting-up restrictions, artificial operation restrictions, etc.) reduce the competitiveness of the country.

The most significant conclusion, though, is that the productivity of enterprises, especially of the bigger fields of the economy, is the key for national competitiveness. This conclusion that business competitiveness is the one leading national competitiveness and not vice-versa will be true if it can be proven in practice. In this way, the approach for improving the competitiveness of the country definitely involves innovation and the effort of the enterprises to improve their productivity.

Technology must constitute the basic parameter for the support of new, more efficient and faster service relation between the citizens and enterprises so that the public sector will support and promote business competitiveness instead of delaying it. This dimension is also the equivalent of technological innovation that the public sector must assume. The targets of the public sector for the development and competitiveness of the country in the international scenario do not differ from the targets of the private sector. The way for improving national competitiveness goes through innovation and business productivity; national competitiveness will be strengthened to the extent Italian enterprises will aim to achieve business and technological innovation so as to improve their productivity. The role of the public sector, in this effort, is important in order to secure some of the prerequisites and to achieve the correct operation of the market.

Acknowledgment We would like to express our special thank to Marco Calabrò and Giancarlo Fiorito for their suggestions. The views expressed in the article are those of the authors and do not involve the responsibility of the institutions in which they work and, as always, the authors of the work are the only responsible for the content of it.

References

Alfó M, Trovato G (2006) Credit rationing and the financial structure of Italian small and medium enterprises. J Appl Econ. Universidad de Buenos Aires, 9:167–184
Bank of Italy (2009) Overview Economic Bulletin No. 58, Rome
Barro R, Sala-I-Martin X (1997) Technological diffusion, convergence, and growth. J Econ Growth 2:1–26
Bozeman B (2000) Technology transfer and public policy: a review of research and theory. Res Policy 29:627–655
Cainelli G, De Marchi M, Leoncini R, Poti B (2003) Ricerca e innovazione nelle imprese. In: M. Scarda (ed) Rapporto sul sistema scientifico e tecnologico in Italia. F. Angeli, Milano, pp. 163–174

Castellacci F, Grodal S, Mendonca S, Wibe M (2005) Advances and challenges in innovation studies. J Econ Iss Bucknell University, Lewisburg, US 39:91–121

Cohen W (1995) Empirical studies of innovative activity. In: Stoneman P (ed) Handbook of the economics of innovation and technological change. Basil Blackwell, Oxford, pp. 182–264

De Marchi M, Poti' BM, Reale E, Rocchi M, Scarda AM (2000) Il Monitoraggio della scienza e della tecnologia. F. Angeli, Milano

European Communities (2007) European innovation scoreboard 2007: comparative analysis of innovation performance. Luxembourg

European Communities (2006) European innovation scoreboard 2006: comparative analysis of innovation performance. Luxembourg

Faber J, Hesen B (2004) Innovation capabilities of European nations: cross-national analyses of patents and sales of product innovations. Res Policy 33:193–207

Gallo R, Mallone M, Zezza V (2008) Trasferimento tecnologico: l'intervento Riditt. In: Oltre lo stato regolatore: scenari e politiche industriali per un'economia globalizzata. A cura di Cesare Pozzi, L'Industria numero speciale 2008, Il Mulino, Bologna

Huergo E, Jaumandreu J (2004) how does probability of innovation change with firm age? small business economics. Springer, New York, NY, pp 187–202

Istat (2006) The Italian innovation survey: methodological issues and operational process, Unit for Innovation and R/D statistics, Rome

Kingsley G, Bozeman B, Coker K (1996) Technology transfer and absorption: an "R&D value-mapping" approach to evaluation. Res Policy 25: 967–995

Klette J, Kortum S (2002) Innovating firms and aggregate innovation, Staff Report 300, Federal Reserve Bank of Minneapolis

Mairesse J, Mohnen P (2002) Accounting for innovation and measuring innovativeness: an illustrative framework and an application. Am Econ Rev, Papers and Proceedings, 92, pp. 226–230

Mayer S, Blaas W (2002) Technology transfer: an opportunity for small open economies. J Tech Transf 27:275–289

Mortensen P (2007) Innovation Indicators: more than technology? 32 CEIES Seminar, Arhus, Denmark, 5–6 Feb 2007

OECD (2008) Oecd science, technology and industry outlook. Paris, France

OECD (2007) Economic survey of Italy 2007. Paris, France

Pianta M, Vaona A (2007) innovation and productivity in european industries, economics of innovation and new technology. Taylor and Francis Journals, Oxford, pp 485–499

Porter ME, Van Opstal D (2001) US competitiveness 2001: strengths, vulnerabilities and long-term priorities. Council on Competitiveness, Washington, DC

Samitas A, Kenourgios D (2005) Entrepreneurship, small and medium size business markets and European economic integration. J Policy Model 27:363–374

Struys W (2004) The future of the defence firm in small and medium countries. Defence Peace Econ 15:551–564

Webster E (2003) Firms' decisions to innovate and innovation routines, Melbourne Institute Working Paper Series 2003, N.5, University of Melbourne, Australia

Chapter 5
Public Policies for Italian SMEs: Instruments, Results and Current Trends

Aurelio Bruzzo

Abstract Following the recent publication of a number of studies on public interventions in Italy regarding SMEs – including crafts firms – this study has a twofold purpose: firstly, to provide a succinct account of the numerous further interventions undertaken for SMEs during the past decade; secondly, to examine the problems apparent in the current phase of structural crisis, also in light of the results obtained to date and those emerging from the official documentation, in order to conduct a critical evaluation of public policies for Italian SMEs. Consequently, the study divides substantially into two parts. The first one provides a survey of the industrial policy measures addressed to SMEs adopted both by the central government and the regional and local administrations during the period considered. The second part describes the state of progress currently achieved by such measures. It dwells in particular on the provision entitled "Industria 2015", in regard to which it estimates the amount of the various financial incentives exclusively allocated to SMEs, thereby making a contribution of particular interest and originality to the scientific debate. Finally, the concluding section outlines the prospects for SMEs in the near future that seemingly emerge from the most recent provisions adopted at national level.

5.1 Introduction: The Assumptions, Aims and Contents of the Study

There is no doubt that, during the past decade, both the European Community institutions and Italian public administrations have continued to issue various provisions in favour of small and medium-sized enterprises (SMEs) operating in Italy. Moreover, recent years have seen publication in Italy of various surveys reporting, amongst other things, the results of industrial policies providing financial incentives (Ministero dello Sviluppo Economico, 2009), for SMEs in particular (Brancati,

---

A. Bruzzo (✉)
Dipartimento di Economia Istituzioni Territorio, Università di Ferrara, Via Voltapaletto, 11, 44121 Ferrara, Italy
e-mail: bruzzo@economia.unife.it

2001; de Blasio and Lotti, 2008). As a consequence, now available is further information with which to update – although they have been conducted very recently – some previous studies by the present author on public policies towards SMEs, including crafts firms.[1]

The study therefore has two purposes: firstly, to describe as succinctly as possible the numerous and differentiated interventions adopted for Italian SMEs during the past decade, seeking to show their critical aspects; secondly, to examine the problems evident in the ongoing phase of structural crisis in light not only of the scientific literature but also of the most recent official documentation, the purpose being to conduct a critical appraisal of public policies for Italian SMEs.

In pursuit of these aims, the study divides into two main parts. The first (Sects. 5.2, 5.3, and 5.4) seeks – also by drawing on such an authoritative international source as the OECD (Organisation for Economic Co-operation and Development) – to furnish a summary description of the industrial policy measures for SMEs adopted by both the central government and the regional and local administrations during the period considered. The second part (Sects. 5.5 and 5.6) deals mainly with the present state of progress of such measures. It dwells in particular on the provision denominated "Industria 2015", in regard to which – owing to the difficulties encountered in determining the tax relief and benefits envisaged for SMEs – a quantitative estimate will be conducted of the amount of the various financial facilities foreseen by the normative provisions concerned exclusively with firms of this type.

Finally, the concluding section outlines the prospects for the near future that seemingly emerge from the provisions most recently adopted at national level for SMEs: a provision issued by the Italian government in regard to Urban Free Zones (UFZs), and a directive implementing the European Community Small Business Act (SBA).

In conclusion this introduction, it should be pointed out that this study does not directly examine the policies for SMEs adopted by the European Community, although they are closely linked with those of the Italian (central and decentralized) administrations. In fact, their numerousness, heterogeneity, and importance preclude their treatment together with those of a single member-country of the European Union (EU); instead, their separate discussion would be required. Hence, they are mentioned here only when they have been implemented jointly with Italian policies and cannot be sharply distinguished from them. Consequently, by analogy, no particular attention will be paid to analysis of the aid given to SMEs within national re-equilibrium policies targeted on the country's late-developing southern regions.

5.2 The Main Provisions on Italian SMEs in the Past Ten Years

According to the OECD, which already in 2000 on the occasion of the first Ministerial Conference on SMEs drew up a document on policies concerning firms of such kind, Italy's economic policy approach to small firms during the first half

---

[1] The reference is to Bernardi et al. (2008) and Bruzzo (2009a, 2009b), works which may also be consulted for an ampler, albeit less recent, bibliography.

of the decade divided into three main strands: reduction and simplification of fiscal constraints in order to stimulate investments; reform of the labour market in order to increase its flexibility; and elimination of excessive bureaucracy (red tape) (OECD, 2005). Whilst it is true that the first two strands seek to remedy two of the main difficulties encountered by SMEs, it is also true that they do not exclusively concern such enterprises: they assume more general significance in that they work to the advantage of the productive system as a whole, and therefore also of large firms.

This observation can be extended to large part of the other measures considered by the last *Outlook* published on the subject by the OECD and concerning: the administrative simplification by creating "one-stop shops" for productive activities; access to infrastructures both basic (transport, etc.) and technological (broadband, computerization of the public administration, etc.); the development of an entrepreneurial society and culture, with particular regard to female entrepreneurship, through specific initiatives especially in training; easier access to financing for investments through the business angels networks proposed by the European Community; e-commerce as a form of organizational innovation through the computerization in this case of the enterprises themselves; and finally the consolidation of networks, clusters and partnerships among enterprises of various sizes, also through simplification of the concept of industrial district.[2]

With the purpose of verifying the existence, and consequently the identity, of policies targeted – exclusively or predominantly – on SMEs, it is necessary to consider the set of legal-institutional instruments devised for their support and development, starting from the division between the state and the regional governments of powers regarding the industrial policies undertaken, not without difficulties, some years ago (Bernardi et al., 2008). In fact, despite the significant reforms enacted in the late 1990s and early 2000s, some years later, the demarcation line established by law among the roles assigned to the central authorities, the regional administrations, and local authorities in the field of industrial policy (which is a concurrent matter among them) is still not entirely clear. In fact, following the administrative devolution implemented towards the end of the 1990s (in application of the Bassanini Law), as well as the more radical institutional amendment made to Title V of the Italian Constitution – in accordance with the subsidiarity principle – one notes the existence, at least in abstract, of the following duality of competence in regard to industrial policies.

(a) The state performs a coordinating and steering role, and assumes responsibility for higher-level actions (those concerning large-scale operators or sectors particularly important for development of the productive system). It also coordinates the actions of the other levels of government by defining rules intended

---

[2]The OECD publication obviously also deals with measures such as the internazionalization of enterprises, access to global markets, and the diffusion of technological innovation. These topics, however, are examined later.

to maximize the effectiveness of policies, preventing overlaps or, vice versa, the crowding-out of roles, as well as the waste of public resources.

(b) The regional administrations and local authorities promote and manage, also in accordance with EC guidelines, interventions concerned mainly with SMEs and the development of local areas, as well as the marketing of local products.

This articulation of public intervention on several levels of governance seems to have increased the role of the Italian Regions in the field of industrial policies: indeed, since 2000 they have managed not only the instruments established by their specific legislations but also those devolved to them: that is, all the government facilitative instruments in being at the moment of their "delegation".[3] The central administration has retained only a limited number of instruments, although they are important ones, such as the regulations on investment incentives for large industrial firms (law no. 488/1992) or those on the Fund for Technological Innovation (Fondo per l'Innovazione Tecnologica, FIT) and the Research Incentive Fund (Fondo Agevolazioni Ricerca, FAR).

However, this fundamental distinction has become less clear under recent legislatures, which have changed the logic of public intervention through adoption by the central government of a series of provisions, the most important of which are now described in chronological order:

(i) the introduction of a support system for firms hinging on the role of the Interministerial Committee for Economic Planning (Comitato Interministeriale per la Programmazione Economica, CIPE), which, also through forms of shared planning with local public and private actors, has become a body working for the development of SMEs and industrial districts;

(ii) the Action Plan for Economic, Social and Territorial Development (Piano di Azione per lo Sviluppo Economico, Sociale e Territoriale, introduced by law no. 80/2005, the so-called "law for competitiveness"), whose implementation has among other things led to reform of financial incentives with a view to superseding their "generalist" nature and to achieve closer accord between firms and banks on access to credit;

(iii) the issue (in 2005) of regulations on the award of a "concentration bonus" to SMEs,[4]

---

[3] The mechanism adopted for transferring the necessary financial resources to the Regions consists in the creation of a single Fund for all the interventions, obviously divided among the Regions themselves. Each Region can add its own resources to these government ones.

[4] In fact, among the difficulties encountered by the SMEs some scholars also include the limited size itself (in terms of employment, etc.) of SMEs, so that another possible policy would be the concentration or merger of several small firms into one of large size. In reality, however, the transformation of the entire small firms' system into companies of medium or large size cannot be considered the best route to follow in a country like Italy, for the simple reason that it would be resisted by entrepreneurs very often unwilling to relinquish their identity and individuality; see Bianchi (2008).

5 Public Policies for Italian SMEs

(iv) the 2006 budget law which, amongst other things, provided for issue of a decree stating the criteria for defining the productive districts to which tax concessions and administrative simplifications were granted,[5]

(v) the 2006–2008 Triennial Plan, which redefined intervention policies, also foreseeing reform of facilities for so-called "under-utilized" areas;

(vi) the identification – within a new industrial policy framework established by the 2007–2011 Economic and Financial Planning Document – of a series of interventions aimed in particular at strengthening material and non-material infrastructures in implementation of the EC strategy for growth and employment (defined in 2000 on the occasion of the European Council in Lisbon);

(vii) the publication of a broad and systematic report entitled "Industria 2015", which delegated powers to the government in regard to reorganization of the public funding system in the field of research and innovation;

(viii) the inclusion in the 2007 budget law of large part of the so-called "Bersani bill", with the creation of funds for the financing of various initiatives (for competitiveness, scientific and technological research, business finance, as well as the rescue and restructuring of firms in difficulties). In regard to this provision, which will be discussed in greater detail in the next section, to be mentioned here is that the implementation of projects involves all the public, national and local administrations, whose actions can contribute to fulfilment of those established at central level. The Regions can contribute on the basis of their productive inclinations, as well as their institutional competences, thereby contributing to projects of national importance. However, it appears evident that these industrial policy choices reverse the roles between State and Regions, in the sense that it is not the regions that expresses their requirements, with which the State conforms, but it is the State that decides, while the Regions merely adapt such decisions to the characteristics of their territory.

A situation substantially similar to the one just described is apparent on considering both internationalization policies (i.e. measures intended to foster foreign trade and to promote the presence of Italian firms on foreign markets) and those concerning innovations (in technology, organization and "product"). In the former case, also because the matter is confused and with overlaps, the practice is for the State to undertake the functions of coordinating and promoting production of national importance, while the decentralized authorities handle the promotion of local products. In the latter case, administrative devolution has transferred to the Regions functions pertaining to the promotion of programmes and projects for applied research and technological transfer, while basic research has remained the competence of the State.

---

[5]For a more detailed description of the 2006 Budget Law containing provisions which may be considered as constituting an outright "statute for productive districts" see Cipollina and Pizzonia (2006).

Panel 5.1 Competences for SMEs support and development

Type of policy	Competence	National	Regional	Local Province	Chamber of commerce
Financial incentives					
a) Internationalization	*Confused*[a]	Framework/ detail/ implementing law	Detail/ implementing	Informative/ implementing	Informative/ implementing
b) Technological innovation	Concurrent	Framework/ implementing law	Detail/ implementing law	Implementing	Informative/ implementing
B1) *Organizational development*	Concurrent	Framework/ detail/ implementing law	Detail/ implementing law	Informative/ implementing	Informative
B2) *Quality*	Concurrent	Framework/ implementing law	Detail/ implementing law	informative implementing	Informative
Context policies					
c) Real and infrastructural services	Concurrent	Programme agreements	Coordination/ implementing	opera-tional	
C1) *Bureaucratic simplification*	Concurrent	Framework/ implementing law	Detail law	opera-tional	

[a] matter exclusive to the State, but also concurrent

At this point it is possible to provide a synopsis (Panel 5.1) which shows the relations effectively operating among the various forms of industrial policy. Two criteria have been used to compile the panel: level of government, and area of intervention.[6] In particular, Panel 5.1 summarizes the roles performed by the various administrations (central and local) in regard to the main types of policy for SMEs. Put extremely briefly, and as has been implied by the foregoing survey, in Italy there prevails an institutional system which is complex and uncoordinated because of the unclear allocation of competences among the various levels of government. This gives rise to interventions whose objectives at least partially overlap.[7]

---

[6] Hence, of the three criteria usually employed for the classification of financial incentives, omitted here is only the typology criterion.

[7] Which level of government is best suited to the efficient development of strategies is still an open question. Considerations concerning economies of scope suggest strong regionalization, albeit within a coordinating framework, while other aspects – such as the connection and linkage – counsel in favour of centralization.

5.3 The Measures for SMEs Envisaged by "Industria 2015"

As said, "Industria 2015" is a palling document that establishes the strategies for the development and competitiveness of the Italian productive system in the future. It is based on:

- an analysis of the future economic-productive scenarios awaiting Italy in a medium-long period perspective;
- a concept of industry extended to the new production chains that integrate manufacturing activity with advanced services and new technologies (www.industria2015.ipi.it).

The government's strategy identifies firms' networks, innovative finance, and especially the Industrial Innovation Projects (Progetti di Innovazione Industriale, PII), the new instruments with which to re-position the Italian industrial system within the now globalized world economy.

This is a strategy that seeks to identify the fundamental drivers of change with a view to innovation and, consequently, to orient economic policy choices. Implementation of the strategy pivots on the capacity to shift the productive system to arrangements compatible with the evolution of competitive scenarios. This capacity for orientation consists, on the one hand, in identification of productive technological areas and specific goals for industrial innovation, and on the other, in mobilization in pursuit of those of the central and local administrations, the universities, research centres, the business world, and the financial system.

Moreover, because the European Commission has approved and announced the new aid regime for research, development and innovation, this strategy represents not only a revolution in the system of incentives for firms, it is also a key factor in realization of the PIIs envisaged by "Industria 2015". The new aid regime, in fact, allows firms to choose both the type and the form of financial support best suited to their needs in regard to activities ranging from industrial research, through experimental development, to the definition of prototypes and demonstration plants for the realization of new products and services able to compete on international markets.[8]

The PIIs – which therefore constitute the main and most innovative instruments with which to relaunch Italian industrial policies – belong within a framework of public policies intended to strengthen the economic system's competitiveness, also through the already ongoing liberalization of various sectors (energy, saving protection, telecommunications, service improvement, restructuring of professional orders), measures to simplify administrative procedures, and general support to the production system, mainly in the form of automatic incentives such as tax credits for

---

[8] Forms of financial aid are the following: funding for R&D projects and technical feasibility studies; aid to SMEs for expenses connected with industrial property rights (IPR); assistance to innovative new firms; the innovation of the processes and organization of services; consultancy and innovation support services; furnishing of qualified personnel; innovation poles.

investments in research and development. These are systematic intervention projects which, on the basis of technological-productive objectives set by the (central) government, seek to foster the development of specific types of highly-innovative products and services in areas considered strategic for the country's development: energy efficiency, sustainable mobility, new life technologies, new technologies for "Made in Italy" products, innovative technologies for cultural goods.

The main novel features of the PIIs are the following: (a) a Project Manager designated for each Industrial Project; (b) re-design of the incentives offered to firms participating in the PIIs; (c) mobilization of a plurality of actors for achievement of the technological-productive objectives; and, therefore, (d) possibility to activate public-private partnerships.

Another instrument for intervention is the Fund for Enterprise Financing (Fondo per la Finanza d'Impresa), whose purpose is to facilitate access to credit and risk capital by firms, especially those of medium and small size. For this purpose, the Fund participates in operations, proposed by banks and/or financial intermediaries, which envisage the adoption of new instruments of credit risk mitigation and private equity. In general, priority is given to "system" operations able to activate further public and private financial resources, as well as involving a plurality of firms in a "portfolio" logic (districts, networks, clusters, etc.).

Finally, Enterprise Networks (Reti di Impresa) are forms of contractual coordination among enterprises obviously intended in particular for SMEs wanting to increase their critical mass and to acquire greater market power, without being obliged to merge or unite under the control of a single subject. In this regard, "Industria 2015" foresees that the government may issue legislative decrees which:

- define forms of stable contracted coordination among enterprises which, because they have distinct decision-making centres, are suitable for the creation of enterprise networks in joint or hierarchical form;
- define the stability, coordination and direction requirements to be fulfilled by enterprise networks;
- define the legal effects of enterprise networks in regard to consequences of an accountancy and taxation nature, if necessary coordinating and modifying the legislation on groups and consortia of enterprises;
- introduce, with regards to networks comprising enterprises with legal offices in different countries, regulations on transnational networks, if necessary distinguishing between European and international networks;
- provide that social enterprises and non-profit organizations may enter into network contracts.

As regards the present state of progress of "Industria 2015", after a rather long gestation phase, PIIs are becoming fully operational with (i) the appointment of those responsible for drawing up the five project plans; (ii) the publication of the project plans relative to the areas of energy efficiency, sustainable mobility, new technologies for the "Made in Italy" sectors, and innovative technologies for cultural goods and tourism; (iii) approval by the State-Regions Conference of four inter-ministerial decrees which, in accordance with the system of the Regions, define the government's strategy in the relative areas of technological intervention; (iv) the publication of three calls for tender (energy efficiency, sustainable mobility, new technologies for the "Made in Italy" sectors); (v) and, finally, the definition – jointly with the Ministry of Universities and Research and the Regions – of the guidelines for actions to boost the effects and the impacts of the projects, also with regard to geographical specificities, concentrating the use of the national and EC resources on the strategic objectives set by the PIIs.[9]

5.4 A Synopsis by Levels of Government and Objectives

Panel 5.2 sets out the distribution by objectives[10] of the measures adopted by each of the three levels of government in regard to SMEs. It shows quite clearly that what has been maintained from a strictly legal point of view on the basis of the institutional order in force does not correspond to the reality. In fact, the measures assumed in recent years by the central government, contrary to what might be expected in light of legislation during the late 1990s and early 2000s, which was characterized by a political endeavour to decentralize large part of the measures for SMEs, tend to pursue the entire range of intervention objectives, thus again assuming a decisive role. Consequently, the previously introduced division of powers among levels of government does not satisfactorily represent the actual ways in which the measures for SMEs have been implemented. In fact, as already pointed out, the lack of both a real division of competences and of coordination among levels of government (by the central level) has led to the overlapping of roles.

One also observes that the various measures adopted are often co-financed by two or more levels of government,[11] so that they are in fact conjoint, even when the individual provisions stem from the initiative or responsibility of a specific level of government. In particular, the majority of measures are addressed to enterprises in general, and only a certain number, as yet indefinite, are targeted exclusively on SMEs. Moreover, some measures are intended for groups or networks of enterprises or productive districts, although it is well-known that these organizational arrangements mainly concern SMEs.

---

[9] See, instead, Bianchi (2008) for an "authentic" interpretation of the objectives (among which that of chaining or networking SMEs with the purpose of recreating the economies of scale enjoyed by traditional large firms), instruments, phases, and the characteristics of the calls for tender connected with "Industria 2015".

[10] This classification differs from the official one usually adopted by the periodic ministerial surveys on interventions in support of productive activities for the simple reason that it derives, not from all the measures enacted, but only the most recent ones.

[11] The co-financing criterion introduced by the European Community and in Italy extended to national policies is intended to give responsibility the several levels of government, especially the decentralized ones, which receive financial resources from the budgets of higher levels.

Panel 5.2 Distribution of SMEs support and development instruments among levels of government

	Level of government		
Policies by type/objective	*National*	*Regional*	*Local*
Financial incentives for:	X	X	X (chambers of commerce)
A1) Internationalization	X	X	X (local authorities)
A2) Technological innovation	X	X	X (agencies)
A3) Organizational development	X (Networks)	X (Districts)	
B) Other policies, of which:			
B1) Bureaucratic simplification	X		X (one-stop shops)
B2) Product quality		X	
B3) Infrastructures and real services			X

Source: Bernardi et al. (2008)

Finally, also the recent "Industry 2015" national scheme tends to confirm both the involvement of the Regions in the financing of projects and, especially, the lack of provisions exclusively concerning the heterogeneous group of SMEs,[12] notwithstanding the priority that should be given to them according the political-economic directives issued by the EU.

5.5 Financial Incentives at National and Regional Level

5.5.1 Overall Assessment

The first assessment of the characteristics of the financial incentives system concerns the quantity of interventions, given that this is one of the most critical aspects of the overall system (national and regional). During the period 2003–2008, there were 91 interventions at national level, and 1,216 at the regional one (Ministero dello Sviluppo Economico, 2009). According to the Ministerial Report, these figures alone suffice to warrant careful reflection on the system of incentives to enterprises and on the possible evolution of public policies in support of the Italian productive

---

[12] In this regard, some commentators have emphasised that SMEs do not constitute a homogeneous group, in that they pursue different strategies and obtain different results. Medium-sized enterprises are achieving the best results, to the extent that they are now considered an essential component of the Italian productive system: see Coltorti (2006), and also Arrighetti and Ninni (2008).

system. The figures evidence redundancy in the system and suggest the overlapping and duplication of incentives, as well as a fragmentation of interventions obviously bound to determine diseconomies in the use of financial resources.

Although there is evidence of some simplification of the system during the period considered, there persist redundancies and criticalities, which concern – besides the large quantity of interventions – the still weak focus on objectives more closely correlated with the factors most decisive for the productive system's competitiveness, such as innovation and research on the one hand, and internationalization on the other.

In other words, analysis of the data contained in the Ministerial Report, apart from the new interventions undertaken in 2008, does not show changes such to signal that the structural problems of the incentives system have been remedied. In general, the fundamental structural problems already stressed by previous reports still persist, and some recent positive results are certainly not enough for those problems to be considered overcome.

In effect, many of the incentive measures, both national and regional, have a high degree of generality, in the sense that they are addressed to a wide array of enterprises different in terms of both size and sector; but above all they often finance diverse types of investments with no particular limitations or conditions apart from the general ones imposed by EC regulations. In short, these are indiscriminate interventions which may therefore be termed "generalized".[13] Another category comprises measures which are instead specifically targeted, in that they are characterized by the selectivity of investments, projects and incentives, and they are more narrowly intended to support development of enterprise competitiveness. These are the interventions that can be called "targeted".[14]

5.5.2 Measures by Level of Government and Objective

In relation to the different possible aspects of analysis, the overall data on the quantity of the interventions largely reflect the values recorded for the national component of the incentives system, which is the one that predominates. Nevertheless, the policies undertaken by the Regions firstly reinforce the general pattern whereby generalized interventions prevail in both geographical areas, and secondly confirm the differences between the two areas recorded for the national component. In fact, features indicative of differences in the organization of public action emerge: on the one hand, national policies appear more articulated and directed to more diversified objectives; on the other, regional policies are centred on a limited number of

---

[13]Tax credits for disadvantaged areas, law no. 488/1992, the central guarantee fund, and many other measures, belong to this category.

[14]This category comprises – besides the already-mentioned measures to support innovation and research and the internationalization firms – also measures for energy saving and environmental protection.

objectives, on which the limited available financial resources, much less substantial than national ones, are concentrated.

Examination of the amount of incentives granted confirms and accentuates the pattern described in regard to the numerousness of national and regional interventions. Again apparent is the concentration of regional resources on consolidation and development of the productive system (over 57% of the total), although the proportion concerning access to credit has increased in recent years, while there has been slight reduction for innovation, research and development. National resources are instead used mainly to reduce differentials in territorial development (44% of the total facilities granted), as well as for innovation, research and development, access to credit, and financial consolidation. The national schemes allocate a greater proportion of incentives to new entrepreneurship and the internationalization of firms, while the regional ones are obviously more concerned with environmental protection and services/infrastructures for enterprises, given that this latter industrial policy objective pertains only to regional interventions.

As regards the average value of investments, the figure is substantially larger for targeted interventions than for generalized ones. This difference is all the more significant if the national interventions are considered, in which case the average investment is more than twice the average one for generalized interventions. These results are largely confirmed by the finding for evaluative interventions: in fact, the national evaluative interventions are characterized by higher average investments, particularly in research and development programmes, which are mainly undertaken by medium- or large-sized firms. Regional evaluative interventions instead finance smaller-scale projects for the simple reason that they refer to SMEs, and, particularly, small firms.

To recapitulate, therefore, the numerous elements which emerge from the foregoing analysis furnish a series of insights and a reference framework which, in extreme synthesis, relate to certain structural characteristics of the incentives system. Firstly, it highlights the numerousness of interventions, particularly at regional level, even though this is mitigated by the fact that the majority of resources are concentrated on a limited number of incentive instruments: 10 interventions, in fact, absorb fully 80% of national resources. Again in regard to the numerousness of instruments, it has also emerged that generalized interventions outnumber targeted ones, as well as those of evaluative and automatic type, just as those that involve capital contributions outnumber those involving other types of incentive. The main recommendation that emerges this respect is logically that of reducing the number of, and the consequent overlaps among, the instruments used at the different levels of government, but preserving the specificities of the policies adopted.

5.5.3 The Guarantee Fund for SMEs

According to figures issued at the end of March 2009, the Guarantee Fund for the SMEs, active since December 2000, had guaranteed more than 60,000 operations and furnished financing to a total of 11.5 billion euros. As shown by Table 5.1,

5 Public Policies for Italian SMEs

Table 5.1 Applications and funding granted by the guarantee fund in the period 2003–2008 (absolute values in millions of euros)

Variables	2003	2004	2005	2006	2007	2008	Total
Applications (a)	4,370	5,636	7,049	8,677	13,239	14,063	53,034
Funding granted (b)	1,128	1,080	1,215	1,649	2,405	2,407	9,884
Incidence % (b)/(a)	25.81	19.16	17.24	19.00	18.17	17.12	18.64

Table 5.2 Overall refinancing of the guarantee fund in the period 2008–2012 (absolute values in millions of euros)

Legislative source	2008	2009	2010	2011	2012	Total
D.l. 185/2008 (art. 11) e D.l. 5/2009 (art.8)	71.0	–	80.5	–	95.9	247.4
D.l. 5/2009 (art.7 –quinquies, c.5)	–	100.0	–	–	–	100.0
Rotating national fund for risk capital schemes	–	65.0	90.0	–	–	155.0
D.l. 5/2009 (art.7 –quinquies, c.8)	–	–	200.0	300.0	500.0	1,000.0
Total	71.0	165.0	370.5	300.0	595.9	1,502.4

however, between 2003 and 2008 the Guarantee Fund progressively reduced its operations, although in the past 2 years – during which the economic-financial crisis has entailed the severe rationing of credit to enterprises – the amount of financing granted has increased considerably compared with previous years.

Important novelties have been introduced by a provision adopted between 2008 and 2009: besides first re-financing up to 450 million euros, the Guarantee Fund has been extended to crafts firms, with the State as guarantor of last resort. Table 5.2 provides an overview of the time schedule of allocations by the Guarantee Fund following the changes introduced by the new regulations. It shows that refinancing the Guarantee Fund for SMEs will make a total of around 1.5 billion euros available, so that it will be able to guarantee bank loans amounting to 70–80 billion euros.

5.5.4 The Most Recent European Community Provisions

In order to boost firms' competitiveness and to accelerate the growth of the European economic system as a whole, new EC regulations have been issued on state aid for innovation, research and development (Communication of European Commission, 2006/C 323/01). On the one hand, the regulations introduce new types of aid in the sector and, on the other, focus closely on the needs of SMEs, which are usually those hardest hit by market failures. The European Commission pays particular attention to SMEs, to the point that – as already mentioned – in June 2008 it adopted the SBA, this being a specific communication expressing the political intent to grant a central role to SMEs in the economies of both Europe and member-states. The distinctive feature of the SBA is its conviction that recognition by society of the role performed by small entrepreneurs is essential for the creation of an environment which encourages individuals to start up their own businesses, and which recognizes the crucial contribution made by SMEs to development of the economy.

This framework of particular attention to SMEs also comprises the new regulation on group exemption (Regulation no. 800 of 6.8.2008), which strengthens the role of member-states in supporting the SMEs through the various phases of their development. All categories of aid exempt from the obligation of notification, among which those for innovation, for the hiring of high-skilled personnel, for investments in machinery in the form of risk capital, can be granted to SMEs with the aim of making them more innovative and competitive in a context of increased international competition.

However, contrary to this position adopted by the EC authorities, the attention paid at formal level by the Italian government to SMEs has diminished in recent years, as evidenced by the fact that, in the most recent Ministerial Report on interventions to support business, specification is no longer made of the proportion allocated to incentives for SMEs. Moreover, interventions by the Regions are no longer distinguished between their own and those conferred.

5.6 An Evaluation of Interventions for SMEs Through Quantitative Estimation of Incentives

Recently published have been the findings of an international seminar on best practices in the evaluation of SMEs and entrepreneurship policies (OECD, 2007). It is evident from the report that the so-called "OECD Istanbul Position" – which emphasises the need to develop an evaluation (*ex post*) culture – has been implemented in Italy with only partly satisfactory results, notwithstanding the presence also in the past decade of a large body of scientific literature on the subject.

A brief survey of this literature on the evaluation of industrial policies shows that, of the various approaches followed, some differ from those adopted in the above-mentioned Ministerial Report, because they appear more directly targeted on the universe of reference for this study, namely SMEs.

A first approach is based on a distinction among fiscal, financial and credit incentives according to whether they are addressed to already existing and operating SMEs, with the purpose of improving their competitiveness, or whether they are targeted on the creation of new small businesses, so as to foster local economic development by increasing employment, etc.

In the former case, the most recent study (D'Aurizio and de Blasio, 2008) evaluating the effectiveness of provisions such as law no. 488[15] argues that the

---

[15] Scanagatta and Riti (2001) have conducted a survey of policies implemented during the 1990s. Their results confirm that incentives had positive effects, especially on the accumulation rate of enterprises, given that this was higher than that of non-financed enterprises. The general findings of the survey, however, suggest that the incentive instruments most widespread among productive enterprises during the 1990s were aimed at accumulation in sectors characterizing the traditional Italian model of specialization, which raises the problem of the capacity of industrial policies to

5 Public Policies for Italian SMEs

stimulation effect of additional investments has been modest, because it has induced mainly inter-temporal substitution effects in entrepreneurial decisions. Apparently more effective has been law no. 388/2000 (budget law for 2001), also because of its different system for the granting of incentives (an automatic mechanism rather than a competitive procedure). Nevertheless, also in this case the additionality of incentives for investment has been scant.

To be cited in regard to policies for new firm creation are the main national provision on the matter (law no. 44/1986, discussed by di Nola and Giacomelli, 2001) and the most recent regional laws for the promotion of new enterprises in Italy. In regard to the latter, it has been shown that they are not particularly effective in promoting the birth of new firms in the various sectors, with the exception of construction, where the policies has had a positive impact on the development of new entrepreneurship (Piergiovanni et al., 2008).

Other approaches, though of lesser interest, are those that distinguish by geographical area on the basis of the distinction introduced for EC cohesion policies between Objective 1 regions (Mancino et al., 2005) and Objective 2 ones (Bondonio and Greenbaum, 2006); or evaluations restricted to incentives of a specific type, such as those for R&D activity in SMEs (Merito et al. 2008) or comparative evaluations of the different types of aid (Bondonio, 2008), which reach conclusions useful mainly for the purpose of defining public interventions for SMEs.

Finally, even more specific studies have been conducted, such as those concerned with strictly technical aspects of the various kinds of incentives (Gai and Rossi, 2009), or those that furnish indications regarding the financial instruments preferable for SMEs, such as private equity, and at the same time deemed more consistent with "Basel 2 Accord" (Ascani, 2007).

A critical feature shared by all these studies, however, is the partiality of their field of inquiry, in the sense that none of them considers the entire range of the numerous and heterogeneous instruments used in favour of SMEs, so that they fail to fill the gap previously mentioned in regard to the Ministerial Report. To remedy this shortcoming at least to some extent, one may estimate the relative amount of aid furnished to Italian SMEs in the period 2003–2008, considering the national incentives reserved to enterprises of this kind (Table 5.3), as well as the regional measures that, by definition, are restricted to SMEs. The amount thus obtained is then compared against the total value of public interventions, obtaining results of a certain significance (Table 5.4).

The first result is that the facilities intended for SMEs in the period considered exceeded 41% of the total, while in terms of actual disbursement the proportion diminished to only just over 35%.[16] When evaluating the relatively limited role of

---

induce the changes necessary to enable the Italian specialization model to respond to the challenges of global competition.

[16] As well known, the difference between the amount of resources disbursed and the amount granted is mainly due to the time lag between the moment of approval of the facilities requested and that of their effective fruition by the recipient enterprises, which in many cases is divided into several instalments, also in function of the multi-year schedule for their investments.

Table 5.3 Incentives granted and disbursed to SMEs, as well as investments facilitated on the basis of national measures in the period 2003–2008 (composition %)

National measures	Incentives granted (contributions)	Incentives disbursed (contributions)	Investments facilitated
Legge 215/1992 (female entrepreneurship)	3.90	8.22	4.76
Legge 488/1992 (crafts firms)	2.37	5.30	4.33
Legge 662/1996, art. 2 (Guarantee Fund)	65.33	2.23	46.14
Legge 266/1997, art. 14 (degraded urban areas)	1.14	2.82	1.91
D.Lgs.185/2000 Tit.I (self-entrepreneurship)	1.80	9.80	2.18
D.Lgs.185/2000, Tit.II (self-employment)	20.80	60.12	25.53
Legge 388/2000, artt.103 e 106 (risk capital)	0.52	0.86	1.44
Legge 388/2000, art.114 (environmental recovery, etc.)	0.09	0.08	0.08
Legge 57/2001, art. 12 (cooperation)	0.91	3.57	0.00
Circolare 946204/2005 (PIA networking)	0.80	0.75	0.80
Legge 13/2006, art. 3, c.12 (naval engineering industry)	0.54	1.30	0.00
Legge 80/2006, art. 34-octies (naval engineering industry)	1.79	4.96	12.83
Total	100.00	100.00	100.00

Source: Author's calculations on ministero sviluppo economico data (2009)

Table 5.4 Incidence of national incentives to SMEs and of regional measures in the total of public measures in the period 2003–08 (absolute values in millions of euros)

Type of incentive	Incentives granted (1)	Incentives disbursed (2)	Investments facilitated (3)	Ratio (3)/(1)
National incentives to SMEs (a)	7,470.53	1,616.77	11,532.40	1.54
Regional measures (b)	17,167.60	10,915.74	59,102.26	3.44
Total (a + b)	24,638.13	12,532.51	70,634.66	2.87
Total public measures (c)	60,014.36	35,703.87	167,963.37	2.80
Incidence % (a+b)/(c)	41.05	35.10	42.05	–

Source: Author's calculations on ministero sviluppo economico data (2009)

SME financing, one should bear in mind that this is also the result of the existence of two sources of facilities for SMEs deriving from the distinction between general laws applying to all enterprises and specific ones which only concern SMEs. In fact, this double financing mechanism, besides being usually considered a duplication, also tends to assume the features of a bias towards large firms, since these are able to prevail over smaller ones in obtaining the facilities provided by the general laws.

A more interesting aspect, however, is the incidence of incentives on facilitated investments: insofar as this is slightly higher than the other two, it confirms that SMEs require a larger amount of financing for their investments than do larger firms, which can obviously rely on other sources of financing.

Finally, on considering national interventions alone, it emerges that almost two-thirds of the total of incentives disbursed concern self-employment, while almost half of facilitated investments relate to the Guarantee Fund, thereby confirming the latter's presumed capacity to generate a "multiplier effect" in a relatively brief period of time.

It is therefore desirable that the resources foreseen for this instrument in the years subsequent to 2008 should be allocated, so that the positive role currently performed by SMEs in the Italian productive system can be further enhanced.

5.7 Conclusions

As anticipated in the introduction, this study concludes with a description of the two provisions for SMEs most recently enacted by the Italian government.

The first consists in the signing by the Minister of Economic Development of the special contracts with the mayors of the towns comprised in the UFZs. The latter have been inspired by a scheme launched in France in 1997, and they represent an innovative example of taxation in favour of underdeveloped areas. This measure, in fact, introduces tax and contributions relief for the creation of new productive activities and new employment in the sectors of micro and small business in municipal areas of a pre-established size.

The idea of experimenting with this new instrument in Italy was first proposed in 2006 by a joint document issued by Confindustria, the trade unions and the Presidents of the Regions of the *Mezzogiorno*, and it was implemented by the Budget Law of 2008. After a period of inactivity, the Ministry of Economic Development initiated the process of creating the UZFs, first by selecting the areas jointly with the Regions, and with the financial allocation presented to the CIPE, and then with notification to the European Commission, from which important and not automatic authorization was obtained.

The European Commission, in fact, considers the renewal of degraded urban districts to be an initiative fulfilling the EC objective of economic and social cohesion. In consideration of both the level of socio-economic difficulties, and the fact that the geographical coverage of the measures anticipated was extremely limited (only 0.58% of the population), the Commission deemed the measures necessary for, and proportionate to, attainment of the objective of urban revitalization, without provoking a distortion of competition contrary to the common interest. The Commission has agreed that the effects on trade would be minor because the measures were essentially intended to combat social exclusion in particularly difficult districts; the regime was exclusively addressed to small and micro enterprises; and the districts had been selected according to objective criteria such as the unemployment and employment rates, the proportion of the population aged under 24, and the schooling rate.

The aim of UFZs is therefore to foster the economic and social development of weaker urban districts but which have potential for development. The provision identified 22 such districts in urban areas with an average population of 14,000 inhabitants. The areas were located on the territories of 23 municipalities distributed among 11 regions: 3 in the Centre-North and 8 in the *Mezzogiorno*; the population concerned amounted to around 310,000 inhabitants. As said, the selection was made by applying a method never previously employed in Italy. The "target areas" within the municipalities were identified by means of objective social and occupational parameters. Besides making it possible to concentrate the intervention on 22 areas selected from among the 70 municipalities that had submitted applications, out of a total of 180 eligible municipalities, the rigour, solidity and transparency of the criteria adopted were important factors in obtaining the European Commission's authorization.

The financial endowment allocated to the start-up of the UFZs by the 2007 budget law amounted to 100 million euros. On the initiative of the Ministry of Economic Development, a "Development Law" (law no. 99/2009) identified further areas and increased the funding for the creation of UFZs by a further 50 million euros a year. Hence, since 1 January 2010, small firms have been able to benefit from tax and contributions relief for a period of up to 14 years.

The second provision consists in the approval by the Council of Ministers of a draft directive transposing the SBA adopted by the European Commission in June 2008 with a view to enhancing the economic role of small medium-sized firms, thereby remedy a discrepancy with respect to the United States, where a similar provision had been in force since 1953. The European institutions showed strong interest in protecting small European firms as regards regulation and, partly, also public contract procurement, by establishing a new economic approach that member-states should adopt.[17]

---

[17] The rationale of the Small Business Act is to enhance the dynamism of SMEs for the benefit that they can also bring to the system of public contracts. SMEs, in fact, have a greater capacity for innovation due to their organizational simplicity and the absence of a bureaucratic structure which enables them to respond more rapidly and efficiently to the needs of the market. Market entry by SMEs offering high-level products and services thus increases the quantitative and qualitative potential of competition for public contracts. The European Union's strategy is based on the 'think small first' principle, according to which it is necessary, as well as advisable, to prioritize small firms in order to facilitate their existence in the business environment. The main objectives are: (a) reduce administrative costs; (b) simplify and accelerate the procedures; (c) improve access to the market and increase competitiveness.

The main actions identified in the document approved by the Council of Ministers are the following: institution of an annual law on SMEs; simplification of administrative procedures so as significantly to reduce the administrative burdens on firms; one-stop shops and online management of relations with the public administration; strengthening the Guarantee Fund and creating new financial instruments for small firm credit and capitalization; programmes to support innovation and internationalization; regulations to encourage participation by SMEs in government and regional incentive schemes through use of the "Network Contract" introduced by the Development Law; evaluation of the economic impact of laws and rules on SMEs, also through specific consultations with sectoral associations; measures to favour access by SMEs to public contracts. The Italian directive, which will involve around 6 million firms, companies, cooperatives and single-owner businesses employing around 9 million people, will be examined by the Joint State-Regions-Local Authorities Conference, and then pass for definitive approval to the Council of Ministers.

It is evident that these are once again provisions adopted by the central government, which thus seems determined, for the near future as well, to assign the leading role in regard to public policies for SMEs to Regions and local authorities, although primary competence for these should attach to the decentralized levels of government. Moreover, provisions similar to the newly-enacted ones are already in force and are managed by such levels of government. Thus reproduced are the negative phenomena of numerousness, duplication and inefficiency already emphasised in regard to the general system of facilities currently enjoyed by Italian SMEs.

References

Arrighetti A, Ninni A (2008) Dimensioni e crescita nell'industria manifatturiera italiana. Il ruolo delle medie imprese. FrancoAngeli, Milano

Ascani P (ed) (2007) Artigianato e politiche industriali. Secondo rapporto sull'artigianato in Italia. Il Mulino, Bologna

Bernardi A, Bruzzo A, Galassi F (2008) Le politiche pubbliche per le PMI in Italia: rassegna degli interventi per livelli di governo e tentativo di verifica dei loro effetti in uno specifico contesto territoriale. Quaderno DEIT 26. Ferrara, October

Bianchi A (2008) Industria 2015: una politica industriale al servizio del cambiamento. Economia e politica industriale 3:225–233

Bondonio D (2008) La valutazione integrata delle diverse tipologie di aiuto. In: de Blasio G, Lotti F (eds) La valutazione degli aiuti alle imprese. il Mulino, Bologna, pp 185–225

Bondonio D, Greenbuam TR (2006) Do business investment incentives promote employment in declining area? Evidence from EU Objective-2 Regions. Eur Urban Region Stud 3:225–244

Brancati R (ed) (2001) Analisi e metodologie per la valutazione delle politiche industriali. FrancoAngeli, Milano

Bruzzo A (2009a) Le politiche pubbliche per le Pmi in Italia: una rassegna degli interventi degli interventi per livelli di governo. Economia e società regionale 1(2):87–121

Bruzzo A (2009b) Le politiche pubbliche per le Pmi in Italia: un quadro complessivo. In: CRIAPI Dalla crisi allo sviluppo: quali strategie per le PMI, Padova, December, 43–47

Cipollina S, Pizzonia G (2006) Un nuovo «statuto» per i distretti produttivi: il modello della Legge Finanziaria 2006. In: Fortis M, Quadrio Curzio A (eds) Industria e distretti. Un paradigma di perdurante competitività italiana. Il Mulino, Bologna, pp 289–313

Coltorti F (2006) Le medie imprese italiane: una risorsa cruciale per lo sviluppo. In: Fortis M, Quadrio Curzio A (eds) Industria e distretti. Un paradigma di perdurante competitività italiana. Il Mulino, Bologna, pp 315–361

D'Aurizio L, de Blasio G (2008) La valutazione degli incentivi agli investimenti. In: de Blasio G, Lotti F (eds) La valutazione degli aiuti alle imprese. il Mulino, Bologna, pp 59–96

de Blasio G, Lotti F (ed) (2008) La valutazione degli aiuti alle imprese. il Mulino, Bologna

di Nola P, Giacomelli P (2001) La valutazione delle politiche per la creazione d'impresa. In: Brancati R (ed) Analisi e metodologie per la valutazione delle politiche industriali. FrancoAngeli, Milano, pp 176–208

Gai L, Rossi F (2009) Le politiche pubbliche di sostegno alle Pmi: una comparazione economica tra gli strumenti attivabili. Bancaria 9:65–70.

Mancino A, Passaro R, Thomas A (2005) Politiche per lo sviluppo dell'imprenditorialità e politiche a sostegno delle PMI: quali contraddizioni? Rassegna Economica 1:177–199

Merito M, Giannangeli S, Bonaccorsi A (2008) L'impatto degli incentivi pubblici per la R&S sull'attività delle Pmi. In: de Blasio G, Lotti F (ed) La valutazione degli aiuti alle imprese. il Mulino, Bologna, pp 97–120

Ministero dello Sviluppo Economico (2009) Relazione sugli interventi di sostegno alle attività economiche e produttive. Roma, June

OECD (2005) OECD SME and Entrepreneurship Outlook 2005. Paris

OECD (2007) OECD Framework for the evaluation of SME and entrepreneurship policies and programmes. Paris

Piergiovanni R, Santarelli E, Vivarelli M (2008) Le politiche per la formazione di nuove imprese. In: de Blasio G, Lotti F (ed) La valutazione degli aiuti alle imprese. il Mulino, Bologna, pp 121–147

Scanagatta G, Riti A (2001) I regimi di aiuto per le piccole e medie imprese. Una valutazione alla luce delle indagini del Mediocredito Centrale sulle imprese manifatturiere. In: Brancati R (ed) Analisi e metodologie per la valutazione delle politiche industriali. FrancoAngeli, Milano, pp 102–140

Part II
The Financing of Small – and Medium – Sized Firms

Chapter 6
SME Financing and the Financial Crisis: A Framework and Some Issues

Gregory F. Udell

Abstract Studies of net job creation generally confirm the importance of the SME sector as an engine that can drive the economy out of a recession. The SME sector cannot perform this role without access to external finance. This article examines new paradigms that have expanded our understanding of how SME loans are underwritten and how underwriting changes during a macro financial shock. We also use these paradigms to examine two interesting issues related to SME financing during the current financial crisis: the behavior of foreign-owned banks particularly in developing economies and the efficacy of government guarantee programs.

6.1 Introduction

Not surprisingly the health of the SME sector during the current global crisis is a major policy concern in both developing and developed economies. In developing economies the reason is obvious – developing economies are highly skewed toward the SME sector. But, even in the largest developed economies, the SME sector is extremely important. For example, the SME sector in the U.S. represents roughly half of the economy in terms of employment.[1] Also in large developed economies it is widely viewed that the SME sector will likely lead the economy out of the recession because it tends to be viewed as the job creation engine of economic performance. This has certainly been the view in the U.S. and it was also the view in Japan during the "lost decade" of the 1990s.

No doubt populist sentiment in favor of helping the "little guy" fuels legislator enthusiasm for pulling policy levers targeted to small business even in large economies. Nevertheless, in general, the existing empirical evidence provides some

---

G.F. Udell (✉)
Chase Chair of Banking and Finance, Kelly School of Business, Indiana University at Bloomington, 1309 E. 10th Street, Bloomington, IN 47405, USA
e-mail: gudell@indiana.edu

[1] The SME's fraction of the U.S. economy is sensitive to the choice of definitions (see Stangler and Litan, 2009)

justification for this view – or a least a more nuanced version. In the U.S., for example, the net addition of jobs appears to be skewed toward younger firms, particularly start-ups and firms that are ages one to 5 years. And, younger firms tend to be smaller. But, there is also a "barbell effect" where the largest and oldest firms also contribute to job creation. In addition, there is a significant amount of destruction of jobs by small firms also (see Stangler and Litan, 2009). But, again, in terms of net job creation, the SME sector deserves the policy attention that it gets in developed economies as well as in developing economies.

One major impediment to the performance of the SME sector is the availability of external finance. SMEs in general do not have access to the capital markets where they can issue publicly traded stock and corporate bonds. Thus, they tend to be dependent on financial institutions (particularly banks and finance companies) and mercantile trade (i.e., trade credit). Even in normal times, access to external finance can be problematic, particularly for those SMEs who are more opaque. This can become acute during a financial crisis that induces a credit crunch in the form of a contraction in the supply of credit.

In this article I would like to discuss several factors associated with how the SME sector might be affected by this financial crisis. In the next section, I discuss a paradigm in the academic literature that provides a useful framework to think about how SMEs obtain financing and how the flow of financing might be affected by a credit crunch induced by the current financial crisis. This paradigm emphasizes that there are a number of *lending channels* through which SMEs obtain financing. The ultimate net effect of this credit crunch on the SME sector will depend on how these lending channels contract and expand.

In the next section, I expand this paradigm to include the foreign sector of the banking system. In some countries the banking system has been substantially acquired by foreign banks. For example, many central and eastern European banks (and banking systems) have been acquired by western European banks. In this section I discuss how foreign ownership of the banking system might affect SME access to finance. In the final section, I will discuss one of the more popular policy levers that have been used to mitigate the effects of credit crunches on the SME sector – government guarantee programs. For example, Japan implemented an enormous government guarantee program to address concern that the financial crisis during the 1990s was severely constraining credit extension to SMEs and the U.S. has significantly expanded its program during this crisis.

6.2 Lending Technologies

Without too much risk of over-simplification, it can be said that the emphasis in the academic literature on SME financing has tended to be focused on *relationship lending*. The genesis of this emphasis can been traced back to the modern theory of the banking firm that emphasized the role of financial intermediaries as delegated producers of information about opaque borrowers (e.g., Diamond, 1984; Boyd and Prescott, 1986), and the early empirical literature on *bank uniqueness* that emphasized the impact on firm value of the renewal of a firm's bank loans (e.g. Lummer and McConnell, 1989).[2] This strand of literature evolved into an emphasis on *soft information* and the strength of banking relationships (e.g. Petersen and Rajan, 1994, 1995; Berger and Udell, 1995; Cole, 1998; Elsas and Krahnen, 1998; Harhoff and Körting, 1998). In the background, there was also some discussion in the literature of (what was viewed as) the opposite of relationship lending, hard information-based *transactions lending* (e.g., Berger et al., 2005). This dyad was formalized in models that connected the delivery of these two types of lending to different types of banks (e.g., Stein, 2002; Berger et al., 2005).

However, more recently some authors beginning with Berger and Udell (2006) have begun to emphasize an alternative view where SME lending comes in many forms. Berger and Udell (2006) applied the label *lending technologies* to these alternative types of lending. An expanded list of these lending technologies is shown in Fig. 6.1.

To be fair, most of the lending technologies listed Fig. 6.1 had been discussed in the academic literature in individual isolation. Moreover, all of these technologies would be familiar to most bankers in countries where they all exist (e.g., the U.S.). Missing from the academic literature on SME financing, however, was a discussion of how these types of lending can be viewed as alternative sources of external funding – and the circumstances where one is preferred over the other.

Figure 6.1 lists each of the lending technologies and: (i) whether it is relationship-based or transactions-based; (ii) the type of SME for whom the technology is best suited (either relatively transparent, or relatively opaque); and, (iii) whether the technology is soft information-based or hard-information based. Soft information is non-quantifiable information such as the loan officer's assessment of an entrepreneur's managerial ability and hard information is quantifiable information such as a financial ratio or a collateral appraisal.

Most of these lending technologies do not need an explanation. But, a few comments are in order here. Financial statement lending is underwritten by an

TECHNOLOGY	TYPE	BORROWER	INFORMATION
Relationship Lending	Relationship	Opaque	Soft
Financial Statement Lending	Transaction	Transparent	Hard
Asset-Based Lending	Transaction	Opaque	Hard
Factoring	Transaction	Opaque	Hard
Leasing	Transaction	Opaque and Transparent	Hard
Small Bus. Credit Scoring	Transaction	Opaque	Hard
Equipment Lending	Transaction	Opaque and Transparent	Hard
Real Estate-Based Lending	Transaction	Opaque and Transparent	Hard
Trade Credit	?	Opaque and Transparent	Soft and Hard

Fig. 6.1 Lending technologies. Based on Taketa and Udell (2006)

---

[2]For a more extensive discussion of the evolution of the literature on SME financing and relationship lending see Udell (2008).

assessment of an SME's financial statements. This type of lending requires that the financial statements be credible – which means they need to be audited. Many SME's, particularly smaller SMEs, cannot afford audited financial statements so this technology is not feasible for them. Asset-based lending is unique to the common law countries of Australia, Canada, New Zealand, the U.K. and the U.S. It is focused on providing working capital finance to relatively highly leveraged SMEs based on a daily (i.e., continuous) assessment of the collateral value of the accounts receivable and inventory. Factoring, which is globally ubiquitous, is a cousin of asset-based lending based on a continuous assessment of the value of accounts receivable. Unlike, asset-based lending, factoring involves the *purchase* of accounts receivable. This protects a lender's position in the event of borrower bankruptcy because the receivables are not part of the bankruptcy estate making this lending technology attractive in countries with weak commercial laws and weak bankruptcy systems (see Bakker et al., 2004; Klapper, 2006). Leasing, equipment lending, and real estate-based lending are all transactions-based lending because their underwriting centers on the appraised value of an underlying fixed asset.

The last lending technology has been the focus of considerable attention in the finance literature. Some argue that relationship lending is transactions-based while others have suggested that it may be relationship-based. Importantly, some have emphasized that it may play an important role in providing financing to SMEs during periods of financial distress.[3] We note in Fig. 6.1 the uncertainty in the literature about whether trade credit is relationship based.[4]

The notion of lending technologies provides a framework to think about how financial shocks will affect SME access to finance. Taketa and Udell (2006) extended the concept of lending technologies to *lending channels* where lending channels are two dimensional combinations of a lending technology and a financial institution. This concept recognizes two fundamental characteristics of lending technologies: first, not all types of financial institutions deliver all types of lending technologies; and, second, the provision of lending technologies may be affected during a crisis by the health of the financial institutions that are capable of providing those technologies. Figure 6.2 shows what lending channels might look like during a normal expansionary period in the U.S.

Note that some lending technologies are very dependent on a single source. Relationship lending may be best (or at least mostly) delivered by small banks where soft information doesn't have to be delivered through different levels of organizational hierarchy located across a spatial divide (e.g., Stein, 2002; Berger et al., 2005; Alessandrini et al., 2009; Kano et al., 2010). Also, trade credit is only extended by commercial enterprises.

It is also interesting to note that some lending technologies that are well suited for both opaque and transparent SMEs are offered by different types of financial

---

[3] See Carbo-Valverde et al. (2009) for a discussion of the literature on trade credit.

[4] For empirical investigations of the mix of technologies in Japan and the U.S. see Uchida et al. (2008) and Berger and Black (2009) respectively.

	Large Banks	Small Banks	Large Com. Finance Cos.	Small Com. Finance Cos.	Corporations
Relationship Lending		o			
Financial Statement Lending	o	o			
Asset-Based Lending	o	o	o	o	
Factoring	o	o	o	o	
Equipment Lending	o	o	o	o	
Leasing	o	o	o	o	
Real Estate-Based Lending	o	o			
Small Bus. Credit Scoring	o				
Trade Credit					o

Fig. 6.2 Lending channels. Based on Taketa and Udell (2006)

institutions. For example, leasing and equipment lending are routinely offered by large and small banks and large and small financial companies. These lending technologies have been utilized by large banks to lend to informationally opaque borrowers even in developing economies (de la Torre et al., 2010).

Importantly, the concept of lending channels allows us to think about how access to SMEs might be affected during a macro shock like the current credit crisis. In particular, some lending channels might shrink during a credit crunch, for example, while others don't. Some might even substitute for others during a credit crunch. That is, some might expand in order to offset those that contract. For example, there is evidence in the U.S. that during monetary shocks or credit crunches large companies might extend more trade credit to SMEs (e.g., Calomiris et al., 1995) or that commercial finance companies might have increased asset-based lending during the 1990–1992 credit crunch (e.g., Udell, 2004). Figure 6.3 shows what the lending channels might have looked like during the 1990–1992 credit crunch in the U.S. where capital shocks to U.S. banks contracted their SME lending. To the extent that commercial finance companies (both large and small) and large company trade creditors picked up the slack, firms "crunched" out of the banking market may have been able to find alternative financing. However, firms dependent on relationship lending that don't have collateral to post (i.e., accounts receivable, inventory, equipment and/or real estate to post) may not have been so fortunate given that relationship lending is only offered by one type of institution – small banks.

	Large Banks	Small Banks	Large Com. Finance Cos.	Small Com. Finance Cos.	Corporations
Relationship Lending		x			
Financial Statement Lending	x	x			
Asset-Based Lending	x	x	o	o	
Factoring	x	x	o	o	
Equipment Lending	x	x	o	o	
Leasing	x	x	o	o	
Real Estate-Based Lending	x	x			
Small Bus. Credit Scoring	x	x			
Trade Credit					o

Fig. 6.3 1990–1992 U.S. Credit crunch

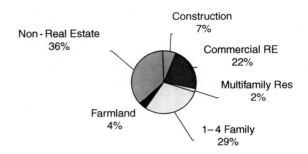

Fig. 6.4 U.S. Lending by Small Banks (2000)

There is reason to be concerned that the situation may be worse in the U.S. during this financial crisis for two reasons. First, while small banks weren't initially the focus of attention in the U.S., they now are. (Again small banks are a particular concern because they are the sole source of relationship lending.) The problem stems from the fact that small banks significantly shifted their loan allocation toward one of the riskiest types of lending, commercial real estate – specifically, commercial real estate mortgages and construction loans. This problem was not initially obvious because the commercial real estate market collapsed in the U.S. with a significant lag relative to the collapse of the residential real estate market. As of this writing it is too early to tell whether small banks will be affected more in this crisis than in the 1990–1992 credit crunch (in which real estate problems were also a factor), but the stunning portfolio shift reflected in Figs. 6.4 and 6.5 is a cause for significant concern.

One hypothesis that might explain this enormous portfolio shift is the deregulation of the U.S. banking system. Spatial constraints on cross-state banking were sequentially removed during the 1980s and 1990s. Thus, small banks found themselves competing with large banks including several giant banks that became powerful nationwide competitors (e.g., JPMorgan Chase and Bank of America). Deregulation of the banking industry may also have an impact elsewhere in the world. Spain is a particularly interesting example. The savings bank industry was spatially deregulated and many of these banks aggressively expanded beyond their

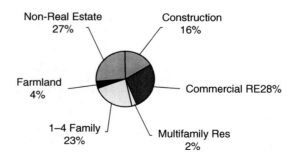

Fig. 6.5 U.S. Lending by Small Banks (2007)

home states at potentially the expense of credit quality – a problem now compounded by a severe deterioration in the Spanish real estate market (just as in the U.S.). To the extent that Spanish SMEs rely on these savings banks for relationship lending, the Spanish credit crunch could be similarly problematic.[5]

Another problem in the U.S. is that most of the large independent commercial finance companies have virtually disappeared since the 1990–1992 credit crunch. They have either been acquired by large commercial banks or they have failed (e.g., CIT). Thus, large commercial finance companies are not likely to provide a safety valve like they appear to have done in 1990–1992. Also, it is too early to tell whether large corporations have offered another safety valve by providing more trade credit to SMEs funded by issuing more commercial paper. Initial problems in the commercial paper market may have inhibited this alternative.[6]

One last comment on lending channels is in order. Figures 6.1, 6.2, and 6.3 describe lending technologies and lending channels as they exist *in the U.S.* Lending technologies and lending channels vary across countries as does their relative size. As we noted above, asset-based lending – while very important in five countries – does not exist in other countries. Recent legislation on security interests (i.e., collateral) in movable assets (e.g., accounts receivable) in countries such as China and Japan allow for the *possibility* that asset-based lending might be introduced in the future. But, other infrastructure improvements are necessary first. Some countries have just recently adopted some lending technologies (e.g., factoring in Vietnam). Also, the institutional landscape varies significantly across countries. For example, in many countries state-owned banks play a very important role. The Indian banking system, for example, is highly influenced by the presence of one very large state bank, The State Bank of India. Hence, lending channels will look very different, and may behave very differently in response to financial shocks, across countries.

6.3 The Financial Crisis and Foreign Bank Ownership

Next we turn to another dimension not addressed in Figs. 6.2 and 6.3, the importance of foreign-owned banks. While this is not a huge issue in either the U.S. or western Europe, it is a significant issue in other parts of the world such as eastern and central Europe and Latin America. In some areas foreign bank entry has been truly dramatic. For example, by 2008 foreign banks controlled about 80% of the banking assets in central and eastern Europe. There are several potential benefits that may be associated with this phenomenon. Large foreign-owned banks may be able to increase access to financing for SMEs through the introduction of

---

[5] See Munoz et al. (2009) for an analysis of savings bank deregulation in Spain.
[6] See Udell (2009a, 2009b) for more detailed discussion of lending channels and SME access to finance in the U.S. during this credit crunch.

the lending technologies that we have described above. For example, there is evidence that this has happened in Latin America (de la Torre et al., 2008).It may also be the case that large foreign owned banks may be able to introduce best practices in the banking system that significantly improve the efficiency of the banking system.

However, there may be a dark side to foreign bank entry if this integration leads to a quicker spreading of financial crises – i.e., if it facilitates contagion across countries. Some recent evidence suggests that this may have happened in central and eastern Europe. One study has found that SMEs in central and eastern Europe were more constrained after the start of the financial crisis if their banks' parents had been affected by the financial crisis including losses in ABS and MBS investments, and that foreign-owned banks shrank their portfolios more in response to financial distress than domestically owned banks (Popov and Udell, 2010). This suggests that lending channels for eastern and central European countries should distinguish between foreign- and domestically-owned banks. Unfortunately, data constraints virtually everywhere make it quite difficult to distinguish among lending technologies and lending channels.

6.4 Bank Guarantee Programs as a Policy Solution

The lending technology and lending channel paradigms are helpful in identifying more precisely how SMEs have access to external finance. But even in large developed economies with sophisticated financial systems it is not clear that bankers have a large enough tool bag to eliminate credit rationing. That is, even economies where are all of the lending technologies that are shown in Fig. 6.1 exist, they may not be collectively sufficient to avoid a *funding gap* caused by informational opacity. The use of government subsidies to the SME sector has long been a popular public policy remedy for this problem. Particularly common among these programs has been government guarantee programs where the government guarantees (or partially guarantees) loans made by private banks. These programs exist across the globe and are predicated under the assumption that this funding gap exists. In addition to informational opacity this funding gap could be caused by gender and racial discrimination.[7]

But the success of government guarantee programs will ultimately depend on a trade-off. Assuming that market imperfections cause credit rationing, then the net benefit of these programs will be determined by whether the aggregate reduction in the funding gap is offset by the perverse effects associated with adverse selection and moral hazard. It is certainly the case that the appetite for these programs can be a political football with critics arguing that these programs provide financing at the taxpayers' expense, on balance, to firms with a negative net present value. Ultimately, this is an empirical question.

---

[7] For a broad discussion of funding gaps and policy implications see Cressy (2002).

It can be argued that the best place to test the efficacy of government guarantee programs would be in the most advanced economies. The argument here is that if it can be shown that government guarantee programs work in economies with the strongest lending infrastructure (i.e., the most, and the strongest, lending channels), then they will likely work anywhere. Recent evidence in the U.S. where the menu of lending technologies is quite broad suggest that the Federal government's loan guarantee program does add value. For example, it has been found in the U.S. that the Small Business Administration's guaranteed lending program has a positive impact on personal income growth, employment, wages and salaries – although the positive effects were not necessarily large (Craig et al., 2005; Hancock et al., 2007).

It is also important to assess how these programs work during periods of macroeconomics shocks. As we note above, many lending channels will likely contract in this financial crisis and it is likely that these will not be offset by the limited number of channels that might be able to expand. Thus, if government guarantee programs are justified during normal times, they might be even more potent during periods of financial distress. There is evidence in the U.S. that government guaranteed lending is less pro-cyclical than non-guaranteed lending suggesting these programs may be relatively more useful during a crisis such as the one we are now experiencing (Hancock et al., 2007). Perhaps more informative is the experience of Japan's government guarantee program during its financial crisis in the 1990s. The importance here derives from two factors. First, the severity of the Japanese financial crisis was comparable to the current crisis today. Second, the guarantee program implemented by the Japanese government from 1998 to 2001 was enormous and unprecedented. Empirical evidence indicates that the positive effect of stimulating small business investment was greater than the adverse selection effect (Uesugi et al., 2006).[8]

Perhaps an answered question regarding government guarantee programs is whether they can be better targeted to SMEs who need it the most. Of course, most programs place an upper limit on the size of loans that can be guaranteed which will effectively target the programs to smaller companies that are likely more opaque and more financially constrained *ceteris paribus*. But the lending technology paradigm suggests that this targeting could be more tightly focused. For example, firms for whom alternative lending technologies are not available may be more vulnerable during a credit crunch. For example, service firms without tangible assets such as inventory, equipment and real estate will not have access to the equipment, leasing and real estate-based lending technologies. If these firms had depended on smaller banks for relationship loans – and small banks were hit by capital shocks – then targeting an expansion in the government guarantee program to these types of SMEs might be appropriate. However, considerably more research is needed in this area. Unfortunately, there is a severe and universal lack of data on the mix of lending technologies across the globe.

---

[8]There is also some evidence that in Japan increases in guaranteed loans induced increases in non-guaranteed loans in the SME sector (Wilcox and Yasuda 2008).

6.5 Conclusion

Studies of net job creation generally confirm the importance of the SME sector as an engine that can drive the economy out of a recession. A key determinant of how well small business can perform this role is its access to external finance. This article examines new paradigms that have expanded our understanding of how SME loans are underwritten and how this can change during a macro financial shock. We also used these paradigms to examine two interesting related issues associated with SME financing during the current financial crisis: the behavior of foreign-owned banks particularly in developing economies and the efficacy of government guarantee programs as a possible solution.

References

Alessandrini P, Andrea FP, Alberto Z (2009) Banks, distances and firms' financing constraints. Rev Finance, 13:261–307
Bakker MHR, Klapper L, Udell GF (2004) Financing small and medium-size enterprises with factoring: global growth and its potential in eastern europe. World Bank Monograph, Washington, DC. http://wbln0018.worldbank.org/html/FinancialSectorWeb.nsf/(attachmentweb)/3342/$FILE/3342.pdf
Berger N, Black L (2008) Bank size, lending technologies, and small business finance. Federal Reserve Board working paper
Berger AN, Miller NH, Petersen MA, Rajan RG, Stein JC (2005) Does function follow organizational form? Evidence from the lending practices of large and small banks. J Financ Econ 76:237–269
Berger AN, Udell G (1995) Relationship lending and lines of credit in small firm finance. J Bus 68:351–381
Berger AN, Udell GF (2006) A more complete conceptual framework for SME finance. J Banking and Finance 30:2945–2966
Boyd J, Prescott EC (1986) Financial intermediary-coalitions, JEcon Ther 38:211–232
Calomiris C, Himmelberg C, Wachtel P (1995) Commercial paper, corporate finance and the business cycle: a microeconomic perspective. Carnegie-Rochester Conf Series Public Pol 42:203–250
Carbo-Valverde S, Rodriguez-Fernandez F, Udell GF (2009) Bank lending, financing constraints and SME Investment. Working Paper
Cole RA (1998) The importance of relationships to the availability of credit. J Bank Finan 22: 959–977
Craig BR, Jackson W, III, Thomson JB (2005) SBA-loan guarantees and local economic growth. Federal Reserve Bank of Cleveland working paper 05–03
Cressy R (2002) Introduction: funding gaps. Econ J 112:1–16
de la Torre A, Martínez Pería MS, Schmukler SL (2010) Bank involvement with SMEs: beyond relationship lending. J Bank Finance 34: 2280–2293
Diamond DW (1984) Financial intermediation and delegated monitoring, Rev EconStud 51: 393–414
Elsas R, Krahnen, J (1998) Is relationship lending special? Evidence from credit-filling data in Germany. J Bank Finan 22:1283–1316
Hancock D, Peek J, Wilcox JA (2007) The repercussions on small banks and small businesses of procyclical bank capital and countercyclical loan guarantees. Federal Reserve Board working paper

Harhoff D, Körting, T (1998) Lending relationships in Germany: empirical results from survey data. J Bank Finan 22:1317–1354

Kano M, Uchida H, Udell GF, WatanabeW (2010) Information verifiability, bank organization, bank competition and bank-borrower relationships. J Bank Finan (forthcoming)

Klapper L (2006) The role of factoring for financing small and medium enterprises. J Bank Finan 30:3111–3130

Lummer SL, McConnell JJ (1989) Further evidence on the bank lending process and the capital market response to bank loan agreements. J Finan Econ 25:99–122

Munoz MI, Norden L, Udell, FG (2009) Liberalization, corporate governance, and savings banks. Working paper

Petersen MA, Rajan RG (1994) The benefits of firm-creditor relationships: evidence from small business data. J Finan 49:3–37

Petersen MA, Rajan RG (1995) The effect of credit market competition on lending relationships. Q J Econ 110:407–443

Popov A, Udell.GF (2010) Cross-Border banking and the international transmission of financial distress during the financial crisis of 2007–2008. Working Paper

Stangler D, LitanRE (2009) Where will the jobs come from? Kaufman Foundation Research Series: Firm Formation and Economic Growth

Stein JC (2002) Information production and capital allocation: decentralized versus hierarchical firms. J Finan LVII:1891–1921

Taketa K, Udell GF (2006) Lending channels and financial shocks: the case of SME trade credit and the Japanese banking crisis. Monet Econ Stud 25:1–44

Uchida H, Udell GF, Yamori N (2008) How do Japanese banks discipline small and medium-sized borrowers? An investigation of the deployment of lending technologies. Int Finan Rev 9:57–80

Udell GF (2004) Asset-based finance. The Commercial Finance association, New York, NY

Udell GF (2008) What's in a relationship: the case of commercial lending. Bus Horiz 93–103

Udell GF (2009a) Wall street, main street, and a credit crunch: thoughts on the current finiancial crisis. Bus Horiz 52:117–125

Udell GF (2009b) How will a credit crunch affect small business finance? FRBSF Econ Lett 2009–09: March 6

Uesugi I, Sakai K, Yamashiro GM (2006) Effectiveness of credit guarantees in the Japaneses loan market. RIETI discussion paper series 06-E-004

Wilcox JA, YasudaY (2008) Do government loan guarantees lower or raise, banks' non-guanranteed lending? Evidence from Japanese Banks. Working Paper

Chapter 7
Access to Bank Financing and New Investment: Evidence from Europe

Larry W. Chavis, Leora F. Klapper, and Inessa Love

Abstract In this paper we study the relationship between firm age, the use of external finance and new investment decisions, in a sample of European firms. We find that younger firms use less bank financing than older firms only in non-EU countries, suggesting that greater financial development and a stronger investment climate offers young firms greater access to bank financing. Next, we show a link between a firm's ability to obtain a loan and make new investments. Furthermore, we find that firms that report a need for credit, but did not apply for a loan, have the lowest incidence and amount of investment. Our results highlight the important role that the business environment can play in supporting wider access to external finance and greater private sector investment.

7.1 Introduction

The ability to pursue new growth opportunities is a key concern for firms, moreover for those that are financially constrained. Not only can missed opportunities keep individual firms from growing, but if large numbers of firms are constrained country-level growth can suffer.[1] Creating a business environment where firm can grow is a major part of encouraging country-level economic growth. Recent research has pointed towards financing as the obstacle in the business environment with the largest impact on firm growth (Ayyagari et al., 2008). In order to better understand

---

L.W. Chavis (✉)
Kenan–Flagler Business School, University of North Carolina at Chapel Hill, CB 3490, McColl Building, Chapel Hill, NC 27599-3490, USA
e-mail: larry_chavis@unc.edu

The opinions expressed do not necessarily represent the views of the World Bank, its Executive Directors, or the countries they represent. The authors would like to thank the organizers and sponsors of the Urbino Conference on SME financing for the opportunity to contribute to this volume and the Cleveland Federal Reserve and the Kauffman Foundation for supporting the development of a related version of this research.

[1] See Levine (2006).

finance as an obstacle to firm growth this research examines the impact of financing on firms' decision to carry out new investments.

In this paper, we analyze the financial structure of a large sample of Eastern European firms, in both EU and non-EU member countries, hoping to shed light on firm characteristics that are associated with greater access to financing, and the relationship between access to bank financing and investment decisions. The focus of our paper is on the relationship between firm age, the incidence of investment in fixed assets and the sources of funds used to finance this investment. We also look at the impact of EU membership on these relationships. These findings can be useful in developing policy recommendations to expand lending to small and new firms.

7.2 The Role of Small and Medium Sized Firms in Eastern Europe

Ninety percent of the firms in this data set have fewer than 220 full-time employees, while the median firm has 25. Thus it is appropriate to give some background on small and medium sized enterprises (SMEs) in Eastern Europe as their emergence in the region was quite different from more developed regions. Unlike the United States, which experienced a natural birth of new, small firms, the SME sector in Eastern European and Central Asian (ECA) countries emerged as a result of the privatization and breakup of large state-owned enterprises, as well as through a large number of new, generally very small firms that came as a consequence of the market liberalization process.[2] While an extensive literature discusses the characteristics and role of SMEs in developed countries, less has been said about SMEs in Eastern Europe. Given the unique nature of the financial development and market structure in Eastern European countries, we would expect to see some distinctions in the firm characteristics and financing choices of SMEs in these countries, relative to developed countries.

Prior to its transition period, the ECA economies were dominated by large state owned enterprises (SOEs), which employed the largest fraction of the labor force, undertook the largest share of investment activities, and received the largest share of bank financing. However, the liberalization process has provided a major role for SME's as a driving force in the continuing transformation of the private sector. The restructuring and downsizing of large firms, the privatization of public utilities and other large companies, the outsourcing of many support services, and the vertical fragmentation of production are all forces that promoted the creation and expansion of SMEs.

Considering the importance of SMEs in promoting growth and dynamism in transition economies, it is critical to analyze the willingness of the banking sector to lend money to SMEs and the degree to which financial intermediaries have

---

[2] See Svejnar (2002).

facilitated their development.[3] Previously, the practice of funding economic activity in transition economies had been mostly directed by the central authorities. It is only after the liberalization process that the banking sector has been able to choose its borrowers and channel a larger share of its funding to companies of different types.[4] In order to make market based loans, commercial banks were required to measure default risk, which includes firm-level measures of profitability, growth opportunities, and available collateral, as well as country-level risk, such as the efficacy of bankruptcy laws and enforcement.

The impact of commercial banks in this transition has varied widely across the region. Johnson et al., (2002) study manufacturing firms in Poland, Romania, Slovakia, Ukraine and Russia based on a survey carried out in 1997. They find a wide degree of variation across these countries in their access to bank finance as well as in their perceived security of property rights. The authors find the highest percentage of borrowers to be in Poland, with bank financing about 2.3% of annual sales (the highest along with Russia within their sample of countries). They also find a high rate of reinvestment of profits in Poland, which they explain is a virtue of strong property rights in the country, relative to neighboring economies.

Additional studies, which more directly analyze the determinants of capital structure, find a significant degree of financing constraints faced by SMEs.[5] The supply of finance seems to be particularly determined by firms' reputation, growth and profitability. For instance, Klapper et al. (2002) use the Amadeus database to analyze patterns of corporate sector development across 15 ECA countries during the transition from planned to market economies. They find that SMEs seem to constitute the most dynamic sector of the Eastern European economies, relative to large firms. In general, the SME sector comprises relatively younger, more highly leveraged, and more profitable and faster growing firms. Firms are more market- and profit-oriented, but these firms appear to have financial constraints that impede their access to long-term financing and ability to grow. This research traces out these financing constraints especially as they relate to access to firm age, bank financing and the ability of small firms to make new investments.

7.3 Data and Summary Statistics

The World Bank Enterprise Survey (WBES) collects information on a range of quantitative and qualitative firm characteristics from a sample drawn to be representative of a country's private sector. Firm owners and managers are asked

---

[3] For additional analysis of the role of SMEs in transition economies see "SME Financing in Eastern Europe" by Klapper et al. (2002).
[4] See "Commercial Bank Lending to SMEs in Poland" by Melanie Feakins (2004).
[5] Konings et al. (2003) find that investment by firms in Poland and Czech Republic is more sensitive to internal financing constraints, as compared to the Romania and Bulgaria case, due to presence of soft budget constraints in the latter. In the same vein, Cornelli et al. (1998) and Weller (2001) observe that Polish industries have operated under hard budget constraints and were finance constrained during the early stages of the transition process.

about a variety of issues including: infrastructure and services provided by the state, firm performance, labor conditions, the financing of new investments, local market conditions, innovation, bureaucracy and crime. The sample is drawn from local business registries and covers a range of industries from basic manufacturing to hotels and restaurants.

This research uses data for 30 countries in Eastern Europe and Central Asia surveyed mainly in 2008 and early 2009.[6] As shown in Table 7.1, there is a range of income levels across this region. Tajikistan had a per capita GNI in 2008 of $600, while Slovenia was 40 times that at $24,010. Overall the average per capita GNI is $7,524, while the 9 members of the European Union have an average of $13,703. These EU members are relatively new members of the EU having joined in 2004 and 2007. Croatia, Macedonia and Turkey are candidates for EU membership, but for the purposes of this research are grouped with the non-EU countries.

For this research we focus on the 10,421 surveyed firms in the dataset are all single establishment firms. As shown in Table 7.2 the mean firm age in the data is 15.3 years, where firm age is based on the year the firm began operations in its current country. Of these firms almost 95% were registered when they began operations. Firm age is capped at 78 years, the 99th percentile, to reduce the influence of outliers. More detail on the distribution of firm age can be seen in Fig. 7.1. We can see that the vast majority of firms are between 1 and 20 years old, with a long tail to the right past 20. This roughly coincides with the end of the cold war and market reforms in the region beginning in the late 1980s and early 90 s. Of the approximately 1,500 firms in data that are more than 20 years old, 53% were privatized from former state-owned enterprises. Only 14% of firms operating less than 20 years were privatized. The analysis below will control for a firm having been privatized and we will show that the main results hold when excluding privatized firms.

The vast majority of firms in the data are small to medium in size, with the median number of full time employees being 25. The WBES over samples large firms in order to have enough large firms in the dataset for comparative purposes. To minimize the influence of very large outlying firms, the variable for the number of full time employees is capped at 1,200, the 99th percentile. Even this with adjustment these large firms pull the mean number of full time employees up to almost 90.

Table 7.2 gives a number of other key descriptive statistics for the data. Almost 60% of the firms are privately held, limited liability companies and 11.5% are publicly listed. Most of the remaining firms are sole proprietorships or partnerships. Firms in which foreign entities (7.1%) or the government (2.3%) hold more than a 20% stake are labeled as foreign and government controlled respectively. The firms are spread across a number of diverse industries, but overall more than 75% of the firms are in either manufacturing or wholesale/retail. Except for firm age and

---

[6] Ninety-eight percent of the firms were surveyed during this time period with a few surveys carried out in 2007 and late 2009.

7 Access to Bank Financing and New Investment

Table 7.1 Survey overview

Country	Firms surveyed	European Union member	2008 GNI per capita ($)
Albania	158		3,840
Armenia	348		3,350
Azerbaijan	319		3,830
Belarus	218		5,380
Bosnia and Herzegovina	332		4,510
Bulgaria	271	Since 2007	5,490
Croatia	136	Candidate	13,570
Czech Republic	211	Since 2004	16,600
Estonia	226	Since 2004	14,270
Georgia	358		2,470
Hungary	258	Since 2004	12,810
Kazakhstan	471		6,140
Kosovo	263		
Kyrgyzstan	202		740
Latvia	219	Since 2004	11,860
Lithuania	257	Since 2004	11,870
Macedonia	339	Candidate	4,140
Moldova	352		1,470
Mongolia	331		1,680
Montenegro	116		6,440
Poland	377	Since 2004	11,880
Romania	488	Since 2007	7,930
Russia	882		9,620
Serbia	337		5,700
Slovakia	246	Since 2004	14,540
Slovenia	260	Since 2004	24,010
Tajikistan	315		600
Turkey	1,027	Candidate	9,340
Ukraine	760		3,210
Uzbekistan	344		910
Total	10,421		

number of full time employees, these variables are all statistically different across EU and non-EU countries.

The research uses two main sets of questions from the WBES to explore the changes in the financing of new investments over the life cycle of firms in ECA. The first set of questions relates to the purchase of fixed assets "such as machinery, vehicles, equipment, land or buildings" in the previous fiscal year (survey instrument). The survey asks if such a purchase was made and if so how much was spent on machinery, vehicles and equipment versus land and buildings. The survey also asks what percentage of the purchase was financed from each of the following sources:

- Internal funds or retained earnings
- Owners' contribution or issued new equity shares
- Loans from private banks
- Loans from state-owned banks

Table 7.2 Firm characteristics

	Observations	Mean	Median	Standard deviation	EU mean	Non-EU mean
Purchased fixed assets last year	10,421	57.7%	1	49.4%	65.5%	54.8%
Ratio of fixed asset purchase to sales	4,492	0.13	0.05	0.20	0.10	0.14
Used retained earning to finance fixed assets	5,896	78.2%	1	41.3%	81.3%	76.9%
Used bank loan to finance fixed assets	5,894	39.8%	0	49.0%	43.2%	38.4%
Used new equity to finance fixed assets	5,895	14.0%	0	34.7%	11.6%	15.1%
Use trade credit to finance fixed assets	5,894	13.0%	0	33.6%	12.4%	13.3%
Firm age	10,258	15.3	12	13.8	15.0	15.4
Full time employees	10,345	89.0	25	176.7	84.3	90.7
Directly exports more than 20% of sales	10,381	11.3%	0	31.7%	15.2%	9.9%
Publicially listed	10,398	11.5%	0	31.9%	5.9%	13.6%
Privately held	10,398	59.2%	1	49.1%	61.6%	58.3%
Sole proprietorship	10,398	16.4%	0	37.1%	14.1%	17.3%
More than 20% foreign ownership	10,326	7.1%	0	25.7%	9.5%	6.3%
More than 20% state ownership	10,326	2.3%	0	14.9%	1.3%	2.7%
Firm was privatized	10,421	19.5%	0	39.6%	13.3%	21.8%
Manufacturing	10,421	45.4%	0	49.8%	35.8%	49.0%
Wholesale/retail	10,421	33.1%	0	47.0%	38.7%	31.0%
Construction	10,421	9.2%	0	28.9%	11.4%	8.4%

Note: All variables except for firm age and employment are indicator variables. All means are statistically different at a 1% level of significance across EU and non-EU countries except for used trade credit, firm age and full time employees

- Purchases on credit from suppliers and advances from customers
- Other (moneylenders, friends, relatives, non-banking financial institutions, etc.)

Each of these sources is analyzed separately in this research, except that borrowing from private or state-owned banks is aggregated in one banking variable. The second set of questions refers to the application for loans or lines of credit during the previous fiscal year. Firms are ask if they applied for a loan or a line of credit in the previous fiscal year and if they did not they are asked their reason for not applying. The firms are presented with the following reasons for not applying:

- No need for a loan – establishment has sufficient capital
- Application procedures for loans or lines of credit are complex
- Interest rates are not favorable
- Collateral requirements are too high

7 Access to Bank Financing and New Investment

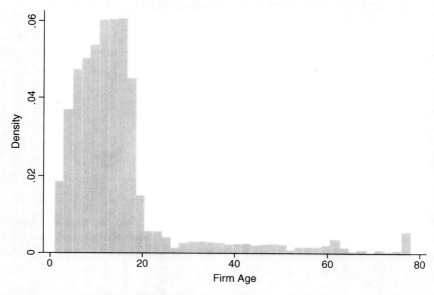

Firm age capped at 78 the 99th percentile.

Fig. 7.1 Firm age distribution

- Size of loan and maturity are insufficient
- It is necessary to make informal payments to get bank loans
- Did not think it would be approved
- Other

In our analysis these responses are categorized in variables presenting no need or sufficient capital for the first response, with remaining response aggregated as needed a loan but did not apply. Firms are also asked if they had a loan or line of credit application rejected in the previous fiscal year. This identifies firms that that had at least one application rejected, though as we will see below this does not mean that all of their applications were rejected or that they had no access to bank financing. Combining these two sets of questions along with the basic firm characteristics from Table 7.2, an interesting picture emerges of how the financing of new investment changes over a firm's life cycle and the different strategies employed by firms with varying levels of access to capital.

7.4 Financing Patterns

In this section we show how both financing patterns and the relationship with banks changes over time. Moreover we analyze how this relationship with banks affects how firms choose to finance their new investments. In Table 7.3 we see that the

Table 7.3 New investment and firm age

	Age 1–2	Age 3–4	Age 5–6	Age 7–8	Age 9–10	Age 11–12	Age 13+
Observations	368	730	933	993	1,062	1,187	4,985
Percentage of firms purchasing fixed assets	57.9	55.1	53.5	54.8	54.0	55.7	61.0
Equipment as a percentage of fixed assets	87.0	88.0	89.8	88.5	86.1	86.2	85.6
Ratio of fixed assets to total revenue (%)	18.4	18.4	14.1	13.8	13.0	12.3	12.4

percentage of firms purchasing fixed assets in the previous year remains relatively constant at around 60% as firms mature. There is not much change over time in the percentage of purchases of equipment versus buildings or land. However the ratio of spending on fixed assets to revenues falls by about one third from 18.4% for firms between 1 and 4 years old to 12.4% for those over 12 years old. This decline could be due to an actual decrease in spending on fixed assets as firms age or revenues could be growing faster than the increase in the spending on fixed assets. We will explore this issue further in the regression analysis below.

While the percentage of firms that purchase fixed assets seems to be fairly stable over time, we would like to see if the sources of financing for fixed assets are changing as firms age. In Table 7.4 we explore the 5 categories of financing that were introduced in the previous section: retained earnings, bank financing, new equity, trade credit and other. This table gives the percentage of firms that use each of sources of financing and also the proportion of total cost of investment that came from each of the source of funds. More than three quarters of the firms useinternal funds, while around 40% use bank financing. Significantly smaller numbers use the other three categories. However if a firm uses a given type of financing, that source generally fills at least half of a firm's financing needs. For example, while only 15% of firms outside of the EU used new equity as a form of financing in the previous year, new equity met 58.1% of those firms financing needs. Retained earnings are especially important for those firms that use this source to finance new investment.

Table 7.4 also highlights the sources of financing that are different in countries in and outside of the EU. A higher percentage of firms in the EU tend to use retained earnings and bank financing while fewer rely on infusions of new equity. On the other hand, firms in the EU tend to fill a lower percentage of their financing needs with retained earnings and new equity if they use these sources. Especially in the case of small firms, retained earnings and new equity could both represent funds coming from the owner of the firm. This could point to firms in the EU having more access to external forms of financing than firms in other parts of Eastern Europe and Central Asia. The patterns in Table 7.4 also indicate that access to various types

7 Access to Bank Financing and New Investment

Table 7.4 Sources of financing of fixed assets by EU membership

	\multicolumn{2}{c}{Percentage of firms using source to fund fixed assets}		\multicolumn{2}{c}{Source as a percentage of fixed asset financing if source is utilized}
	Not part of EU	EU member		Not part of EU (%)	EU member (%)
Retained earnings	76.9	81.3	***	77.6	71.6	***
Bank financing	38.4	43.2	***	59.5	60.6
New equity	15.1	11.6	***	58.1	48.9	**
Trade credit	13.3	12.4		43.6	46.3
Other sources	5.9	8.1	***	48.7	51.6

"Retained earnings" are generated within the firm. "New equity" is described in the survey as "owners' contribution or issued new equity shares". "Bank financing" is financing from private or state-owned banks. "Trade credit" are funds from "purchases on credit from suppliers and advances from customers. "Other sources" is the residual category described as "other (moneylenders, friends relatives, non-banking financial institutions etc)"
**Significant at 5% level; ***significant at 1% level. Based on a z-test of the difference between proportions

of financing may be a key aspect of financing. It is in the percentage of firms that use banking that non-EU firms seem to be at a disadvantage, suggesting that banking access is more widely available in EU countries. However, the total amount of investment financed with banks is not different in EU and non-EU countries for those firms that utilize this source of funds.

The percentage of firms accessing the various types of financing also varies by firm age. Table 7.5 lays out these trends by EU status. In non-EU countries, we see a slight increase in the percentage of firms using retained earnings and trade credit as firm age increases and a substantial increase in the percentage using banking. Fewer firms rely on new equity as they age. For EU members we see a stronger increase

Table 7.5 Sources of financing for new fixed assets

	Age 1–2 (%)	Age 3–4 (%)	Age 5–6 (%)	Age 7–8 (%)	Age 9–10 (%)	Age 11–12 (%)	Age 13+ (%)
Panel A: countries not in the European Union							
Retained earnings	72.5	73.9	72.9	78.0	79.0	76.6	77.5
Bank financing	28.8	34.2	33.2	34.0	37.5	40.9	41.5
New equity	20.6	20.2	17.7	15.9	15.3	14.7	13.4
Trade credit	6.9	13.4	10.0	12.2	11.1	13.8	15.0
Other sources	11.3	7.8	6.6	6.4	5.4	4.1	5.6
Panel B: European Union members							
Retained earnings	72.5	78.6	77.2	80.0	79.1	76.9	84.0
Bank financing	45.1	40.5	44.7	38.4	46.2	44.4	43.4
New equity	25.5	15.5	17.9	10.4	11.4	10.6	10.2
Trade credit	13.7	10.7	9.8	14.4	14.6	10.0	12.4
Other sources	9.8	9.5	6.5	8.0	8.9	8.8	8.0

in the percentage using internal funds, while for each of the other four sources a lower percentage of the oldest firms use these sources than 1–2 year old firms do. The contrast in the trends between EU and non-EU is strongest in the case of new equity. 25.5% of the newest firms in the EU use new equity versus 20.6% out of the EU. For firms over 12 years old these numbers have reversed to 10.2% (EU) and 13.4% (non-EU). It could be that firms in the EU have access to more private capital during the startup phase but with stronger growth opportunities and more access to banking they do not have to rely on new equity as much as they mature.

What is most interesting is that in non-EU countries we observe gradual increase in usage of bank finance as firms grow older, while no such increase is observed in EU countries. This may suggest that younger firms are relatively more restricted in their access to bank finance in non-EU countries. In other words, in EU countries usage of bank finance is more "democratic" and less depends on firm age than it is in on-EU countries.

Similar patterns arise when we compare our proxies for a firm's relationships to the banking sector by EU status. Table 7.6 explores our banking variables across by EU status. The percentage of firms that apply for loans across the two groups is relatively similar, with firms outside of the EU being slightly more likely to apply for a loan. However the rate of rejection is significantly higher in non-EU countries were firms are about 50% more likely to have a loan rejected. A higher percentage of EU firms state they have sufficient capital while far fewer claimed that they needed bank financing but did not apply. Fourteen percent of the firms said they needed financing but did not apply in the EU while 22% of the firms outside of the EU stated that this was the case. Overall 46% of those that did not apply did so because of high interest rates while 16% said applications were too complex and 15% pointed to collateral requirements. These results suggest that firms in non-EU countries have more difficulty with access to financing than firms in EU countries.

Firms that did not apply for a loan often rank financing as a severe obstacle to growth. As shown in Table 7.7, 41.9% firms that needed a loan but did not apply feel like access to financing is a major or severe obstacle to their current operations. This percentage is even higher, 48.1%, for those that have applied for a loan or line of credit and have had at least one rejection. As one might expect fewer firms with sufficient capital, 12.9%, felt the same way.

Table 7.6 Regional effects on loan application status

	Non-EU countries (%)	EU members (%)	
Applied for loan	43.6	41.6	*
Loan rejected if applied	17.0	11.3	***
No need for loan	33.9	42.9	***
Need but did not apply	21.8	14.0	***

Table gives the percentage of firms that fall into each category. *significant at 10% level; **significant at 5% level; ***significant 1% level. These are the results of a z-test of the difference between proportions

7 Access to Bank Financing and New Investment

Table 7.7 Bank loan application status and financing

Percentage of firms that feel financing is a major or severe obstacle				Percentage of firms purchasing fixed assets in previous year			
Applied for loan	30.9	23.1	Did not apply for loan	Applied for loan	72.6	46.6	Did not apply for loan
Applied and loan rejected	48.1	27.7	Applied and loan not rejected	Applied and loan rejected	64.8	74.0	Applied and loan not rejected
No need for loan	12.9	34.2	needed loan	No need for loan	48.9	62.9	Needed loan
Needed loan but did not apply	41.9	22.7	Applied for loan or had sufficient capital	Needed loan but did not apply	42.2	61.6	Applied for loan or had sufficient capital

All pairs are statistically different at less than a 1% level of significance based a z-test of the difference of proportions

While a firm's experience with the banking sector affects their perception of financing as an obstacle, these experiences also have real effects on a firm's likelihood of purchasing fixed assets and on how purchases are financed as seen in Table 7.7. Only 42.2% of firms that needed a loan but did not apply purchased fixed assets in the previous year. This is compared with 61.6% of firms that applied for a loan or had sufficient capital. Seventy-four percent of firms that applied for a loan or line and credit and were not rejected purchased fixed assets. As one would expect, these experiences with loan applications affect the way that firms finance their new investments.

The relationship between loan application status and sources of financing for fixed assets is laid out in Table 7.8. As we might expect a high percentage (60.6%) of firms that applied for loans used bank financing. Even more than half of those that applied and were rejected at least once use bank financing. This suggests that these firms were able to eventually file a successful application for a bank loan, or perhaps used an existing line of credit. More than 85.9% of those firms that stated they had

Table 7.8 Correlation between fixed asset financing patterns and loan applications

	Applied for loan (%)	Loan rejected if applied (%)	No need for loan (%)	Need but did not apply (%)
Retained earnings	73.7	74.4	85.9	78.5
Bank financing	60.6	52.4	14.5	17.5
New equity	14.0	15.6	12.3	18.5
Trade credit	16.4	14.5	7.3	12.1
Other sources	7.0	7.7	4.8	8.7

This table shows the percentage of firms that use these five sources of financing for the purchase of fixed assets in the previous year as a function of their need for credit and their relationship with banks

no need for a loan used retained earnings to fund their new investment. Overall a higher percentage of these firms used retained earnings and a lower percentage used the other four types of financing than any other type of firm. A firm that needed a loan but did not apply was far less likely to use a bank loan that those firms that applied and more likely to use retained earnings, new equity or other sources of financing.

In Table 7.5, we saw some changes in the financing patterns of fixed assets by firm age and EU status. Table 7.9 does a similar comparison of firms' loan application status. In the non-EU countries as firms age they are more likely to apply for loans and fewer loan applications are rejected with age. In the EU countries these proportions are more similar for older and younger firms. This again points to the more universal access to bank finance in firms of different age and more restricted usage of bank finance by younger firms in non-EU countries. However there is little change in the percentage of firms that needed loans but did not apply as firms age, while this percentage tends to decline among firms in the European Union. As illustrated above, it is these firms that tend to have the most difficulty getting the capital they need for investments. Given that we see the decline in the percentage of these

Table 7.9 Status of bank loan in the last fiscal year by firm age

	Age 1–2 (%)	Age 3–4 (%)	Age 5–6 (%)	Age 7–8 (%)	Age 9–10 (%)	Age 11–12 (%)	Age 13+(%)
Panel A: countries not in the European Union							
Applied for loan	36.4	40.0	39.7	40.4	39.8	46.8	46.9
Applied for loan and at least one loan rejected	27.1	21.3	20.1	21.0	15.1	13.4	15.7
No need for loan sufficient capital	40.8	35.7	35.6	36.6	35.0	31.8	32.1
Needed loan but did not apply	21.8	23.3	24.0	22.3	24.6	20.5	20.5
Panel B: European Union Members							
Applied for loan	40.3	38.1	35.8	37.4	36.3	41.2	44.4
Applied for loan and at least one loan rejected	13.8	11.3	13.4	18.2	14.0	14.8	9.3
No need for loan sufficient capital	36.1	44.6	46.0	45.6	46.1	43.7	41.8
Needed loan but did not apply	22.2	13.7	16.6	15.5	17.2	12.9	12.4

This table reports on the mean of indicator variables related to questions regarding applications for loans or lines credit during the fiscal year before the survey. Firms where ask if they applied for a loan or line of credit and if they did not apply, firms were asked why they did not apply

firms only in the EU, it seems less likely that the decline is only due to survival bias. It could be that firms are better able to solve their financing problem in the EU as they age than in the less developed countries.

7.5 The Determinants of Investment Incidence and Financing Strategies

The analysis so far has shown the challenges faced by younger firms and those without strong relationships with the banking sector. We have also seen that these challenges can vary with the quality of the institutional environment, as measured by being a member of the European Union. In this section we will aim to calculate a more precise measure for the impact of age, banking relationships and EU membership on the financing of fixed assets. Using multiple regression analysis will also allow us to control for the other factors like size of the firm or country specific factors that affect the financial choice sets that firms face.

In addition to looking at the effects of firm age and the status of loan applications the regressions also control for a comprehensive set of firm characteristics. These variables were discussed above and are summarized in Table 7.2. The regressions also contain country, survey year and sector fixed effects. Thus our results represent the average within country and sector effects. Two basic types of effects will be estimated in this section. The first is the effect of age and loan application status on the percentage of firms that purchase fixed assets. We are assuming here that banking options affect the likelihood of purchasing fixed assets and not vice versa. While we cannot completely rule out edogeneity of financing and investment decisions, the descriptive statistics we have looked at so far suggested that the status of loan applications is correlated withboth – the ability to purchase fixed assets and the types of financing that are available. The second type of regression will focus on the effect of firm age and banking relationships on the types of financing used in the recent purchase of fixed assets. Here again we are assuming that a firm has a range of choices and that those choices are affected by the status of the loan application or the firm's need for capital.

Table 7.10 gives the regression results for the both the likelihood of purchasing a fixed asset and for using the four main sources of financing. In each case the dependent variable is an indicator variable and the results are the probit regressions, except for specification 2 which as a continuous dependent variable and uses OLS. The reported coefficients for the probit regressions are marginal effects calculated at the average value of the variables for continuous variables and for a 0 to 1 transition for indicator variables (all variables expect for Ln Firm Age and Ln Full Time Employees are indicator variables). In specification one, we can see that as firms age the likelihood of purchasing a fixed asset decreases. Going from a firm of 1 year to a 12 year old firm decreases the likelihood of purchasing a fixed asset by about 6 percentage points. That is about a 10% decrease from the likelihood based on the average percentage of firms purchasing assets (58%).This seems reasonable given

Table 7.10 Affect of firm age on fixed asset purchase and financing patterns

	(1) Fixed assets	(2) Ratio of a FA to sales	(3) Retained earnings	(4) Bank financing	(5) Equity financing	(6) Trade credit
Ln firm age	−0.025	−0.010	0.015	−0.007	−0.016	−0.002
	[0.01]***	[0.02]**	[0.09]*	[0.56]	[0.06]*	[0.69]
Sufficient capital	−0.130	−0.60	0.106	−0.369	−0.026	−0.065
	[0.00]***	[0.00]***	[0.00]***	[0.00]***	[0.13]	[0.00]***
Needed loan did not apply	−0.147	−0.041	0.037	−0.275	0.025	−0.019
	[0.00]***	[0.01]***	[0.28]	[0.00]***	[0.21]	[0.30]
Applied and not rejected for loan	0.088	−0.006	−0.013	0.107	−0.019	0.009
	[0.00]***	[0.62]	[0.60]	[0.00]***	[0.20]	[0.49]
Ln full time employees	0.094	−0.013	0.018	0.034	−0.009	0.006
	[0.00]***	[0.00]***	[0.00]***	[0.00]***	[0.05]*	[0.14]
Exporter	0.013	0.001	0.006	0.001	−0.006	0.016
	[0.64]	[0.95]	[0.75]	[0.95]	[0.76]	[0.27]
Publically listed	−0.044	0.021	−0.033	−0.017	0.021	0.029
	[0.03]**	[0.03]**	[0.11]	[0.59]	[0.11]	[0.2]**
Sole proprietorship	−0.025	0.019	−0.031	0.030	0.020	−0.003
	[0.27]	[0.12]	[0.24]	[0.08]*	[0.24]	[0.76]
Foreign owners	0.030	−0.018	−0.020	−0.077	0.017	−0.031
	[0.31]	[0.10]*	[0.39]	[0.01]***	[0.26]	[0.06]*
State owners	−0.085	0.020	0.015	0.028	0.000	−0.009
	[0.02]**	[0.27]	[0.60]	[0.53]	[1.00]	[0.68]
Privatized	−0.062	−0.011	−0.007	−0.058	−0.021	−0.013
	[0.00]***	[0.09]*	[0.64]	[0.00]***	[0.16]	[0.25]
Observations	9,996	4,388	5,694	5,692	5,693	5,692
Censored Obs	58%		78%	40%	14%	13%
Pseudo R2	0.14		0.07	0.21	0.09	0.10
R2		0.09				

Specifications 1, 3-6 report the marginal effects of probit estimates, while specification 2 uses OLS. Marginal effects are calculated at the average value of the variables for continuous variables and for a 0 to 1 transition for indicator variables. The dependent variables in the first column is a dummy equal to one if the firm purchased fixed assets in the previous fiscal year; the second column is a the ratio of fixed assets purchased in the previous year to sales for the year; the third column uses a dummy equal to one if the firm uses retained earnings, the four the column is a dummy equal to one if the firm uses government of private bank financing, the fifth column is a dummy equal to one if the firm uses new equity; and the sixth column is a dummy equal to one if the firm uses trade credit. All regressions include sector fixed effects (manufacturing, services, and construction), country-level fixed-effects, and survey year fixed effects. Standard errors are clustered by country

Asterisks *, **, and *** indicate significance at 10, 5 and 1% respectively

7 Access to Bank Financing and New Investment

that as firms age they need less equipment and buildings as they accumulate a stock of assets over time.

The access that a firm has to capital seems to have a strong relationship with the likelihood of purchasing new assets. Firms with sufficient capital are 13 percentage points less likely to purchase fixed assets than those that applied and were rejected, which is the omitted category. This would indicate that many of these firms feel they have sufficient capital because they are not looking to increase their stock of fixed assets. On the other hand, firms that have applied for a loan or line of credit and were not reject in the previous year are almost 9 percentage points more likely to purchase a fixed asset than those that applied and were rejected. The group appears to least likely to make purchases of fixed assets are those firms that did not apply for loans despite their need for capital. They are 14.7 percentage points less likely to invest in new assets. This is a 25% decline in the probability of investment, again based on the average observed likelihood of purchasing fixed assets. Thus, again the firms with the most precarious relationship to bank financing are the least likely to be able to pursue new opportunities. Similar effects are seen in specification 2, where the dependent variable is the ratio of fixed assets purchased in the previous year to total sales in that year.

Examining specifications 3 through 6, we see that firm age positively effects the probability of using retained earnings but is negatively associated with equity financing. In both of these cases the absolute size of the change in probability based on going from a new firm to a 12 year old firm is approximately 4 percentage points. This is a relatively small impact on the likelihood of using retained earnings since 78% of the firms use some internal funds, however this is more than a 25% decrease in the likelihood of using new equity. Thus firms seem to be shifting from the funds of the owner or other private individuals to retained earnings as they age.

Although firms indicating they have sufficient capital are less likely to invest, those that do invest are 10.6 percentage points more likely to use retained earnings. Since they did not apply for a loan or line of credit they are significantly less likely to use bank financing and also rely on trade credit less often. Those that needed loans but did not apply are almost 70% less likely to use bank financing and those they were never rejected for a loan are 25% more likely. Neither of these variables has a significant effect on the likelihood of using other types of financing. Thus, for firms that needed a loan but did not apply, the absence of bank financing is leaving a hole in their financing choices.

Table 7.11 extends the regressions in Table 7.10 by adding an interaction between firm age and EU status. This interaction is statistically significant in all 6 specifications, except for the specification 2. Adding the EU interaction gives us a clearer picture of the relationship between firm age, their investment decisions and different financing strategies that firms employ both inside and outside the EU. As in Table 7.10, the coefficient on Ln Firm Age is negative and significant; however, the coefficient on the EU interaction term is positive. Thus firms in the EU do not become less likely to purchase fixed assets as they age. However, the ratio of fixed

Table 7.11 Effect of instituions on fixed asset purchases and financing patterns

	(1) Fixed assets	(2) Ratio of FA to sales	(3) Retained earnings	(4) Bank financing	(5) Equity financing	(6) Trade credit
Ln firm age	−0.032	−0.013	0.007	0.008	−0.008	0.005
	[0.00]***	[0.01]***	[0.55]	[0.56]	[0.44]	[0.54]
Ln firm age	0.039	0.008	0.038	−0.055	−0.037	−0.027
EU status interaction	[0.07]*	[0.32]	[0.00]***	[0.03]**	[0.01]**	[0.03]**
Observations	9,996	4,388	5,694	5,692	5,693	5,692
Censored Obs	58%		78%	40%	14%	13%
Pseudo R2	0.15		0.07	0.21	0.09	01
R2		0.09				

Table 7.11 features the same regressions as Table 7.10, expect the interaction of Ln Firm Age and EU status is added. All the same control variables are included (sufficient capital, needed loan, not rejected, ln full time employees, exporter publically listed, sole proprietorship, foreign owned, state owned, privatized and survey year, sector and country fixed effect) but only the coeffients on the firm age variables are reported. The coefficients in specification 1 and 3–6 are the marginal effects of probit estimates. Specification 2 uses OLS. Marginal effects are calculated at the average value of the variables. The dependent variable in the first column is a dummy equal to one if the firm purchased fixed assets in the previous fiscal year; the second column is a the ratio of fixed assets purchased in the previous year to sales for that year; the third column uses a dummy equal to one if the firm uses retained earnings, the fourth column is a dummy equal to one if the firm uses government or private bank financing, the fifth column is a dummy equal to one if the firm uses new equity; and the sixth column is a dummy equal to one if the firm uses trade credit. All regressions include sector fixed effects (manufacturing, services, and construction), country-level fixed-effects, and survey year fixed effects. Standard errors are clustered by country
Asterisks*, **, and *** indicate significance at 10, 5, and 1% respectively

assets purchases to sales declines across both groups of countries. At the same time, firms in the EU become more likely to use retained earnings as they mature and less likely to use bank financing, new equity and trade credit. The affects are both statistically and economically significant. This suggests that firms in the EU are able to maintain the frequency of new investments as they age, but they are likely to do so using internally generated funds.

In unreported results these differences based on EU status are robust to excluding both privatized firms and firms in Central Asia. As we outlined above there is a strong correlation between privatization and firm age with firms over 20 years of age being more likely to have been privatized. Also one might be worried that the poorer countries on Central Asia are a poor comparison group to countries with vastly higher incomes. Thus it is reassuring to see the results hold when removing these subgroups. It also seems less likely that it is solely survival bias that is driving these results. If survival bias were a main driver of the results we might expect to see similar results across EU and non-EU countries. One might even expect for the survival bias to be worse in the less developed countries, yet it is only in the EU countries that we see firms becoming less reliant on external funds as they age.

7.6 Conclusions

We study the relationship between access to external finance and new investment in a sample of European firms. We investigate firm behavior over the age cycle of firms and focus on young firms, as these are most likely to be the most entrepreneurial firms that will drive the future progress and growth. We focus on the impact of the institutional environment, proxied by EU membership, on the use of external finance and the real effect on firm investment behavior.

We find several interesting patterns. Firms in EU have are more likely to use bank financing for their investment purchases. We also find that in non-EU countries older firms are more likely to apply for loans and their applications are less likely to be rejected than for younger firms. However, we do not find the same effects in EU countries, meaning that in EU countries older firms do not have significant advantage over younger firms in getting loans. This suggests that credit access is more "democratic" in the EU countries.

We also find that a firm's ability to secure a loan is related to real behavior, measured by incidence of investment and the amount invested. Not surprisingly, firms that were able to obtain a loan are more likely to make any investment than firms that were rejected for a loan, or firms that did not even apply because they thought to be rejected. More importantly, we find that firms that did not apply even when they needed a loan are the most negatively affected with respect to incidence of investment and investment amounts. These results suggest that these firms are the most constrained in their investment behavior by inability to obtain financing. These firms are the important category for policy interventions.

Finally, we find that older firms are less likely to purchase fixed assets and when they do, they spend smaller amounts on fixed assets purchases. However, this impact is most pronounced in non-EU countries. This suggests that in those countries larger firms are not investing as much as their younger counterparts. In addition, firms in the EU are more likely to use retained earnings and less likely to use other sources of external finance. This suggests that as firms in the EU mature they are able to maintain the frequency and amount of investment using their internal funds, while firms in non EU countries have to decrease their investment with age and rely relatively more on external funds.

Our results confirm a link between availability of external finance and firms investment behavior and highlight the important role business environment can play in supporting wider access to external finance and hence an increased incidence of investment.

References

Ayyagari M, Demirgüç-Kunt A, Maksimovic V (2008) How important are financing constraints? The role of finance in the business environment. World Bank Econ Rev 22(3):483–516

Cornelli F, Portes R, Schaffer M (1998) The capital structure of firms in central and eastern Europe, Paris, France pp. 171–188. In: Bouin O, Coricelli F, Lemoine F (eds) Different paths to a market economy: China and European Economies in transition. CEPR/CEPII/OECD

Feakins M (2004) Commercial bank lending to SMEs in Poland: an empirical investigation. Small Bus Econ 23:51–70

Johnson S, McMillan J, Woodruff C (2002) Property rights and finance. Am Econ Rev 92(5): 1335–1356

Klapper L, Saria-Allende V, Sulla V (2002) Small- and medium-size enterprise financing in Eastern Europe. World Bank Policy Research Working Paper 2933, December

Konings J, Rizov M, Vandenbussche H (2003) Investment constraints in transition countries. Econ Lett 18:253–258

Levine R (2006) Finance and growth: theory and evidence. In: Aghion P, Durlauf S (eds) Handbook of economic growth. Elsevier North-Holland, New York, NY, pp 865–934

Svejnar J (2002) Transition economies: performance and challenges. J Econ Perspect 6(1):3–28

Weller C (2001) The finance investment link in a transition economy: evidence for Poland from panel data. Comp Econ Stud 43:31–52

Chapter 8
Basel II and Changing Bank-Firm Relationship: A Survey

Chiara Bentivogli, Emidio Cocozza, Antonella Foglia, and Simonetta Iannotti

Abstract This chapter analyzes the results of a business survey on the changes in the bank-firm relationship in view of Basel II carried out in 2006. A non-negligible share of firms was aware of the possible effects of the new regulation and some of them were implementing relevant organizational changes. In general firms did not perceive any relevant change in banks' behavior, but there was some dispersion in the answers on credit availability and conditions. A trend towards reduction in multiple bank relationships emerged, particularly among firms participating in the national survey. The local survey aimed also at evaluating the impact of bank-firm relationship on growth plans of Italian SMEs. Firms located in Emilia-Romagna showed a higher growth propensity. Among the main obstacles to growth, firms emphasize bank financial and consulting support, and managerial and organizational problems.

8.1 Introduction

At the beginning of 2007 the new rules on banks' capital requirement (Basel II) have come into effect. The main purpose of the new regulation is to reconcile capital requirements on credit portfolios to banks' own assessment of risk and therefore to adjust capital rules to management practices of the operators.

It is difficult to establish a priori the impact of Basel II on bank-firm relationships. The sound practices expected as a result of the introduction of the new rules are, on the one hand, a spur to banks to use more sophisticated instruments for the effective knowledge of businesses as well as to improve the evaluation of investment projects; on the other hand, Basel II should provide an incentive for firms to make a more thorough disclosure of their own financial condition and growth prospects. Greater knowledge of firms by banks may imply a better credit pricing and an increasing

---

C. Bentivogli (✉)
Banca d'Italia, Bologna Branch, Piazza Cavour 6, 40124 Bologna
e-mail: chiara.bentivogli@bancaditalia.it

differentiation in credit availability for firms. Moreover, there could be an incentive for more exclusive and long-lasting bank-firm relationships, thus reducing the scope for multiple lending relationships, a phenomenon widespread in Italy and linked to the presence of switching costs (Detragiache et al., 2000).

The new regulation hinges on a better exploitation of information. The theory of financial intermediation shows that banks have a specific advantage in the acquisition of private information during their credit relationship (Gordon and Winton, 2003). The specialization of banks in the evaluation, selection and monitoring of investment projects is central to explain their function in innovation and growth projects. King and Levine (1993), for example, emphasize the role of intermediaries in reducing the costs of identifying the entrepreneurs more capable of generating innovation. Herrera and Minetti (2007) find that the length of the lending relationship, a proxy for the intensity of the relationship with the main bank, has a positive effect on the probability that firms invest in process innovation. The literature on relationship lending does not give a clear-cut answer on the effect of exclusive and long-lasting bank-firm relationships on the availability and cost of credit. Some authors find a trade-off in lending relations: on the one hand the solution to information asymmetries can increase credit supply by the main bank to the more opaque clients (protection effect), on the other hand the holding up effect of exclusive relations can increase credit costs (Boot, 2003).

The final impact of Basel II should not be taken for granted, but will depend on the balance of the expected benefits and the costs envisaged by the agents. The possible final market equilibrium is not unique and it could be a sub-optimal one. For example, if banks limited themselves to a bureaucratic use of automatic procedures, based mainly on data from firms' balance sheets, without exploiting adequately the qualitative information deriving from the relationship with firms, or if they based the lending decision only on the presence of suitable collateral, then there could be credit rationing and/or higher credit costs (Calcagnini, 2004). Moreover, if firms perceived the introduction of the new rules as a burden in terms of higher information costs or more difficult credit access, then they could increase the number of banking relationships in order to keep some flexibility and bargaining power with respect to the banks. Finally, it is not clear whether the instruments given by the regulator could be adequate to favor the correct evaluation of start-ups, the youngest firms without a business history, which are more difficult to distinguish from the inefficient firms.

In other terms, it is the "interpretation" of the new rules by economic agents that will determine whether they will be effective in improving the relationship among banks and borrowers. Such "interpretation" has more relevance in periods of economic crisis, when credit supply can be constrained by the availability of bank capital. In this situation, the extent to which banks can extend credit depends on their ability to evaluate and select investment projects based on an effective use of soft information (information on the quality of management, for example) or difficult-to-process information (such as forecasts for the sector of economic activity in which the firm is operating). If banks adopt an automated processing of the lending relationship, and firms maintain an excessive degree of opacity, credit becomes a commodity, that risks to evaporate rapidly when external conditions are not favorable. In sum, a valuable lending relationship can be maintained also in period of economic crises if both banks and firms invest in increasing the quality of the information exchanged.

In order to verify if and how the relationship between banks and firms were evolving in view of the introduction of the new rules on bank capital adequacy, in 2006 the Bank of Italy carried out a survey, adding a special section on Basel II to the yearly survey on a sample of private non-agricultural firms with 20 and more employees.[1] The survey focused on three aspects:

1. The actual degree of knowledge of the new regulation by firms, their awareness of the repercussions for their activity and the initiatives taken to adapt to these changes. In particular, the survey verified whether the firms had carried out some organizational changes in order to provide banks with additional and more detailed information on their activity and on their economic results;
2. The changes in banks' behavior perceived by firms as specifically related to Basel II, in order to verify whether the new rules could determine some sort of credit rationing;
3. The changes in the firms' financial structure and in lending relationship. More specifically, the survey aimed at checking whether the greater transparency required by Basel II could induce firms to reduce multiple lending and to concentrate credit on their main bank.

The impact of Basel II may be different depending on firm size. In this context, the effect of new rules on the relationship between banks and small firms could vary depending on their geographic location, the characteristics of the bank, and how widespread becomes among intermediaries the use of the more sophisticated methods stimulated by the new regulation.

The Italian productive structure is dominated, more than in other European countries, by small firms. In 2003 95% of Italian firms and 47% of total industrial employment was concentrated in firms with less than 20 employees. The average firm dimension was about 4 employees, against 7 in France and about 12 in Germany and in the United Kingdom (Istat, 2006). In 2005 bank loans to small firms (with less than 20 employees) represented less than a fifth of the total. In this segment small local banks showed a high degree of specialization, with a market share of 27%, about twice the share they had in total firm credit market.

Since the impact of Basel II may differ according to firm size, the national survey was supplemented by a local survey on small and very small firms localized in Emilia-Romagna (Northern Italy), Puglia and Basilicata (Southern Italy). The local

---

[1] The survey was conducted before the financial crises of 2007–2008 and, in particular, does not cover the following period of economic recession. Preliminary empirical analysis elaborated after this chapter was drafted shows that the strength of the lending relationships – and, presumably, the intensity of soft information exchanged – is an important factor in ensuring a continued supply of lending.

survey was carried out with the help of the local Associations of small and medium firms (API). In addition to these topics, the local survey on small firms dealt with bank-firm relationship when the firm decides to expand its scale of operation: the type of financing involved, the non-financial support by the main bank, the obstacles met by firms that decided to drop the growth project.

The new regulation is likely to have an impact on the firms' funding choices regarding their investment plans and more generally on the link between "finance" and "growth and development" of the economy (Calcagnini, 2004). Greater knowledge of the firm and the adoption of assessment processes more oriented to the prospective evaluation of economic viability of the firm should allow banks to better evaluate not only their client's creditworthiness in the short-term but also the impact of the different types of funding on the financial stability of the firm in the long-term. As a result, the role of the banks would evolve from mere financing institutions to that of financial partners, with a positive effect on credit expansion and firms' growth.

After a short a description of the main characteristics of the samples of the two surveys (Sect. 8.2), Sect. 8.3 outlines the results of the survey on Basel II. Section 8.4 analyzes the results of the local survey on firms' relationship with the banking system and on growth financing. Some conclusions are reported on Sect. 8.5.

8.2 Characteristics of the Surveys

The national survey has been conducted on a sample of 3,231 firms of industry (excluding construction) and 1,159 firms of non-financial services with 20 and more employees. The sample represents 8.4% of the universe for industry and 4.3% for the service sector. These percentages double in the case of firms with more than 50 employees; the sample distribution is therefore relatively unbalanced towards big firms, as 60.8% of interviewed firms has more than 50 employees (Bank of Italy, 2006). In order to relate the sample to the universe, data were weighted by the number of businesses in the reference population.

The firms in the sample have an average dimension of 85.5 employees, €314,000 sales per employee, about one fifth of which are abroad (29.3% for industry and 8.7% for services), and in 2005 invested about €12,000 per employee. The firms are on average 30 years old and in 90% of case are public companies.

The local survey has been conducted on a sample of 214 firms, mostly of small dimension, with a relatively balanced distribution with respect to the universe: 80% of them has less than 20 employees, against 98% in the relevant universe. The average dimension, 13.9 employees, is smaller for the regions of Puglia and Basilicata, while sales per employee are about €245,000 and are not very different geographically. A significant gap between Emilia-Romagna and the South is found in foreign sales (16.2% for Emilia-Romagna and 5.6% for Puglia and Basilicata) and in average investment per worker (37.3 and 18.3 thousand euros, respectively).

Southern firms are relatively younger and were founded on average around 1995, 11 years after those of Emilia-Romagna; 7.8% of the first group of firms was founded before 1980, against 36.1% of the second group. A similar difference is found in the year of control acquisition (1998 against 1988) and in the age of the controlling subject, 43.1 against 54.7 years. The controlling subject is descendant of the founder in 45% of cases (50% for the firms of Puglia and Basilicata, and 35.7% for those of Emilia-Romagna). In the firms' history the change of control occurred only in a limited number of cases, probably because firms are relatively young, and it is absent in 76.2% of cases. This percentage diminishes when the firm dimension increases.

As far as the participation to the property of the firm is concerned, the greater diffusion of joint stock companies in Emilia-Romagna (95.1% of the total against 70.6%) is not matched by a larger number of partners, who are about 3 in both cases and does not change substantially in higher dimensions.

8.3 The Knowledge of Basel II and the Initiatives Taken

8.3.1 The National Survey

38.6% of respondents said they already knew Basel II and were aware of its effect on the firm (Table 8.1). This share does not seem negligible, considering that the new regulation had not came into force yet when the survey was carried on and that the question was not just about the sheer knowledge of Basel II but about the firms' evaluation of the effects on their relationships with banks. Knowledge of the new rules is above average for firms with 50 and more employees (46.4%), for joint stock companies (44.2%) and for those operating in manufacturing and energy (43.4%). From a geographical point of view, firms in the Southern Italy show the lowest degree of knowledge (35.5%).

Changes in firm behavior. – About half of the firms which said that they knew the new regulation also declared that they had already adopted some initiatives to adapt to Basel II or had the intention to adopt them during 2006. While there are no substantial differences among firms of different size, the decision to take initiatives is more frequent in Centre and South and Islands (62.2 and 54.1%, respectively) and in the service sector (53.1% against 47.8% in manufacturing and energy). There is also a considerable gap between the firms of the North-East (more than 50%) and those of the North-West (less than 40%).

Further disclosure of information is deemed necessary by the firms more aware of the effects of Basel II, which in 32.7% of cases envisaged an enrichment of the information about the firm. The second action envisaged, in order of importance, is the raise of capital to debt ratio (23.7% of the respondents).

Poor disclosure and undercapitalization are therefore perceived by the firms as a limit that should be overcome through skills and organizational means that are already available inside the firm. The strengthening of specialized skills in finance, either within the firm or hired from outside, is pointed out by only 19.8% and 16% of the respondents respectively. There are no substantial differences among size classes, except for a higher role given to external specialists by smaller firms,

Table 8.1 Knowledge of the effects of Basel II on firm operations and planned initiatives[a] *(percentages)*

Class size and geographical area	Knowledge of the effects of Basel II	% of positive answers	Initiatives taken or envisaged in view of Basel II — of which:[b]					
			Increase information on the firm	Creation/ strengthen. of financial dept.	Increase involv. of external specialists	Request of valuation by specialized agencies	Decrease the debt/equity ratio
National survey	**38.6**	**49.6**	**32.7**	**19.8**	**16.0**	–	**23.7**
20–49 employees	35.1	49.4	32.3	18.9	18.6	–	23.3
50 employees and more	46.4	50.1	33.5	21.2	11.4	8.9	24.4
North-West	38.5	38.9	25.0	12.7	9.4	7.4	14.6
North-East	39.6	51.7	35.1	20.5	15.7	7.8	26.3
Centre	39.9	62.2	43.6	26.8	26.2	9.4	32.3
South and Islands	35.5	54.1	32.8	26.2	19.0	16.2	29.2
Industry[c]	43.4	47.8	31.0	18.2	14.0	8.3	23.3
Services	31.6	53.1	36.1	22.9	19.8	10.3	24.6
Local survey	**61.7**	**43.9**	**26.6**	**21.0**	**23.8**	**19.6**	**23.4**
1–9 employees	64.1	44.4	26.6	21.0	23.8	19.6	23.4
10–19 employees	57.7	44.2	24.8	16.2	27.4	19.7	23.9
20–49 employees	60.6	39.4	26.9	32.7	26.9	23.1	25.0
50 employees and more	77.8	66.7	27.3	18.2	9.1	12.1	21.2
Emilia-Romagna	47.5	24.6	16.4	9.8	11.5	8.2	16.4
Puglia and Basilicata	67.3	51.6	30.7	25.5	28.8	24.2	26.1

[a]Data from the national survey are weighted. [b]Multiple answers are possible. [c]Excluding construction
Source: Bank of Italy (2006) and Bank of Italy-API, *Local survey on Basel II and firm growth*, 2006

which in general already hire professional financial advisers when they take long term decisions. From a geographical point of view, the firms in Central Italy are more active in taking the initiatives illustrated above: more than 40% intend to improve disclosure about the firm (against 25% in North-West) and more than 30% want to strengthen capital to debt ratios (as opposed to 15% in North-West). Moreover, 9% of larger firms want to receive a credit rating from a specialized agency. The percentage is higher among Southern firms (16%) and among those operating in the service sector (10%).

The intention to increase the capital ratio shows that a non negligible number of firms wants to ease indebtedness, presumably to receive a more favorable rating. Indeed, rating systems that are totally or partially based on quantitative indicators put a lot of weight on balanced capital positions and on the ability to generate enough cash flows to cover financial costs.

Changes in banks behavior. – Most of firms which had already examined the effects of Basel II did not perceive in the previous year relevant changes in banks' behavior attributable to the next introduction of the new rules (Tables 8.2 and 8.3).

More than 80% did not notice changes in the length of credit inquiries and in loans' maturity. Among the remaining firms, the share of those who perceived a lengthening in credit inquiries and in loans' maturity is slightly higher. This could signal an ongoing adjusting process to the new rules.

A lower percentage (62%) of the firms that said to be aware of the effects of Basel II did not notice any change in bank behavior in granting larger or new loans. A non-negligible share did not obtain the loan requested (9.4%, which rises to 10.4% for small firms). Almost 30% instead perceives a higher availability of bank credit.

Banks did not change financing terms (interest rate, charges and collateral) for 73% of the sample. This share rises to 75% for firms with 50 and more employees and decreases to 69% for those with less than 50 employees. Moreover, 18% of the large firms (and 14% of the small ones) were subject to a rise in interest rates connected to the imminent introduction of Basel II and/or were required to increase their collateral. On the contrary, 13% of large firms (and 11% of small ones) paid a lower interest rate or gave less collateral.

Data show high variability in the responses on credit availability and on changes in credit terms, with high percentages both of firms perceiving an improvement and of those perceiving a worsening, suggesting that banks, by using more sophisticated techniques, can better evaluate their borrower's risk and consequently can adjust credit availability and terms. This interpretation is confirmed by the fact that differentiation is stronger among firms belonging to larger size classes, which probably have relationships with banks that use internal ratings.

Twenty seven percent of firms said they were asked to supply more qualitative (for example on shareholders and management) and quantitative information, on their financial situation and prospective profitability. This seems to confirm that, in applying the regulation, the firm could have already seized the opportunity to strengthen bank-firm relationship on the grounds of a deeper cooperation on information exchange.

Table 8.2 Changes in the financing relationships accomplished by banks and related to Basel II[a] *(percentages)*

Type of change	Decrease	No change	Increase
	National survey		
Availability of the bank to grant loans	9.4	61.8	28.8
Change in loans conditions (interest rate and costs) and/or request of collateral	11.6	72.7	15.7
of which: *change in conditions*[b]	*9.4*	*75.7*	*14.9*
request of collateral[b]	*7.0*	*84.4*	*8.6*
Request of qualitative and quantitative information	2.0	70.9	27.0
Change in length of proceedings, loan maturity or other changes	4.6	84.5	10.9
of which: *change in length of proceedings*[b]	*6.8*	*84.1*	*9.1*
change in loan maturity[b]	*2.5*	*92.0*	*5.5*
	Local survey		
Availability of the bank to grant loans	17.2	57.8	25.0
Change in loans conditions (interest rate and costs)	11.3	67.0	21.7
Request of collateral	1.8	67.6	30.6
Request of qualitative and quantitative information	1.9	73.8	24.3
Change in length of proceedings	5.4	46.0	48.7
Change in loan maturity	1.0	82.9	16.2
	Emilia-Romagna		
Availability of the bank to grant loans	21.7	52.2	26.1
Change in loans conditions (interest rate and costs)	4.8	85.7	9.5
Request of collateral	4.8	81.0	14.3
Request of qualitative and quantitative information	–	81.0	19.1
Change in length of proceedings	9.5	76.2	14.3
Change in loan maturity	4.8	95.2	–
	Puglia and Basilicata		
Availability of the bank to grant loans	16.1	59.1	24.7
Change in loans conditions (interest rate and costs)	12.8	62.8	24.5
Request of collateral	1.1	64.4	34.4
Request of qualitative and quantitative information	2.3	72.1	25.6
Change in length of proceedings	4.4	38.9	56.7
Change in loan maturity	–	79.8	20.2

[a]Data from the national survey are weighted. [b]Only for firms with 50 employees and more
Source: Bank of Italy (2006), and Bank of Italy-API, *Local survey on Basel II and firm growth*, 2006

Table 8.3 Changes in the financing relationships accomplished by banks and related to Basel II – national survey[a] *(percentages)*

Type of change	Decrease	No change	Increase
	Firms with 20–49 employees		
Availability of the bank to grant loans	10.4	61.2	28.4
Change in loans conditions (interest rate and costs) and/or request of collateral	10.6	75.1	14.3
Request of qualitative and quantitative information	2.0	70.0	28.1
Change in length of proceedings, loan maturity or other changes	2.7	86.5	10.8
	Firms with 50 employees and more		
Availability of the bank to grant loans	7.6	62.8	29.6
Change in loans conditions (interest rate and costs) and/or request of collateral	13.3	68.7	18.0
of which: *change in conditions*	*9.4*	*75.7*	*14.9*
request of collateral	*7.0*	*84.4*	*8.6*
Request of qualitative and quantitative information	2.1	72.5	25.4
Change in length of proceedings, loan maturity or other changes	7.5	81.5	10.9
of which: *change in length of proceedings*	*6.8*	*84.1*	*9.1*
change in loan maturity	*2.5*	*92.0*	*5.5*
	Industry[c]		
Availability of the bank to grant loans	9.1	61.2	29.6
Change in loans conditions (interest rate and costs) and/or request of collateral	11.7	73.8	14.4
of which: *change in conditions*[b]	*8.7*	*77.9*	*13.4*
request of collateral[b]	*8.1*	*83.5*	*8.4*
Request of qualitative and quantitative information	1.3	71.6	27.0
Change in length of proceedings, loan maturity or other changes	4.6	85.3	10.1
of which: *change in length of proceedings*[b]	*7.0*	*83.2*	*9.8*
change in loan maturity[b]	*3.5*	*91.3*	*5.2*
	Services		
Availability of the bank to grant loans	9.9	62.8	27.3
Change in loans conditions (interest rate and costs) and/or request of collateral	11.4	70.2	18.3
of which: *change in conditions*[b]	*11.1*	*71.0*	*17.9*
request of collateral[b]	*4.7*	*86.3*	*9.0*
Request of qualitative and quantitative information	3.4	69.6	27.0
Change in length of proceedings, loan maturity or other changes	4.7	82.7	12.5
of which: *change in conditions*[b]	*6.4*	*86.0*	*7.6*
change in loan maturity[b]	*0.4*	*93.5*	*6.2*

[a]Weighted data. [b]Only for firms with 50 employees and more. [c]Excluding construction
Source: Bank of Italy (2006)

Table 8.4 Changes in the relationship with banks that the firm intends to undertake *(percentages of positive answers)*

Class size and geographical area	Change of the main bank	Reduction in the number of financing banks	Increase in the number of financing banks
National survey	**4.9**	**26.0**	**10.4**
20–49 employees	5.0	25.7	..
50 employees and more	4.5	26.4	10.4
North-West	3.3	23.1	9.5
North-East	4.8	28.0	10.9
Centre	6.6	25.8	11.6
South and Islands	6.3	28.8	10.1
Industry[a]	3.9	25.4	10.1
Services	6.9	27.1	11.0
Local survey	**24.8**	**32.0**	**28.1**
1–9 employees	33.8	34.3	38.2
10–19 employees	10.3	37.9	21.4
20–49 employees	10.5	21.1	11.1
50 employees and more	28.6	14.3	–
Emilia-Romagna	10.7	28.6	12.0
Puglia and Basilicata	28.7	33.0	32.3

[a]Excluding construction
Source: Bank of Italy (2006) and Bank of Italy-API, *Local survey on Basel II and firm growth*, 2006

From a geographical point of view a slight difference emerges for Central Italy's firms, which, compared to the average, show: (i) a lower bank readiness in granting larger or new loans (12% of cases against 9%); (ii) a worsening in credit terms (20% of cases against 16%); (iii) more frequent requests for information (31% of cases against 27%).

Changes planned by the firms in the relationships with banks. – Just above one fourth of firms showed the intention to reduce the number of lending relationships, as a result of the introduction of the new rules. This ratio is roughly the same in all areas and among firms of different size (Table 8.4). A substantial share of the sample thinks that strengthening the relationships with intermediaries is the best strategy in view of Basel II. This strategy is consistent with further evidence resulting from the survey. Firms seem to take actions to obtain favorable ratings from banks, and such actions are more effective if they are concentrated on just one intermediary and seem to be justified by the more accurate evaluation by the banks that derives from that.

However this strategy is not unique: a small percentage of firms stated that they want to change the main bank (almost 5%, a percentage that becomes slightly higher for smaller firms and for those in Central and Southern Italy). A non negligible share of the firms with 50 employees and above (about 10%, without sharp differences among areas and sectors) said they wanted to increase the number of lending banks. These data show that for some firms the gains from stable bank relationships, potentially more efficient in exploiting information, are relatively modest compared to those resulting from new credit relationships.

8.3.2 The Local Survey

The firms interviewed in the local survey showed a better knowledge of the effects of Basel II. 61.7% of the sample had already closely examined the effects of Basel II on firm's operations. Knowledge of the new rules is higher among companies, among firms with 50 employees or more and for those located in Southern Italy.

Changes in firms behavior. – The differences in responses between the national and the local surveys become less evident when one looks at the propensity to adopt specific measures. Among the firms that said they knew Basel II, 43.9% stated they had already taken or would take actions related to the coming into force of the new rules. The share is much higher among Southern firms (51.6% against 24.6% of the firms of Emilia-Romagna) and among those with 50 employees or more.

As in the national survey, disclosing more information about the firm and increasing the ratio of capital to total debt are the main actions, envisaged by one out of four firms, with a slightly lower share among Southern firms. The raise of capital to debt ratio which is deemed necessary to adequately cope with the new context is non-negligible: 61.2% of firms said they would increase the ratio by a rate ranging from 11 to 50%, whereas 12.2% of the respondents anticipated a raise of more than 50%.

Changes in banks behavior. – Opposite to the changes underway or expected inside the firms, few of the interviewees perceived relevant changes in banks' behavior attributable to next introduction of the capital agreement (Table 8.2). Among the main changes, the most noticeable are the lengthening of credit inquiry, especially highlighted by Southern firms, and the request of more information on the state of business. There is no overall agreement on the effects of Basel II on banking credit supply: a fourth of the respondents perceives an easing, while 17.2% perceives a rationing.

Changes planned by the firms in the relationships with banks. – According to the firms interviewed in the local survey, the relationships with banks could in prospect undergo deeper changes in the behavior of entrepreneurs towards intermediaries. Less than a third of the firms stated they would reduce the number of lending banks, and this share is roughly uniform in both geographical areas (Table 8.4). The intention of reducing the number of intermediaries is more marked among smaller firms (but 38.2% of firms with less of 10 employees want to increase it) while it involves only 14.3% of the larger ones. A substantial share of the sample believes that strengthening the relationship with few intermediaries is the better strategy in view of the introduction of Basel II. Nevertheless in Puglia and Basilicata 32.3% of firms showed the intention to increase the number of lenders and 28.7% of changing the main bank. These responses could be interpreted as signs that in Southern regions, where firms are younger, relationship with banks are less stable.

8.4 Bank-Business relationship and Growth: The Local Survey

8.4.1 Banking Relationship

In the local survey the reasons underlying firms' choice of the main bank and of multiple banking relationships were closely examined in order to understand how they could be influenced by the introduction of Basel II. Firms in the sample have on average relationships with 3 banks and the number grows up to 5 banks for firms with 50 employees and more (Table 8.5). Only one firm out of four borrows from just one bank.

The firms motivated multiple relationships with financial intermediaries as a mean to receive more credit by fractioning banks' risk, with the possibility to stimulate more competition among the financial partners so as to achieve better credit terms. Another reason given by firms is that it is difficult to receive from a single intermediary all financial services needed at better terms; this is particularly true for firms more active on foreign markets, which ask for services not always available with all banks. Finally, some firms reported heterogeneity in the valuation of balance sheet data and cash flows by banks. The possibility of divergent interpretations of the same set of data is recognized and considered rational in economic theory (Boot and Thakor, 2003).

The role of the main bank is prevalent, with an average share of firm total banking debt of around 57%. The share is lower for larger firms (from 63.2% on average for those with less than 10 employees to 37.2% for those in the largest size class). The length of the relationship with the main bank is on average of 9 years.

There are sharp differences of behavior connected with geographic location. The firms of Emilia-Romagna generally borrow from a higher number of intermediaries and establish longer credit relationships, on average 13 years compared to 7 for the firms residing in Puglia e Basilicata. Those differences could reflect the smaller

Table 8.5 Local survey: main features of the relationship with the banks *(means and percentages)*

Class size and geographical area	Number of banks	Share of total loans granted by the main bank	No. of years of the relationship with the main bank	No. of years in which the current bank has been the main bank
1–9 employees	2.4	63.2	7.4	6.8
10–19 employees	3.3	57.6	12.8	10.6
20–49 employees	4.2	45.6	12.7	11.2
50 employees and more	5.2	37.2	10.6	8.0
Emilia-Romagna	4.2	47.1	15.2	12.8
Puglia and Basilicata	2.6	61.7	7.7	7.0
Total	3.0	57.4	9.9	8.6

Source: Bank of Italy-API, *Local survey on Basel II and firm growth*, 2006

size and younger age of firms in the latter regions, as 64% were founded over the last 10 years, compared to 16.3% of firms interviewed in Emilia–Romagna. Several empirical studies show that there is a positive relation between the age of the firm and the number and the length of credit relationship with banking partners (Farinha and Santos, 2002; Ongena and Smith, 2001). The length of the relationship with the main bank however does not appear to reflect the size of the firm.

For Southern firms the choice to borrow from a lower number of banks could reflect the existence of higher informational asymmetries which make access to credit market less easier and stricter relationships with lenders more advantageous. Asymmetric information however could considerably raise the costs of switching to a different lender when the bank develops an informational monopoly on the firm. These last effects could be substantial and may have induced the higher turnover of the main bank observed among Southern firm.

Another important factor influencing the different behavior observed among firms in the two areas could be the presence of a lower number of intermediaries (of different bank groups) operating in Southern regions.

8.4.2 Growth Financing

The choice to grow reflects the singling out of a market opportunity and the willingness to exploit it by accepting changes, even substantial, in the management and in the ownership of the firm. More than two thirds of the firms interviewed in the local survey regard their size as adequate (66.4%; Table 8.6), even though more than half of them has less than 10 employees. A similar evaluation emerged in a survey carried out by the Bank of Italy in 2005 in the province of Brescia: the firms interviewed, albeit convinced that business growth was a fundamental competitive factor in the long run, frequently judged their own size as optimal (Schivardi, 2005; Rossi, 2006). Even a survey on small firms conducted by Unioncamere shows that the 54% of respondents did not reinvest profits on firm growth (Unioncamere, 2005). Firms interviewed in Emilia-Romagna show the highest dissatisfaction for their scale of production (65.6% against 20.3% of Southern respondents).

More than 80% of Southern firms and two thirds of those of Emilia-Romagna said that they had considered the possibility of increasing the business scale during the last 10 years. The reasons underlying this choice are quite diverse and mainly reflect demand factors in the South (49.7%). In the North supply factors connected with technological and quality improvement of products seem to play an important role (41.2 and 43.1%, respectively). Less frequently the choice of increasing the size is motivated by a change in the type of product (16.2%).

The growth plan was carried out in most cases, but the accomplishment rate is higher in Emilia-Romagna (91.2% against 79.0%). The rate rises with firm size, going from 72.9% for the lowest size class to the 100% for the highest. These results could indicate the existence of obstacles to growth which could be either institutional or financial and could be connected to a smaller variety of financial instruments available to small firms. Small size mostly explains the generalized

Table 8.6 Local survey: decision to grow[a] *(percentages of positive answers)*

Questions	Emilia-Romagna	Puglia and Basilicata	Total
Evaluation of firm's dimension with respect to the one considered optimal:			
Too small	65.6	20.3	33.2
Adequate	34.4	79.1	66.4
Too big	–	0.7	0.5
Opportunity to growth considered in the last 10 years	62.3	81.7	76.2
Main reason:			
Increase in demand	41.2	49.7	47.5
Qualitative and technological improvement of the product	43.1	34.0	36.4
Change in the type of product	15.7	16.3	16.2
Implementation of the growth project	91.2	79.0	81.7
Construction of a plant in Italy	100.0	100.0	100.0
Construction of a plant abroad	7.7	–	1.6
Horizontal acquisition	23.1	10.4	13.1
Vertical acquisition	15.4	6.3	8.2

[a]For the questions on the ways of implementation of the growth project, the total is not 100 because multiple positive answers are possible
Source: Bank of Italy-API, *Local survey on Basel II and firm growth*, 2006

choice of carrying out the growth plan through greenfield investment in Italy; no firm in Puglia e Basilicata has chosen to build a plant overseas, an option adopted by 7.7% of the firms of Emilia-Romagna. Almost one fourth and one tenth of firms of the two areas respectively made a horizontal acquisition, while the acquisition of a supplier it is not so widespread in either areas, although it is more frequent in Emilia-Romagna.

There are substantial geographic differences in the ways growth is financed. For Southern firms self-financing is the main form of funding (45.5% of total funds; Table 8.7), while in Emilia-Romagna bank credit is the main source (49% of total funds, increasing with firm size). Almost one fourth of funds come from new capital placements, mainly among existing shareholders. This share decreases by 8 percentage points in Emilia-Romagna. As for self financing, loans from relatives (6.2% of total funds) are more important among smaller firms.

The mix of funds used to finance the growth shows how, especially for small firms, the opportunity to grow can be exploited only when there are enough internal resources. The banking system seems to support only firms which are over some size thresholds. This could represent a substantial obstacle for start-ups, which, according to a survey carried on by Unioncamere in 2005, are financed for 81.9% by their own capital (88% in the South; Unioncamere, 2005).

A mixture of growth financing in which internal sources are more relevant could however reflect the intention to avoid a deep change in the ownership and managerial structure of the firm (Bianchi et al., 2005).

8 Basel II and Changing Bank-Firm Relationship

Table 8.7 Local survey: Financing the dimensional growth *(average shares of total financing)*

Type of financing	Emilia-Romagna	Puglia and Basilicata	Total
Capital increase	15.3	25.5	23.0
Of which: *placed to partners*	*51.2*	*43.1*	*44.9*
Bond issues and other medium/long term issues	–	–	–
Issues of other securities	–	0.2	0.2
Change in bank debt	49.0	22.4	28.9
Self-financing	30.0	45.5	41.7
Relatives' loans	5.7	6.3	6.2

Source: Bank of Italy-API, *Local survey on Basel II and firm growth*, 2006

Table 8.8 Local survey: contribution of the main bank to the growth project *(percentages)*

Type of contribution	Emilia-Romagna None	Emilia-Romagna Little	Emilia-Romagna Large	Puglia and Basilicata None	Puglia and Basilicata Little	Puglia and Basilicata Large	Total None	Total Little	Total Large
Increase of financing	33.3	50.0	16.7	28.0	57.0	15.1	28.6	56.2	15.2
Consulting for eventual market access	100.0	–	–	50.8	30.2	19.1	52.3	29.2	18.5
Contacts with other financial intermediaries	100.0	–	–	54.4	10.5	35.1	55.2	10.3	34.5
Consulting on the industrial plan	75.0	25.0	–	92.3	7.7	–	88.2	11.8	–
Consulting with other firms of the sector	100.0	–	–	85.0	15.0	–	86.7	13.2	–
Identification of the firm to acquire	100.0	–	–	98.3	1.7	–	98.5	1.5	–

Source: Bank of Italy-API, *Local survey on Basel II and firm growth*, 2006

The banking system, and particularly the main bank, can play an important role in supporting the growth process of small firms. Besides lending, the intermediaries can be advisers guiding firms in their choices and helping to reduce the risks of the project. The survey shows that financial backing of the main bank is often negligible. The majority of the firms pointed out that the main bank offered little or no support in terms of higher credit availability (56.2 and 28.6%; Table 8.8). The adviser role played by the intermediaries is even less remarkable. For the firms of Emilia-Romagna this role concerns only the industrial plan.

Table 8.9 Local survey: factors contributing to the quitting of the growth project[a] (*percentages of positive answers*)

Reasons	Emilia-Romagna	Puglia and Basilicata	Total
Fear of losing the control of the firm	–	15.8	15.8
Lack of financial support	–	100.0	100.0
Excessive cost of financing	50.0	63.2	68.4
Difficulty of finding qualified managers	100.0	31.6	42.1
High uncertainty on investment results	50.0	57.9	63.2
Low transparency of the firm to be acquired	–	–	–
Too high legal and bureaucratic constraints	–	21.1	21.1

[a]The column totals are not equal to 100 because multiple answers are possible
Source: Bank of Italy-API, *Local survey on Basel II and firm growth*, 2006

The survey confirmed the existence of obstacles to growth. Financial constraints are among the main factors: the firms which abandoned the growth project ascribed it mainly to the lack of financial support (Table 8.9).

However credit availability is not the only constraint to growth. Other relevant factors reported by the interviewees are the financing cost and the uncertainty of the outcomes of the investment, pointed out by the 60% of the respondents. Other obstacles are connected to the governance of firms (15.8% abandoned the project since they were afraid of losing the control of the firm) and to bureaucratic delays (21.1%). Even more important are the problems firms encountered in finding the staff able to manage a larger firm. This was reported by all firms in Emilia-Romagna and by more than 30% of those located in Puglia and Basilicata.

8.5 Conclusions

The national survey shows that a non negligible share of firms is aware of the effects of the new regulation on relationships with lenders. The share is higher among the respondents to the local survey (which are of smaller size). About one half of the firms which answered they knew the new regulation thinks it is necessary to carry out some organizational changes, mainly consisting in enriching information about the firm, increasing the capital to debt ratio and strengthening the financial area. Firms' answers to the perceived changes in banks' behavior connected with the new regulation are ambiguous. A high share of respondents to the national survey did not notice any change in the length of credit inquiries and in loans' maturity. Both surveys show that banks are asking for more qualitative and quantitative information. There is a wide dispersion in the answers on perceived changes in credit availability and terms, which could signal either differences in the way banks are adapting to the new regulation or in the ability to better evaluate borrowers' creditworthiness and to better differentiate credit supply, with advantages for some borrowers and disadvantages for others.

In the national survey a trend in reducing multiple banking relationships is emerging. The local survey shows that a high share of small firms, located mainly in the Southern regions, has planned to increase the number of lending banks and/or to change the main bank. Qualitative responses signal that multiple banking relationships have still substantial advantages.

The section on firm growth of the territorial survey shows that the perception of limitations connected to small size is more widespread among firms residing in Emilia-Romagna than among those located in the South. In Emilia-Romagna the accomplishment rate of growth projects is also higher, with an important financial support by the banks. However it seems that there is not a wider backing by the intermediaries in terms of assistance and counseling, and that there are obstacles to growth connected to problems in finding management and in the governance of the firm.

Acknowledgments We thank Enrico Beretta, Sergio Cagnazzo, Leandro D'Aurizio, Massimo Omiccioli, Antonio Giuseppe Perrelli, Anna Maria Tarantola and Sandro Trento for the useful comments, the Associations of small and medium firms (API) of the provinces of Bologna, Puglia and Basilicata for the precious cooperation in the survey organization, and in particular Paolo Mascagni, Carlo Rossini, Paolo Parlangeli, Erasmo Antro and Riccardo Figliolia. The usual disclaimer applies. The opinions expressed are those of the authors and do not involve the responsibility of the Bank of Italy and of API. The authors only are responsible for any mistake in this paper. A previous version of this paper has been published in the review *Banca Impresa Società*, 1, 2007.

References

Bank of Italy (2006) Indagine sulle imprese industriali e dei servizi. Supplementi al Bollettino statistico 41:20–22
Bianchi M, Bianco M, Giacomelli S, Pacces AM, Trento S (2005) Proprietà e controllo delle imprese in Italia. Il Mulino, Bologna
Boot, AWA. (2003) Relationship banking: what we know? J Finan Intermed 9:7–25
Boot AWA, Thakor A (2003) The economic value of flexibility when there is disagreement. CEPR Discussion Paper in Financial Economics, 3709
Calcagnini G (2004) Finanza e sviluppo economico: il ruolo di Basilea 2. Argomenti 11:5–24
Detragiache E, Garella P, Guiso L (2000) Multiple versus single Banking Relationship: theory and evidence. J Finance 55(3):1133–1161
Gorton G, Winton A (2003) Financial intermediation. In: Constantinides GM et al (eds) Handbook of the economics of finance, vol 1, chap 8.). Elsevier, Amsterdam, pp 431–552
Herrera A, Minetti R (2007) Informed finance and technological change: evidence from credit relationships. J Finan Econ 83:223–269
Istat (2006) Rapporto annuale, La situazione del Paese nel 2006, Roma. 64–79
King R, Levine R (1993) Finance, entrepreneurship and growth: theory and evidence. J Monet Econ 32:513–542
Ongena S, Smith DS (2001) The duration of bank relationship. J Finan Econ 61:449–475
Rossi S (2006) La regina e il cavallo. Quattro mosse contro il declino. Laterza, Bari
Schivardi F (2005) Indagine su innovazione, organizzazione e governance nelle imprese bresciane, survey organized by a working party coordinated by Anna Maria Tarantola, Bank of Italy, mimeo
Unioncamere (2005) Basilea 2. L'affidabilità delle imprese minori, survey coordinated by S. Pettinato, giugno

Chapter 9
Financial Models of Small Innovative Firms: An Empirical Investigation

Giorgio Calcagnini, Ilario Favaretto, and Germana Giombini

Abstract This paper aims at analysing financial models of innovative firms in Italy by means of a sample of firms located in the Marche region. While it is well known that innovative firms have different financial needs and more severe problems in accessing funds than traditional firms, our analysis shows that only a small number of the interviewed firms have faced problems in raising external funds for innovation, even during the current economic and financial crisis. Policy recommendations point towards the improvement of firms' levels of financial culture and the dilution of firms' ownership by means of external private equity.

9.1 Introduction

The current economic crisis is the worst since the post-war period. Between the second quarter of 2008 and the second quarter of 2009 the Italian GDP fell to its 2001 level, while industrial production fell to its mid-Eighties levels. Therefore, it is strategic to understand which firms (having which characteristics) have been suffering from the crisis, and those that are withstanding the economic recession.

As different sources have pointed out, (Bank of Italy, 2009; Bugamelli et al., 2009), the effects of the international crisis on the Italian economy were firstly observed in the fall of the demand for goods, mainly in the manufacturing sectors open to international competition, and in the instrumental goods industry. Then the crisis spread widely to other sectors both because of subcontracting linkages and the credit restrictions imposed by banks.

Firms that started up and have carried out deep reorganization since the beginning of the last decade have better stemmed the negative effects of the crisis. These firms

---

G. Calcagnini (✉)
Dipartimento di Economia e Metodi Quantitativi, Università di Urbino "Carlo Bo",
Via Saffi 42, 61029 Urbino, Italy
e-mail: giorgio.calcagnini@uniurb.it

have been able to adopt active responses to the crisis such as market and product diversification. Innovation has once more been a key element of economic strength and resulted in the creation of new products that stimulated final demand and higher international competitiveness.

Therefore, even if innovative firms are a small share of all Italian firms, they may substantially contribute to the economic recovery.[1]

The increase in the number of innovative firms should be realized by means of economic policies that promote and finance R&D investments, improve high-quality research with universities, the provision of incentives to make the linkages between high level education and the economy stronger. Last but not least, economic policies should promote the development of venture capital and foreign direct investments in Italy.

Credit access is one of the key elements in the life of firms. In the event of a credit crunch, firms' ability to undertake new investment projects is seriously compromised. Financial constraints and credit rationing undermine firms' profit and growth. On one hand, countries' financial development affects the GDP level and growth rate (Levine, 1997; Papaioannou, 2007). On the other, the quality of the legal system improves the efficiency of the financial system (Beck and Levine, 2008).

A recent survey of the European Central Bank (ECB, 2009) provides evidence on the access to finance of small- and medium-sized enterprises (SMEs) in the euro area in the first half of 2009. Results show that almost half of the euro area SME respondents reported a decrease in turnover and profits during the previous 6 months. Moreover, in the same period, about 40% of them experienced an increase in production costs. This assessment appears more negative than that for large firms and suggests that SMEs have been relatively more affected by the economic downturn.

The survey highlights some of the main differences in the financing model of SME versus large-sized firms. On one hand, SMEs largely rely on banks: 32% reported having used a bank loan in the previous 6 months and 30% a bank overdraft or credit line. Leasing, hire purchase and factoring (used by 27%), and trade credit (15%) also played a relatively important role. On the other hand, market-based financing played a minor role: 0.9% had issued debt securities in the previous 6 months and 1.3% had issued equity or relied on external equity investors. However, it is likely that the financial crisis and the difficult market conditions were also to blame for such low demand for market-based financing.

Financial systems play a crucial role for all firms, but they may substantially foster the start-up and development of new innovative firms.

This chapter aims at analyzing the financial models of innovative firms in Italy by means of a sample of firms located in the Marche region. Compared to traditional firms, innovative firms may have different financial needs and, due to their characteristics, usually face more severe problems in searching for funds.

---

[1] Italian patents are only one-fortieth of the European average (Persico, 2009). Indeed, the technology content of Italian productions is generally low and, therefore, they suffer relatively more from competition of emerging economies.

First, innovative firms may be subject to negative cash flows or high return volatility. Therefore, they are riskier than traditional firms.

Second, innovative firms typically base their activity on intellectual capital and intangible assets that amplify the problem of financial opaqueness i.e. investors find it more difficult to evaluate the profitability of their investment projects and, therefore, firms' current and future market value.

The consequence of these characteristics is twofold. On one hand, innovative firms usually incur in higher financing costs than traditional firms. On the other hand, innovative firms have a higher probability of being credit rationed than traditional firms. Therefore, because of moral hazard problems and riskier activity, innovative firms should mainly base their financing on internal funds and equity.

At the beginning of 2009, at the peak of the economic and financial crisis, we carried out the empirical analysis on a sample of innovative firms located in the Marche region to provide more evidence on financing innovative firm models. The Marche region represents an interesting case study because it is characterized by a relatively large number of innovative, small-sized firms and long-lasting relationships between banks and firms. The latter is one of the critical success factors of its economy. Indeed, it has been shown that in Italy bank development positively affects firms' innovative processes, especially for small-sized firms and those that operate in high-tech sectors (Benfratello et al., 2006).

Our empirical analysis shows that none of the firms in our sample faced problems in raising external funds for innovation activity. Only 9% of firms declared that banks refused to fund their growth process, and 16% of firms obtained only a share of the requested amount. However, the analysis also shows that the regional bank industry is more willing to finance traditional than innovative firms. Indeed, only 50% of innovative firms obtained the whole amount of the required funds compared to 63% of non-innovative firms.

The importance of innovative firms for economic growth suggests that all economic and institutional actors should cooperate to increase the number of innovative firms. Firms can do so by pursuing dimensional consolidation and the adoption of organizational models that favour financial strategies oriented to supporting innovation. Banks can do so through new financial instruments suitable to promote innovative processes and sustain firm growth. Trade associations and local governments can do so by identifying firms' need for a new breed of employee, and supporting the educational system in its design of new curricula. Universities can do so by strengthening their research activities, while politicians should design economic policies oriented to promote long-run investments in industries such as energy, transportation, communications, the health sector and collective security.

The chapter is organized as follows. Section 9.2 reviews the theoretical and empirical literature on innovative firms' financial problems with a special focus on small-sized and innovative firms. Section 9.3 describes the sample selection and the questionnaire used for the survey, while Sect. 9.4 analyzes our main empirical findings. Section 9.5 concludes.

9.2 Theoretical and Empirical Models of Small Firm Financing: A Review

Financial models of innovative firms are an issue of great interest in the economic literature and have generated a huge amount of research work. The starting point is that, compared to traditional businesses, innovative firms typically face financial constraints or credit rationing because their investments are riskier, and due to the presence of more severe problems of asymmetric information and informational opaqueness. These problems are generally bigger in the case of small-sized innovative firms.

Theoretically, the analysis of firms' financial structure starts with the pioneering work of Modigliani e Miller (1958). In a situation of perfect capital markets and in the absence of transaction costs, the market value of firms is independent of their debt and equity mix. However, capital markets are generally characterized by both high transaction costs and asymmetric information. In these situations, firms are better informed than potential investors, and there is a pecking order of financial sources: firms find it most convenient to finance their investment projects with internal sources, followed by debt, and finally with equity finance (Myers, 1984; Myers and Majluf, 1984). Moreover, asymmetric information may discourage potential investors because of agency costs that give rise to monitoring costs that the external investors should bear to control the financed firm (Barnea et al., 1981; Jensen and Meckling, 1976). Indeed, moral hazard problems may arise in the case of asymmetric information because the entrepreneur (or the firm manager) could make choices that do not necessarily maximize profits (and the utility) of external investors. Furthermore, even if we assume the absence of moral hazard, in case of asymmetric information the firm could decide to issue new equity only if overvalued (Leland and Pyle, 1977).

Finally, to maintain firm control, the owner may prefer internal funds or debt to external equity when financing investment projects (Aghion and Bolton, 1992; Aghion et al., 2004). In this case, the lower the amount of tangible assets the firm can use as collateral is, the higher is the share of firm control that external investors require to finance investment projects. As a consequence, the entrepreneur reluctant to lose firm control typically decides to finance the firm, first by using internal funds, second with debt and, eventually, by issuing equity.

Asymmetric information problems may also generate adverse selection problems when the firm decides to finance its investment projects by debt finance. Indeed, in the case of firms of differing quality, banks may find distinguishing between high-risk and low-risk firms difficult or too expensive. Therefore, banks may decide to increase the cost of debt to all potential borrowers to a level that makes credit rationing profitable (Stiglitz and Weiss, 1981).

From the perspective of investment theory, R&D expenses have a number of characteristics that make them different from fixed investment (Hall, 2009): (i) they need to be smoothed in order to retain valuable employees and their knowledge; (ii) they are highly uncertain and information about success or failure is revealed over time; and (iii) they create an idiosyncratic intangible capital with a limited resale market.

Therefore, in the case of innovative firms, financial problems may become particularly tough due to the following reasons.

First of all, the success of innovative firms depends on the evaluation of their growth potential that is derived from scientific knowledge and intellectual property; second, innovative firms, especially in the first stages of their life cycle, usually have limited physical capital to use as collateral to mitigate moral hazard or adverse selection problems; finally, innovative firms produce goods subject to quick depreciation and, therefore, they are riskier. These problems are amplified in the case of small innovative firms.

Berger and Udell (1998) analyze a life-cycle theory of firm financial models. The theory assumes that the optimal strategy for firms is to use different sources of funding at different stages of their dimensional/age/informational growth.

The authors assume that small firms suffer informational opaqueness problems more heavily and, therefore, mainly finance themselves through internal funds, trade credit or informal investors. The latter are known as business angels. Informational opaqueness problems decrease along firms' life cycle so that they may start using external equity provided by institutional investors, such as the venture capitalists or debt finance provided by banks and other financial institutions. Eventually, if firms keep being profitable and continue to grow, they may gain access to public equity and debt markets.

Therefore, the financing of innovative firms may be particularly difficult and onerous, and consequently two opposite effects have to be kept in mind.

On one hand, the innovative nature of the their activity implies a higher opaqueness and more severe asymmetric information problems. Then external funds become particularly costly. On the other, innovative firms, as opposed to traditional ones, tend to experience rapid growth rates and the need to attract increasing amounts of external funds, especially risk capital.

The theoretical literature analyzed emphasizes that debt financing is less suitable than other sources to finance innovative, small-sized firms, especially during their start up phase. This is due to the presence of tougher moral hazard problems, riskier activity, lower collateral, and therefore to potential investors' difficulties in valuing their investment projects.

Brierley (2001), O.E.C.D. (2006), and (Coleman and Robb 2010) review the main empirical research findings on the financing of innovative firms and underline how the results are not unique. On one hand, there are outcomes that also confirm the pecking order theory for innovative firms; on the other, there are studies that support the life-cycle theory of financial sources. Eventually, other studies point out that equity finance is more important for innovative firms than for traditional firms (Coleman and Robb 2010).

Chavis et al. (2010) analyze financial models of new firms in more than 100 countries. The authors find that younger firms systematically finance their projects by using internal sources of funds and by referring to informal investors, such as business angels. They also find that firms that operate in countries where the quality of their legal system is higher, and asymmetric information problems are less severe, are able to access bank funding more easily.

Finally, other works analyze the financial models of Italian innovative firms.

Guidici and Paleari (2000) analyze a sample of 46 small- and medium-sized innovative Italian firms. The authors find support for the pecking order theory. Indeed, a firm owner's wealth is the main source of funds, followed by short-term debt. The entrepreneur's fear of losing control of the firm is the main obstacle to issuing new equity. Indeed, outside equity finance is used only if the new investors also provide new financial skills.

Pozzolo (2003) does not find substantial differences between the financial structure of traditional and innovative Italian firms, i.e., firms linked to the new economy industry or characterized by a higher share of technological immobilizations.

Nucci et al. (2004) find an inverse relationship between firms' leverage and their share of intangible assets; i.e., most innovative firms are those with lower leverage.

Colombo and Grilli (2007) study the determinants of financing sources for a sample of 386 small-sized innovative Italian firms and find confirmation of the pecking order hypothesis. Indeed, only a small share of firms finances investment projects by using external equity or debt. The main financing source is the entrepreneur's personal wealth, followed by bank loans and, finally, private equity. Moreover, the authors find that small innovative firms may experience a higher likelihood of credit rationing if they heavily rely on debt.

Magri (2007) finds that small-sized innovative firms: (i) show a lower degree of leverage than small-sized traditional firms; (ii) rely more heavily on equity; (iii) and are less sensitive to cash-flow fluctuations than small-sized traditional firms. Finally, small-sized innovative firms face more difficulties in using external equity than innovative larger firms.

Therefore, empirical findings concerning the financial models of Italian innovative firms are not unique. Indeed, while some analyses show the presence of a hierarchy of financial sources in which debt capital is preferred to equity finance, other analyses find that innovative firms show lower leverage levels and a higher recourse to external equity finance than traditional firms.

9.3 The Empirical Investigation: Sample Selection and Questionnaire

The non-unique findings on the financial structure of Italian innovative firms, as it appears from the review of the literature in the previous Section, stimulated us to carry out a new survey. We focused on a sample of small- and medium-sized (SME) located in the Marche region, traditionally known as the "SME region". We started from the outcomes of a previous research project on innovation (Favaretto and Zanfei, 2007) that allowed us to identify 346 innovative firms located in the Marche region. These firms emerged to carry out, in 2007, at least one of the innovative activities listed in Table 9.1 and constituted a large share of all innovative firms located in the Marche region. Indeed, they represented around 58% of all residents registered in the national register of research projects (universities and state-owned laboratories of research were the remaining 42%) and 50% of all patents registered

9 Financial Models of Small Innovative Firms: An Empirical Investigation

Table 9.1 Variables used to identify innovative firms

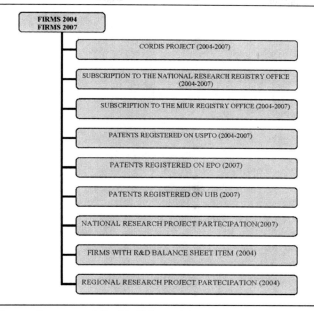

Source: Favaretto and Zanfei (2007), p. 351

with the United States Patent and Trademark Office (USPTO) between 1991 and 2007 by residents in the Marche region.

According to Favaretto and Zanfei (2007) firms are concentrated in a few and often non-front-rank innovative activities. Most of the firms (192 over 346, that is 55% of all firms) are included in the sample because they are registered with the national register of research projects.

Together with the dataset containing innovative firms, we built a control sample with firms owned by young entrepreneurs and not necessarily located in the Marche region (for simplicity's sake we will also call them traditional firms). Overall, our dataset included almost 500 firms to which we emailed a link to a webpage containing the electronic questionnaire. We opted for this modern survey procedure hoping to reduce the bother to firms and thus increase the number of answers. Only 66 innovative firms and 44 non-innovative firms filled in the questionnaire (i.e., around 20% of the original dataset).

Instead of developing a new questionnaire from scratch, we received permission to use a questionnaire previously used by the O.E.C.D. and the Kauffman Foundation for a pilot research project on innovative and high-growth SMEs (O.E.C.D., 2008).

The questionnaire is made up of five sections. The first section collects general information on the firm such as the type, the year of foundation, etc. The second and the third sections focus on the growth strategy implemented by the firm and its financing, respectively. Finally, sections four and five collect information on the relationships existing between the firm and its financers and especially with its equity finance providers.

9.4 Empirical Findings

9.4.1 Firm Characteristics

The innovative firms of the Marche region are mainly limited liability companies (89.4%), followed at a distance by partnerships (6.1%) and by sole proprietorships (3.0%), (Table 9.2). Therefore, innovative firms possess a more structured organization compared to our control sample; the latter is made up of non-innovative firms, and the distribution of firms is by type at the national level. The latter may be reconnected to the more specific and riskier activity carried out by firms, firm size, or the number of years from the firm's foundation. Indeed, Berger and Udell (1998) showed that a sole proprietor often owns small-sized and recently-established firms.

Information on firm size supports the hypothesis that innovative businesses are generally larger than traditional ones. Innovative firms with fewer than 10 employees make up only 23% of the total, compared to 72.5% and almost 95.0% in the cases of the control sample and Italy, respectively (Table 9.3). Innovative firms in our sample are mainly concentrated in the two size classes 10–49 and 50–249 employees. The two shares are similar and add up to over 70% of all firms. This value compares with 27.5% in the case of the control sample, and 5.1% in that of the whole Italian economy.

Table 9.2 Distribution of firms by type (%)

Type of firm	Innovative firms	Control sample	Italy 2008
Sole proprietorship	3.0	25.0	56.2
Partnership	6.1	36.4	19.7
Limited Liability	89.4	36.4	20.8
Others	1.5	2.3	3.3
Total	100.0	100.0	100.0

Table 9.3 Distribution of firms by size (%)

Size	Innovative firms	Control sample	Italy 2007
1–9	23.0	72.5	94.8
10–49	37.7	22.5	4.6
50–249	34.4	5.0	0.5
> 249	4.9	0.0	0.1
Total	100.0	100.0	100.0

9 Financial Models of Small Innovative Firms: An Empirical Investigation

As already pointed out, size plays an important role in firms' financial structure (Berger and Udell, 1998). Small-sized firms mainly have access to the debt and private equity markets, while larger firms have more opportunities to be listed on the stock exchange market. Indeed, asymmetric information and informational opaqueness are generally more severe for small-sized firms than larger ones. Further, issuing costs are characterized by economies of scale that once more favor larger firms.

The number of years passed from firm foundation is another determinant of firms' financial structure. According to Berger and Udell (1998) younger firms may have more difficulties accessing capital markets than older firms. The latter have had time to build up a reputation compared to younger firms that, therefore, are considered riskier.

Innovative firms, besides being on average larger than those included in the control sample, are also older.[2] The number of innovative firms established before 1970 is almost three times larger than that of the control sample. Overall, almost 86% of innovative firms were established before year 2000 versus 39.5% in the case of the control sample (Fig. 9.1).

One question in the survey aimed at discovering if and how important participations in other firms are. Indeed, the existence of even minority participations among firms may generate positive externalities that financial markets do not always fairly price.

Innovative firms located in the Marche region only hold control shares in other companies in 14% of the cases, while almost 48% own minority participations. Finally, only 6% of innovative firms show some state-owned participations. Brierley (2001) shows that state-owned participations may play an important role in supporting innovative firm start-ups and growth.

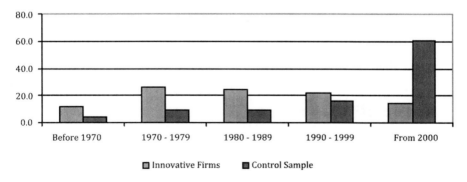

Fig. 9.1 Distribution of firms by year of foundation (%)

---

[2]This is not surprising since young entrepreneurs own most of the firms included in the control sample.

Table 9.4 Distribution of innovative firms by industry (%)

Industry	%
Utilities	3.1
Construction	6.2
Manufacturing	58.5
Wholesale trade	6.2
Technical, scientific, and professional services	12.3
Educational services	1.5
Other industries (public administration excluded)	12.3
Total	100.0

As noted above, most of the firms located in the Marche region are not concentrated in front-rank innovative activities. Indeed, a large share of firms is concentrated in Manufacturing (58.5%), while only 12.3% belongs to the Technical, Scientific, and Professional Services industry (Table 9.4).

The distribution of innovations by type sheds light on the differences between innovative and traditional firms. Overall, 30.4% of innovations are concentrated

Table 9.5 Distribution of innovations by type (%)

Activity	Innovative Firms	Control Sample
Intramural (in-house) R&D: creative work undertaken on a systematic basis to increase the stock of knowledge	23.7	12.4
Extramural R&D: same activities as in-house R&D but purchased from research organizations or other firms	6.7	3.1
Acquisition of other external knowledge: acquisition of patent rights, non patented inventions, trademarks, know-how and other types of knowledge, other than R&D, from other enterprises or institutions	3.6	5.2
Acquisitions of advanced machinery, equipment, computer hardware and software, land and buildings for the purpose of product or process innovation	16.5	16.5
Internal design, planning or testing activities, that are not already included in R&D, for new or significantly improved products, production processes and delivery methods	13.9	8.2
Market preparations for product innovations: activities aimed at the market introduction of new or significantly improved goods or services	12.4	13.4
Training: training (including external training) linked to the development or implementation of product or process innovations	12.4	18.6
Preparations for marketing innovations: activities related to the development and implementation of new marketing methods specifically related to marketing innovations	2.1	8.2
Preparations for organizational innovations: planning and implementation of new organization methods, or acquisition of external knowledge and other capital goods related to organizational innovations	8.8	14.4
Total	100.0	100.0

in intramural (23.7%) and extramural (6.7%) R&D investments. In contrast, only 15.5% of innovations of the control sample are of the R&D type.

Both firm types (innovative and traditional) consider it important (16.5%) to acquire advanced-technology machinery and equipment, and hardware and software that support product and process innovations, while the percentage of innovations such as internal design for new or significantly improved production processes and methods is significantly larger among innovative firms than among traditional ones (13.9% and 8.2%, respectively) (Table 9.5).

As expected, traditional firms invest relatively more resources (18.6%) in training. In other words, on average, innovative firms have employees with more developed professional skills and thus find it more convenient to invest in R&D and fixed capital. The opposite is true for traditional firms that are likely less capital intensive than innovative firms, but need to improve their employees' professional skills by means of training.

Finally, innovative firms are more oriented towards international markets than traditional firms, even though only 18% of the former shows a foreign-sales-to-total-sales ratio larger than 50%. Further, 27% of innovative firms do not (directly) export at all (Fig. 9.2), while in the case of traditional firms this value is over 73%.

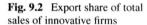

Fig. 9.2 Export share of total sales of innovative firms

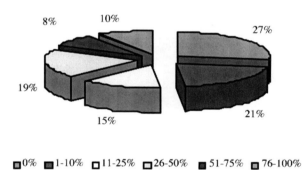

9.4.2 Firm Growth Strategies

This section describes our survey outcomes concerning innovative firms' growth strategies.

In 2008 almost 79% of innovative firms, and 78% of traditional firms, made investment decisions oriented towards supporting their economic growth.[3] The analysis of the types of investment sheds light on the differences in growth strategies between innovative and traditional firms.

---

[3] All firms with some state-owned participations made growth-oriented investments.

Table 9.6 Distribution of investment by type (%)

Investment type	Innovative firms	Control sample
ICT	2.0	0.6
Creation of new products	7.8	2.9
Improvement of existing products	5.2	4.5
Improvement of existing processes	2.1	2.4
Marketing	2.7	4.0
Land, buildings and other facilities	28.2	43.1
Machinery and equipment	33.9	34.4
Patents, licences and other intangible assets	2.0	0.9
Human resources	13.4	5.4
Other	2.7	1.8
Total	100.0	100.0

As expected, investments are concentrated in the acquisition of machinery and equipment, and in land, buildings and other facilities. However, while the former have the same importance for innovative and traditional firms, the latter are significantly larger in the case of traditional firms (Table 9.6). Investment in ICT, human resources, and the creation of new products are, instead, larger in the case of innovative firms. It is surprising that investments in patents, licences and other intangible assets are only 2% of total investment even for innovative firms (0.9% for traditional firms).

9.4.3 The Financing of New Growth Strategies

Given the observed differences in the type of business organization, size and type of investment between innovative and traditional firms, it is now interesting to analyze their financial structures. As discussed in Sect. 9.2, the group of traditional firms should show a financial structure in accordance with the pecking order theory, while innovative firms should rely relatively more on equity.

Information from our survey clearly shows that the role of equity finance is significantly larger in the case of innovative firms than in that of traditional firms. The former fund themselves mainly by means of debt (57.5%), but equity still plays an important role (42.5%). The latter make use of debt for a share slightly larger than 83% and equity for the remaining 17% (Fig. 9.3).[4]

The fact that even innovative firms make large use of financial debt is not necessarily in contrast with the theory that stresses the role of equity for these types of firms. Indeed, we already noted that innovative firms included in our sample belong to traditional industries and are still SMEs. Further, not being particularly young,

---

[4]There are not significant differences if the analysis is broken down according to firm size or age.

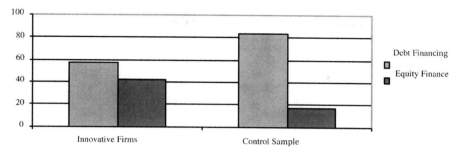

Fig. 9.3 Investment financing (%)

they had time to build a reputation by means of which they are able to access the bond and bank loan markets (Berger and Udell, 1995).

As for the different types of debt finance, innovative firms prefer leasing (35.8%), followed by short- and medium-term bank loans (26.5%) and lines of credit (24%). Differently, traditional firms – finding access to the equity market more difficult – mainly rely on long-term bank loans (55.3%), and then leasing (31.6%) (Table 9.7).

Innovative and traditional firms are also different with respect to their equity composition. In the former case, almost 80% of equity is represented by the risk capital staked by firm owners, and 20% by capital provided by private investors (venture capitalists). In the latter case, risk capital is almost completely represented by funds staked by the owners, and for a very small share (0.4%) by capital provided by their relatives and friends (Table 9.8).

For both type of firms, and more surprisingly in the case of innovative firms, the provision of capital by business angels is nil. In other countries business angels are informal investors who represent a proven solution for early stage ventures and a source of funds available to develop innovative and emerging technologies. Further,

Table 9.7 Distribution of financial debt (%)

Debt finance	Innovative firms	Control sample
Long term bank loans	7.7	55.3
Short and medium term bank loans	26.5	11.3
State-guaranteed bank loans	0.0	0.0
Loans from family members and friends	0.0	1.8
Loans from other third parties (shareholders, companies, etc.)	1.7	0.0
Lines of credit	24.0	0.0
Credit cards	0.0	0.0
Leasing	35.8	31.6
Other types of long term debt financing	1.1	0.0
Other types of short and medium term debt financing	3.1	0.0
Total	100.0	100.0

Table 9.8 Distribution of the equity finance (%)

Equity finance	Innovative firms	Control sample
Own Capital	79.5	99.6
Equity from employees	0.0	0.0
Equity from family members or friends	0.0	0.4
Equity from Business Angels	0.0	0.0
Equity from Venture Capital firms	20.4	0.0
Equity from other private equity sources	0.1	0.0
Equity from government capital transfers through business supporting policies and incentives	0.0	0.0
Total	100.0	100.0

business angels invest locally, and their proximity with innovative firms helps to reduce asymmetric information problems. Differently form venture capitalists, business angels are less interested in the acquisition of firm control, but they generally provide fewer financial skills and resources.

A likely explanation for the lack of business angels in the Marche region is that most firms in our sample are not in their early stage of development. Indeed, as already shown, our innovative firms are long established ones for whom it is more convenient to turn to formal investors such as venture capitalists.

Innovative firms are often growth oriented and characterized by high investment dynamics and are, therefore, riskier. Their riskier nature may be reflected in stricter liquidity constraints and, then, in more obstacles to investment. However, only 24% of innovative firms belonging to our sample were prevented from making the desired growth investment due their inability to borrow, as opposed to 44% in the case of traditional firms (Fig. 9.4). This different behavior between the two groups of firms may be explained by the composition of their investment financing: innovative firms are, on average, less dependent on debt than traditional firms (Fig. 9.3).

There are several reasons why firms did not invest in innovation and, of course, they are different for the two groups of firms. Recalling that the survey was carried out in January 2009, when the economic and financial crisis started to bite, innovative firms reported that the two most important reasons were their (a) insufficient

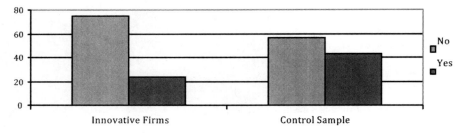

Fig. 9.4 Firm growth investment and financial constraints (%)

9 Financial Models of Small Innovative Firms: An Empirical Investigation

Table 9.9 Reasons why firms did not invested in innovation (%)

Motivation	Innovative firms	Control sample
The firm has insufficient revenues or assets to support growth-oriented policies	11.8	12.5
The firm does not think it can raise the required funds through external finance providers	0.0	0.0
The firm does not feel there is the potential to increase demand enough to support a growth strategy	5.9	37.5
At the present time, the firm has no interest in expanding production, changing processes or exploiting new markets	5.9	0.0
The firm prefers to retain revenues and assets for future operational expenditures	11.8	0.0
The firm is consolidating activities and a growth-oriented strategy is premature	5.9	12.5
None of the above	58.8	37.5
Total	100.0	100.0

revenues or assets to support growth-oriented policies (11.8%) and (b) preference for retaining revenues and assets for future operational expenditures (11.8%). Firms belonging to the control sample – that are more dependent on the business cycle than innovative firms – pointed out their feeling that demand would not have been enough to support a growth strategy as the most important reason to not invest in innovation (37.5%) (Table 9.9). Therefore, even though firms belonging to the control sample are not classified as innovative, they understand the importance of innovations, but only ones that are limited to periods with expectations of expanding markets.[5] The lack of revenues or assets to support growth-oriented policies (12.5%), and the beginning of consolidating activities (12.5%) are the next main reasons mentioned by traditional firms for not investing in innovations (Table 9.9).

9.4.4 Firm Relationships with Their Debt Finance Providers

Relationships with debt finance providers are another issue that needs to be analyzed to better understand innovative firms' funding decisions.

Notwithstanding equity appears to be the preferred financial source to support innovation, debt (especially bank) finance is always one of the main sources of funds for all types of firms. Therefore, the question requires some closer scrutiny. Our information shows that only 50% of innovative firms obtained all funds requested of the bank, as opposed to 62% in the case of firms belonging to the control sample.

---

[5] Unfortunately, almost 60% of innovative firms and 38% of firms belonging to the control sample answered that none of the motives shown in the questionnaire was responsible for their decision to not invest in innovations. Therefore, this interpretation should be taken with some caution.

Table 9.10 Firm-bank relationship and investment (%)

Type of relationship	Innovative firms	Control sample
Banks provided all the funds that were requested	50.0	62.5
Banks provided only partial funding	15.9	15.6
Banks refused to provide the requested funds	9.1	6.3
The firm did not apply to banks for financing	25.0	15.6
Total	100.0	100.0

Moreover, banks refused to provide finance to 9.1% of innovative firms, but only to 6.3% of other firms. Finally, a larger share of innovative firms (25%) decided not to apply to banks for loans compared to traditional firms (15.6%) (Table 9.10).

However, information from our survey does not help us in determining why the relationship between banks and innovative firms should be different from that with traditional firms. Indeed, in a larger number of cases (12.5% versus 0%) banks seem to consider traditional firms' investment riskier than those of innovative firms. Further, traditional firms are denied credit because of insufficient collateral (25% versus 0%) and the requested loan has been considered too large (25% versus 7.1%). Finally, firms find the access to bank loans difficult because of their low credit rating score, more frequently in the case of traditional firms (12.5%) than in that of innovative firms (10.7%) (Table 9.11).

Table 9.11 Main reasons why banks provided no credit e or only part of the requested amount (%)

Type of reason	Innovative firms	Control sample
Project considered to be too risky	0.0	12.5
Firm considered to be over-exposed to lenders	3.6	0.0
Firm had weak business plan	0.0	0.0
Firm had insufficient collateral	0.0	25.0
Firm had low credit rating score (Basel II)	10.7	12.5
Firm had insufficient growth potential	0.0	0.0
Too large a loan was requested	7.1	25.0
Banks gave no explanations for decision	10.7	0.0
Other reasons	67.9	25.0
Total	100.0	100.0

9.4.5 The Relationship of Firms with Their Equity Finance Providers

Firms' equity finance providers, as discussed in Sect. 9.4.3, may be formal investors, such as venture capitalists, or informal investors, such as business angels. Formal and informal investors are not necessarily alternatives. Indeed, they are often

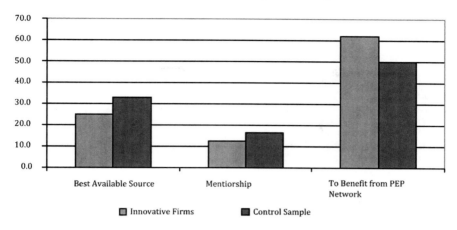

Fig. 9.5 Reasons why firms applied for finance with Private Equity Providers (%)

complementary: business angels seldom come before venture capitalists, and the arrival of the latter is the prelude to stock exchange listing.

Innovative firms apply for finance with private equity providers (PEP) mainly because, through their network, they also provide connections with other finance providers (62.5%). Only 25% of innovative firms find private equity providers the best available source of funds. They also represent for 12.5% of firms a source of professional financial skills (Fig. 9.5).

Differences between innovative and traditional firms can also be traced back from the analysis of why firms refrained from involving private equity providers in their financing.

Two issues are worth mentioning given that they are the most important ones and show the largest differences between the two groups of firms. The first issue concerns the knowledge of private equity providers: almost one out of two traditional firms do not know of their existence. Private equity providers, as expected, are instead better known among innovative firms: only one out of five declared to have refrained from contacting PEPs because they had no information on them (Table 9.12).

In many cases, (45.5% in the case of innovative firms and 25% in that of the firms belonging to the control sample) private equity providers provided no explanations for their decision to not fund the firm. When these explanations are available, they point to the existence of a weak business plan, insufficient growth potential, and the size of the requested loan for innovative firms, and to personal incompatibilities of firm founders and private equity providers and, again, the size of the requested loan for traditional firms (Table 9.13).

Finally, we tried to understand why firms would decide to turn to informal investors to fund themselves. However, we should recall that – at the time of the survey – only 0.4% of traditional firms' equity was in the hands of their family and friends, and none was in the case of innovative firms.

Table 9.12 Main reasons why firms refrained from involving private equity providers (%)

Motivations	Innovative Firms	Control sample
Firm has no knowledge of private equity providers	19.4	44.0
Concern that founders would loose control by sharing firm ownership	6.5	8.0
Concern that private equity providers' "exit" strategy would affect firm's stability	9.7	8.0
Firm's size and sector of activity	6.5	8.0
No interest in private equity providers as a financing source	25.8	16.0
Others	32.3	16.0
Total	100.0	100.0

Table 9.13 Main reasons why PEPs provided none or only part of the requested amount (%)

Motivation	Innovative firms	Control sample
Project considered to be too risky	0.0	0.0
Firm had weak business plan	9.1	0.0
Firm had insufficient collateral	0.0	0.0
Firm had insufficient growth potential	9.1	0.0
Personal incompatibility of firm founders and private equity providers	0.0	50.0
Too large a loan was requested	9.1	25.0
Private equity providers gave no explanations for their decision	45.5	25.0
Other reasons	27.3	0.0
Total	100.0	100.0

Innovative firms only bring up two reasons: to allow increased involvement of family and friends in the firm management (20%) and to overcome procedural difficulties encountered with traditional fund providers (10%). Unfortunately, in 70% of the cases answers point to reasons not present in the questionnaire (Table 9.14).

Table 9.14 Main reasons why firms would seek informal and individual investors' involvement (%)

Motivation	Innovative firms	Control sample
Family and friends were the only available source in the current stage of development	0.0	11.1
To overcome procedural difficulties encountered with traditional fund providers	10.0	22.2
To reduce the firm's exposure towards external fund providers	0.0	66.7
To allow family and friends an active and operational role in the firm's management	20.0	0.0
Other reasons	70.0	0.0
Total	100.0	100.0

In the case of firms belonging to the control sample, the main reason for turning to informal investors is to reduce the firm's exposure towards external fund providers (66.7%), followed by the need to overcome procedural difficulties encountered with traditional fund providers (22.2%), and the fact that family and friends were the only available source in that specific stage of development (11.1%).

9.5 Conclusion

Our survey of innovative SMEs in the Marche region at the beginning of 2009 brings to the fore some interesting conclusions about the role of finance in the development of these ventures. Innovative firms are riskier than traditional firms, and they have less collateral to provide to financial markets since their capital stock is often made up of intangible capital, or the proportion between intangible and tangible favors the former. These two characteristics, when accompanied by small dimensions, make innovative firms' financial market access more difficult and onerous than that of traditional firms. In this work we analyzed how 66 innovative firms located in a specific region, well known for being a small business laboratory, funded themselves and compared the outcomes with those of a control sample of 44 small-sized traditional firms.

Several outcomes from our analysis are worth recalling.

First, debt also plays an important role as a finance source for innovative firms. It contributes to financing almost 60% of investment. However, this share is significantly lower than that (83%) observed in the case of non-innovative firms. Leasing, bank loans, and lines of credit are the main components of firms' financial debt. All three types of debt imply relationships with banks that, overall, continue to represent a main financial supporter of firms. Indeed, even in the middle of the current economic and financial crisis, banks refused to provide the requested funds to only 9% of innovative firms. Reasons behind bank loan refusal were the firm's low credit rating score and the size of the loan requested.

Second, innovative firms need to fund their investment by means of equity. On average, it represents 40% of all funds. However, most equity (80%) comes from owners and only one-fifth from external equity providers. This result is a further confirmation of the attitude of Italian entrepreneurs to not dilute their ownership of companies that, in most cases, are family owned. We also reported that external private equity providers are in most cases venture capital firms; that is, firms tend to mainly use formal channels of equity provision, while informal providers – such as business angels – are completely missing from the regional economic context. This is true even though entrepreneurs declared that business angels would be useful to overcome procedural difficulties encountered with traditional fund providers. Further, in most cases private equity providers become firms' co-owners because, through their network, they allow original owners to enter into contact with other finance providers, and because PEPs provide financial skills that are lacking within firms. Finally, one of the main reasons for which external equity providers refused to provide funds is that firms had weak business plans.

If innovation is still the key issue for the economic development of the future, and if finance is believed to play a central role in supporting innovation especially in those economies characterized by the presence of small-sized firms, then a few specific and effective policy recommendations can be drawn from the conducted survey. They mostly center on the low level of firms' financial development. Therefore, actions should be taken to (a) improve entrepreneurs' and firm managers' financial culture (business plans, rating, etc.); (b) favor the dilution of firms' ownership by means of external private equity; (c) increase the rate of firm transformation from partnerships into limited liability companies since the latter are, in modern economies, usually associated with both concerns raised under a) and b).

Acknowledgments We thank the Pesaro-Urbino Chamber of Commerce for funding the survey through the Laboratory of Regional Economics at the Department of Economics and Quantitative Methods, Università di Urbino "Carlo Bo".

References

Aghion P, Bolton P (1992) An incomplete contracts approach to financial contracting. Rev Econ Stud 59:473–494

Aghion P, Bond S, Klemm A, Marinescu I (2004) Technology and financial structure: are innovative firms different? J Eur Econ Assoc 4:277–288

Bank of Italy (2009) Indagine sulle imprese industriali e dei servizi. Supplemento al Bollettino Statistico di Luglio

Barnea A, Haugen RA, Senbet LW (1981) Market imperfections, agency problems, and capital structure: a review. Finan Manage 10:7–22

Beck T, Levine R (2008) Legal institutions and financial development. In: Ménard C, Shirley MM (eds) Handbook of new institutional economics. Springer-Verlag (Berlin Heidelberg)

Benfratello L, Schiantarelli F, Sembenelli A (2006) Banks and innovation: microeconometric evidence on Italian firms. IZA Discussion Paper No. 2032. Available at SSRN: http://ssrn.com/abstract=848950 Accessed 3 November 2010

Berger AN, Udell GF (1995) Relationship lending and lines of credit in small firms finance. J Bus 68(3):351–381

Berger AN, Udell GF (1998) The economics of small business finance: the roles of private equity and debt markets in the financial growth cycle. J Bank Finan 22:613–673

Brierley P (2001) The financing of technology-based small firms. A review of the literature. Bank Engl Q Bull 41(1):64–76

Bugamelli M, Cristadoro R, Zevi G (2009) La crisi internazionale e il sistema produttivo italiano: un'analisi su dati a livello di impresa. Bank of Italy, Questioni di Economia e Finanza n. 58

Chavis LW, Klapper LF, Love I (2010) Entrepreneurial finance around the world: the impact of the business environment on financing constraints. In: Calcagnini G, Favaretto I (eds) The economics of small business. An international perspective. Springer-Verlag (Berlin Heidelberg)

Colombo MG, Grilli L (2007) Funding gaps? Access to bank loans by high-tech start-ups. Small Bus Econ 29:25–46

Coleman S, Robb A (2010) Sources of financing for new technology firms: evidence from the Kauffman firm survey. In: Calcagnini G, Favaretto I (eds) The economics of small businesses. An international perspective. Springer-Verlag (Berlin Heidelberg)

ECB (2009) Survey on the access to finance of small and medium-sized enterprises in the Euro area. September 2009

Favaretto I, Zanfei A (2007) Rapporto Finale 2007 – Innovazione e Centri di Ricerca nelle Marche. Progetto Inter-universitario, Università di Urbino

Guidici G, Paleari S (2000) The provision of finance to innovation: a survey conducted among Italian technology-based small firms. Small Bus Econ 14(1):37–53

Hall BH (2009) The financing of innovative firms. Eur Invest Bank Papers 14(2):8–28

Jensen M, Meckling WH (1976) Theory of the firm: managerial behavior, agency costs and ownership structure. J Finan Econ 3:305–360

Leland H, Pyle D (1977) Information asymmetries, financial structure, and financial intermediation. J Finan 32:371–387

Levine R (1997) Financial development and economic growth: views and agenda. J Econ Lit 35(2):688–726

Magri S (2007) The financing of small innovative firms: the Italian case. Temi di Discussione Bank of Italy, n. 640

Modigliani F, Miller MH (1958) The cost of capital, corporate finance and the theory of investment. Am Econ Rev 48(3):261–297

Myers SC (1984) The capital structure puzzle. J Finan 39(3):575–592

Myers SC, Majluf NS (1984) Corporate financing and investment decisions when firms have information that investors do not have. J Finan Econ 13:187–221

Nucci F, Pozzolo A, Schivardi F (2004) Is firm productivity related to its financial structure? Evidence from microeconomic data. Rivista di Politica Economica 95:269–290

O.E.C.D. (2006) Risk capital and innovative SMEs. In: The SME financing gap (Vol. I): theory and evidence. OECD Publishing (Paris)

O.E.C.D. (2008) High growth SMEs, innovation, intellectual assets and value creation project: module on financing. Centre for Entrepreneurship, SMEs, and Local Development. Statitiscs Directorate

Papaioannou E (2007) Finance and growth a macroeconomic assessment of the evidence from a European angle, European Central Bank WP

Persico N (2009) Il nostro problema è la tecnologia. www.lavoce.info Accessed 3 November 2010

Pozzolo AF (2003) Il ruolo della finanza nello sviluppo della nuova economia. In: Rossi S (ed) La Nuova Economia. I fatti dietro il mito. Il Mulino, Bologna

Stiglitz J, Weiss A (1981) Credit rationing in markets with imperfect information. Am Econ Rev 71:393–410

Chapter 10
Sources of Financing for New Technology Firms: Evidence from the Kauffman Firm Survey

Susan Coleman and Alicia Robb

Abstract This article uses data from the Kauffman Firm Survey to explore the financing sources and strategies of new technology-based firms. Findings reveal that technology-based firms, and particularly high tech firms, raise larger amounts of capital at startup than firms on average. These findings also suggest that, contrary to the Pecking Order and Life Cycle theories, owners of high tech firms are both willing and able to use external equity as a financing source.

10.1 Introduction

Technology-based firms have been and will continue to be important contributors to the U.S. economy. For the last two decades, technology firms have been a major source of innovation, business development and growth, and new jobs. Securing funding for new technology-based firms is particularly problematic, however. Many such firms are built upon intellectual capital rather than on physical assets, so it is difficult to determine the value and prospects of the firm. The problem of asymmetric or incomplete information is especially acute (Brierley, 2001), often resulting in a shortage of capital or capital that can only be obtained under unfavorable terms and conditions.

Prior research suggests that the owners of new technology-based firms use a combination of personal equity and debt that is often secured by the personal assets of the entrepreneur. In this sense, new technology-based firms are not that different from new firms in general. As technology-based firms grow, however, it becomes increasingly important for them to attract external sources of capital. External debt in the name of the business is often a problem, since many of these firms have few tangible assets that can be used as collateral (Colombo and Grilli, 2007). There is

S. Coleman (✉)
The Barney School of Business, University of Hartford, 200 Bloomfield Ave, West Hartford, CT 06117, USA
e-mail: scoleman@hartford.edu

also a higher risk of failure for firms based on new technologies, which serves as an added deterrent to bank lending (Guidici and Paleari, 2000). Some technology-based firms may be able to attract external equity in the form of angel investor and venture capital (Audretsch and Lehmann, 2004). This can also be a challenge as well, since it is difficult for investors to evaluate the demand for new technologies and products.

In this paper we will examine the financing sources and strategies of new technology-based firms using the Kauffman Firm Survey data. We identify not only sources of financing, but also financing gaps which may impede the launch, growth, and survival of technology-based small firms. Finally, we compare the patterns of financing observed in the data with the patterns prescribed by theory.

10.2 Capital Structure Theory

Capital structure refers to the mix of debt and equity used by firms to finance their long-term (fixed) assets. Debt is capital that has been loaned by other parties and must be repaid. In contrast, equity represents the investment made by owners or shareholders and is a permanent source of capital. As with other inputs to the firm, i.e. labor, equipment, facilities, both debt and equity have a cost. The mix of long term debt and equity is referred to as the firm's capital structure. The blended cost of the various sources of long term debt and equity is referred to as the firm's weighted average cost of capital (WACC).

Within the field of finance, capital structure theory is grounded in the work of Modigliani and Miller (1958) who initially wrote on the subject of capital structure in the electric utility industry. This theory, henceforth referred to as M&M, contends that firms will select the mix of debt and equity that maximizes the value of the firm and minimizes its weighted average cost of capital, both of which, in their theory, occur simultaneously. M&M's work was groundbreaking at the time, and has served as the basis for capital structure theory for almost 50 years.

Unfortunately, however, M&M does not necessarily hold for new, privately held firms, because it is based on the assumptions that there are no transaction costs of any kind and that investors and managers have the same information about the firm. M&M also assumes that firms have access to the full range of debt and equity alternatives. In the case of new firms in general, and technology-based firms in particular, however, informational asymmetries abound. Further, unlike, larger, publicly held firms, small firms typically do not have the option of issuing stocks and bonds, because the costs of doing so are prohibitive for smaller firms. Alternatively, they tend to be heavily reliant on other sources of capital including personal sources, bank loans, supplier credit, funding from private investors, venture capital, and, in some instances, government sources of funding.

Since M&M, several additional capital structure theories have emerged which may, in fact, be more applicable for small, new firms. Myers (1984) and Myers and Majluf (1984) developed a "pecking order" theory of finance. According to this theory, insiders have information about the firm that outsiders do not necessarily have. Because of this informational asymmetry, outside share purchasers will tend to under-price a firm's shares. In light of that, insiders prefer to use internal equity in the form of retained earnings or debt before they resort to issuing external equity. Thus, there is a "pecking order" of financing sources geared toward allowing the business owner to retain the maximum amount of control for as long as possible. According to this theory, firm owners prefer to use internal equity first, followed by short-term debt, long-term debt, and, finally, new external equity.

As noted by Coleman and Cohn (2000), the pecking order theory is particularly applicable to firms that are small and privately held, precisely because the informational asymmetries are so large. Since small, privately held firms do not publish annual reports or submit reports to the Securities and Exchange Commission, their financial statements are not publicly available. Thus, outsiders have no way of knowing the financial condition of the firm. Their response to this lack of information is to assume a higher level of risk, and in turn, to demand a higher cost for equity capital. External equity is very costly for small, privately held firms, and is typically their last choice in terms of financing alternatives.

Berger and Udell (1998) put forth a "life cycle" theory of financing which contends that firms use different types of financing for different stages of growth. They noted that small, privately held firms, in particular, are "informationally opaque". Thus, they have a difficult time obtaining external sources of financing and tend to be more reliant on insider financing such as the personal financial resources of the firm owners, and, in instances where the firm is profitable, retained earnings. According to Berger and Udell, when firm owners do have to turn to external sources of financing, their preference is for debt rather than equity because debt does not require them to give up ownership or control of the firm. Informational asymmetries are particularly severe for early stage firms, those in the seed or developmental stages. As the firm moves through its life cycle, however, it becomes less "opaque" and has access to a broader array of funding sources.

If we consider these three theories of capital structure, we can understand why the case of new technology-based firms is particularly problematic. These firms are often informationally opaque because many are built upon new and proprietary technologies making it difficult to attract external sources of capital. At the same time, however, new technology-based firms are often subject to the pressures of rapid growth as they move through their life cycle, particularly if they focus on products, services, or markets that experience dramatic increases in demand. In light of these characteristics, it would seem inevitable that new technology-based firms would have to draw upon both internal and external sources of capital to launch, develop their products and services, manage rapid growth, and survive. This research will attempt to determine if their use of debt and equity is consistent with previously articulated theories of capital structure, or if it differs in substantive ways.

10.3 Prior Research

To date, there have been few research studies specifically targeting the financing strategies of new technology firms. A review of literature done by Brierley in 2001 (Brierley, 2001) cited a small number of studies conducted prior to that time. Those studies that had been done, however, suggested that new technology-based firms face particular difficulties. These difficulties are associated with a lack of tangible assets that can be used as collateral, products that have little or no track record, and entry into untested markets. Brierley (2001) noted that angel investors and venture capitalists who might serve as funding sources to this sector have a difficult time identifying and evaluating the potential of high tech companies. He observed, however, that firms that were capable of securing SBIR (Small Business Innovation Research) awards or other external sources of funding were more likely to survive.

Brierley's findings were supported by an earlier study of firms that had received SBIR funding conducted by Lerner (1999). Lerner made use of a data set of firms that received SBIR funding between 1983 and 1997 compiled by the U.S. General Accounting Office. He found that SBIR awardees enjoyed substantially greater employment and sales growth than firms that did not receive awards. He also observed that SBIR awardees were more likely to receive venture capital funding. Lerner concluded that receipt of an SBIR award may convey information to potential investors thereby at least partially reducing the informational asymmetries associated with new technology-based firms. Audretsch (2002) also addressed the importance of SBIR funding, noting that a significant number of new technology-based firms would not have been started without its support.

Several studies have stressed the prominence of personal financing for new technology-based firms. They note that technology ventures are more risky than traditional businesses, and their prospects for success are more difficult to predict. In light of that, it is often difficult to obtain either external debt or equity. Moore (1994) surveyed a sample of high technology firms in Britain and found personal financing was the most important source of financing at startup. In his study, only 7% of technology startups were able to secure bank financing compared with 40% of all firms. Moore further noted that as the firms in his study matured, their financial constraints became less severe, and the firms in his study relied increasingly on banks and external equity as sources for expansion capital. Westhead and Storey (1997) also addressed the problem of financial constraints in a study of small high tech British firms. Twenty-five percent of the firms they surveyed reported that financing was a "continual" problem. In analyzing the results of their survey, the authors found that more technologically sophisticated firms were more likely to report continual financial constraints than firms based on less complex technologies.

These findings were echoed in a subsequent study of Danish information technology and biotechnology companies conducted by Bollingtoft et al. (2003). Their findings revealed that personal savings were the principal source of capital for new technology firms. The authors concluded, however, that different technology industries rely on different sources of capital. Bollingtoft et al. found that while firms in IT relied on personal savings and bank loans to some extent, those in biotechnology were much more reliant on external equity in the form of venture capital. Like Westhead and Storey (1997), Bollingtoft et al. concluded that it is more difficult to assess the risks associated with complex technologies. Thus, entrepreneurs in those fields have to put more effort into searching for capital and may have to rely more on external equity obtained from investors who have knowledge and expertise in that field.

Guidici and Paleari (2000) found evidence of financing constraints in a study of Italian technology-based small firms, particularly for newer firms. In their study, 73% of startups were financed exclusively with the entrepreneurs' personal wealth. Short and long term debt represented the next most frequently used source, and only a small percentage of firms used external equity. In interviews with their sample firms, Guidici and Paleari found that the entrepreneurs were reluctant to open the firm to outside investors. In instances when outside equity was considered, it was typically used as a means to gain not only additional capital but additional competencies in the areas of technology or managerial expertise. The authors concluded that their findings provided support for the "Pecking Order Theory" of financing.

In another study of Italian firms, Columbo and Grilli (2007) also found that a financing hierarchy existed. The vast majority of firms in their study relied on internal sources of funding at startup and sought outside financing only when their personal financial resources were exhausted. At that point, the entrepreneurs turned to bank loans as a source of financing, and, finally, to outside private equity. Columbo and Grilli found that firms that relied on debt financing as an alternative to external equity raised dramatically less capital leading the authors to conclude that new technology-based firms suffer from credit rationing. They concluded that even if technology-based firms were able to get access to bank loans, the amounts provided were not sufficient to fund their growth.

In a study of German firms, Audretsch and Lehmann (2004) tried to establish a link between financing sources for technology-based firms and subsequent performance. Their findings revealed that venture capital-backed firms outperformed firms that did not receive venture capital. In contrast, firms that were financed by friends and family exhibited substantially lower growth rates. They concluded that venture capitalists specialize in a small group of targeted industries such as biotech and technology, thus leveraging their expertise in exchange for higher returns. Finally, Audretsch and Lehman found an inverse relationship between the amount of debt and the amount of equity used by technology-based firms leading them to conclude that traditional banks alone are not sufficient as a source of financing for innovative firms and particularly technology-based firms.

Several studies provide support for a "life cycle theory" of financing. Freear and Wetzel (1990) conducted an early study of new technology-based firms to find that sources of equity capital shifted as firms matured. They studied 284 technology-based firms launched in New England and found that 38% used no outside equity. Of those firms that did use outside sources of equity, private individuals were the most common source, followed by venture capitalists. However, venture capitalists provided much larger amounts of equity capital on average, compared with private individuals. Freear and Wetzel also found that while private investors dominated in the earliest stages of firm development, venture capitalists were more prominent in later rounds of financing.

Manigart and Struyf (1997) conducted an exploratory study of financing sources for a sample of high technology startups in Belgium. Their results revealed that the most important source of financing was the entrepreneur himself, followed by bank financing because it did not require the entrepreneur to relinquish control. In the case of bank financing, however, substantial amounts of collateral were required to combat informational asymmetries. The firms surveyed also used funding from private individuals, venture capitalists, non-financial companies, and universities. Manigart and Struyf found that only a small number of startups used venture capital, because they did not want to give up control to outside parties, even if that meant hampering the growth of the firm. For those firms that survived, however, almost half used venture capital to fund later stages of growth. The authors concluded that the roles of private investors and venture capitalists are complementary with private investors playing a larger role in startup financing while venture capitalists play a greater role in funding early growth.

These findings were echoed in a more recent study by Bozkaya and De La Potterie (2008), which examined a sample of new Belgian firms to find support for both the life cycle and pecking order theories. Initially, development funding almost always came from personal savings and family and friends. As firms matured and became less informationally opaque, however, they were able to attract angel investors and venture capital financing. The authors concluded that the longer the entrepreneurial firm was able to survive on its own with internally generated funds, the lower the cost of external capital and the more control retained by the entrepreneur. In this sense their findings are consistent with Myers' pecking order theory of finance. They also concluded that, as the firm matures and moves through different stages of its "life cycle", different sources of funding become substitutes for each other. Thus, personal sources of financing are replaced by bank financing which is in turn replaced by angel and venture capital funding.

In contrast, Hogan and Hutson (2005) concluded that the pecking order theory does not do a good job of explaining the capital structure strategies of new technology-based firms. They surveyed a sample of Irish software companies to find that those firm owners not only used more external equity than debt but actually preferred external equity to debt. They noted that banks are not particularly appropriate sources of capital for high tech firms, because most of their loans are collateralized, and technology firms are based on intellectual rather than physical capital. Hogan and Hutson observed the venture capitalists and angel investors specialize by industry and are able to provide not only capital but also time and expertise. In their study, they found that entrepreneurs were willing to trade off ownership and control in exchange for the longer term goals of growth and value. Their findings are consistent with earlier work done by Hustedde and Pulver (1992) using a sample of U.S. firms seeking equity capital. In that study the authors found that those entrepreneurs who were willing to surrender a higher percentage of equity to outside investors were more successful in raising equity capital.

This study, using the Kauffman Firm Survey data, will be one of the first studies of small technology firms using a large, longitudinal database of new U.S. firms. We will identify the financing sources, both debt and equity, used by new technology firms at startup and in subsequent years. We will also determine the amounts of

10 Sources of Financing for New Technology Firms 179

financing used, and the relative importance of internal versus external sources of debt and equity. In this fashion, we hope to identify not only financing sources but also financing constraints that may impede the growth and development of new technology firms. We will also determine if the capital structures of these new firms are consistent with previously articulated theories of capital structure.

10.4 Data

The Kauffman Firm Survey (KFS) is a longitudinal survey of new businesses in the United States. This survey collected information on 4,928 firms that started in 2004 and surveys them annually. This cohort is the first large national sample of firm startups that will be tracked over time. These data contain detailed information on both the firm and up to ten business owners per firm. In addition to the 2004 baseline year data, there are 3 years of follow up data (2005–2007) now available. Additional years are planned. Detailed information on the firm includes industry, physical location, employment, profits, intellectual property, and financial capital (equity and debt) used at startup and over time. Information on up to ten owners includes age, gender, race, ethnicity, education, work experience, and previous startup experience. The detail provided by these data allows us to compare the financial strategies and the use of both debt and equity for new firms over the period 2004 through 2007. For more information about the KFS survey design and methodology, please see Robb et al. (2009a). A public use dataset is available for download from the Kauffman Foundation's website and a more detailed confidential dataset is available to researchers through a data enclave provided by the National Opinion Research Center (NORC). For more details about how to access these data, please see www.kauffman.org/kfs.

The sampling frame for the KFS is based on the Dun & Bradstreet (D&B) database, which was partitioned into sampling strata defined by industrial technology categories (based on industry designation). The high and medium technology strata were defined based on categorization developed by Hadlock et al. (1991), which took into account the industry's percentage of R&D employment and classified the businesses into technology groups based on their Standard Industrialization Classification (SIC) codes. High technology businesses were oversampled. Specifically, the original sampling design called for 2,000 interviews to be completed among businesses in two categories of high-technology businesses and 3,000 interviews to be completed among businesses in all other industrial classifications. The industries that make up each technology strata are listed in Table 10.1. Firms are defined as high tech, medium tech, and low tech. For more information on the survey methodology and sampling frame, see Robb et al. (2009a). A subset of the confidential dataset is used in this research – those firms that have data for all four survey years and those that have been verified as going out of business over the 2004–2007 period. This reduces the sample size to 3,974 businesses.

Table 10.1 Technology strata definitions

Technology stratum	SIC Code	Industry
High tech	28	Chemicals and allied products
	35	Industrial machinery and equipment
	36	Electrical and electronic equipment
	38	Instruments and related products
Medium tech	131	Crude petroleum and natural gas operations
	211	Cigarettes
	291	Petroleum refining
	299	Miscellaneous petroleum and coal products
	335	Nonferrous rolling and drawing
	371	Motor vehicles and equipment
	372	Aircraft and parts
	376	Guided missiles, space vehicles, parts
	737	Computer and data processing services
	871	Engineering and architectural services
	873	Research and testing services
	874	Management and public relations
	899	Services, not elsewhere classified
	229	Miscellaneous textile goods
	261	Pulp mills
	267	Miscellaneous converted paper products
	348	Ordnance and accessories, not elsewhere classified
	379	Miscellaneous transportation equipment
Low tech/non tech		All other industries

10.5 Descriptive Statistics

Tables 10.2, 10.3, 10.4, 10.5, and 10.6 provide descriptive statistics for 2004 and 2007 for high tech and low tech firms included in the Kauffman Firm Survey. These statistics reveal some striking differences between the two groups. Table 10.2 demonstrates that high tech firms were less likely to be organized as sole proprietorships or partnerships (27.4% vs. 43.2%) than as limited liability entities or corporations (72.7% vs. 56.8%) at startup. High tech firms were also less likely to be home-based (38.4% vs. 47.8%). In terms of revenues, profits, assets, and employment, high tech firms outperformed low tech firms in all four measures during the startup year. In fact, the employment potential for high tech firms was particularly noteworthy. Although 41% of low tech firms had employees in 2004, 46.9% of high tech firms had employees. Further, high tech firms employed a larger number of employees on average than low tech firms (2.9 vs. 1.9).

These differences persisted into the third follow-up year. By 2007, only 20.4% of high tech firms were organized as either sole proprietorships or partnerships compared to 40.5% of low tech firms. High tech firms were thus much more likely to start and to evolve into a more complex organizational structure. By 2007 also, two-thirds (68.3%) of high tech firms had employees compared to 56.7% of low tech

10 Sources of Financing for New Technology Firms   181

Table 10.2 Firm outcomes in 2004 and 2007

	2004 High tech	2004 Low tech	2007 (Surviving) High tech	2007 (Surviving) Low tech
Sole Proprietorship	0.238	0.372	0.192	0.352
Partnership	0.036	0.06	0.012	0.053
Corporation	0.409	0.269	0.465	0.297
Limited Liability Corporation	0.318	0.299	0.331	0.295
Home Based	0.384	0.478	0.331	0.471
Employer Firm	0.469	0.41	0.683	0.567
Employment	2.893	1.898	6.438	3.692
Revenues	78096.84	53775.27	258237.43	151357.81
Profits	31916.13	22743.11	84169.00	53146.17
Assets	107241.65	72694.78	215022.36	123665.12

Source: Kauffman Firm Survey Microdata. Sample includes only surviving firms over the 2004–2007 period, and firms that have been verified as going out of business over the same period. The original sample size in 2004 was 4,928

Table 10.3 Firm innovation

		2004 All firms	2004 Just those with x > 0	2004 % of firms w/x > 0	2007 All firms	2007 Just those with x > 0	2007 % of firms w/x > 0
High tech firms							
Number of	Patents	0.57	4.44	0.133	0.77	4.53	0.176
Number of	Copyrights	0.88	7.91	0.119	0.86	8.4	0.112
Number of	Trademarks	0.42	2.03	0.214	0.55	2.52	0.238
Employees		2.89	6.17		6.44	9.42	
Low tech firms							
Number of	Patents	0.13	7.74	0.018	0.15	7.78	0.022
Number of	Copyrights	0.88	12	0.077	1.45	18.99	0.083
Number of	Trademarks	0.27	2.1	0.134	0.35	2.92	0.134
Employees		1.9	4.62		3.69	6.51	

firms. The average number of employees was 6.4 and 3.7 respectively. In terms of revenues, profits, and assets, the gap between high tech and low tech firms increased. High tech firms had average revenues of $258,237 and profits of $84,169 compared with $151,358 and $53,146 for low tech firms. Finally, by 2007, high tech firms had 75% more assets than low tech firms ($215,022 vs. $123,665).

Table 10.3 provides a comparison of the level of innovation and intellectual property in high tech and low tech firms. It demonstrates that a higher percentage of high tech firms had some type of intellectual property at startup; 13.3% had patents, 11.9% had copyrights, and 21.4% had trademarks compared to 1.8%, 7.7%, and 13.4% for low tech firms. Interestingly enough, however, low tech firms that had

Table 10.4 Financial capital structure in 2004

By technology strata, credit score, and conditional on getting outside equity

	All firms	High tech High CS	High tech w/outside equity	Low tech High CS	Low tech w/outside equity
Owner equity	29567.36	65228.91	52415.68	47867.59	94223.14
Informal equity	1907.16	3692.44	9708.28	4174.6	7462.68
Formal equity	7628.91	128688.36	317297.64	12581.9	146379.39
Owner debt	3509.68	3163.6	6114.33	3457.86	8284.52
Informal debt	8021.2	26087.16	33276.47	18359.19	15405.46
Formal debt	33358.9	88526.29	130886.33	71897.51	109723.67
Total financial capital	83993.21	315386.75	549698.73	158338.66	381478.85
Zero financial capital	0.1	0.06		0.12	
Owner equity	0.35	0.21	0.09	0.30	0.25
Informal equity	0.02	0.01	0.02	0.03	0.02
Formal equity	0.09	0.41	0.58	0.08	0.38
Owner debt	0.04	0.01	0.01	0.02	0.02
Informal debt	0.09	0.08	0.06	0.11	0.04
Formal debt	0.40	0.28	0.24	0.45	0.29
Total financial capital	1	1	1	1	1
N	3974	81	61	271	103

Source: Kauffman Firm Survey Microdata. Sample includes only surviving firms over the 2004–2007 period, and firms that have been verified as going out of business over the same period. The original sample size in 2004 was 4,928

10 Sources of Financing for New Technology Firms

Table 10.5 Detailed financial capital structure in 2004

By technology strata, credit score, and conditional on getting outside equity

	All firms	High tech High CS	High tech w/out.equity	Low tech High CS	Low tech w/out.equity
Owner equity	29567.36	65228.91	52415.68	47867.59	94223.14
Informal equity	1907.16	3692.44	9708.28	4174.6	7462.68
Spouse equity	544.22	871.16	690.88	249.26	1364.07
Parent equity	1362.94	2821.28	9017.4	3925.34	6098.61
Formal equity	7628.91	128688.36	317297.64	12581.9	146379.39
Other informal investors	3004.85	37395.45	82960.02	5695.9	64037.65
Other business equity	2058.04	16558.18	65486.75	0	41634.42
Government equity	501.63	14062.45	31982.31	1086.8	8667.3
Venture capital equity	1686.16	60672.28	136017.96	5575.63	22656.63
Other equity	378.23	0	850.59	223.57	9383.39
Owner debt	3509.68	3163.6	6114.33	3457.86	8284.52
Personal credit card –owner	3182.36	2997.14	5891.34	3296.44	7277.35
Personal credit card-other owners	301.77	166.46	222.98	161.42	418.02
Other personal owner loan	25.55	0	0	0	589.14
Informal debt	8021.2	26087.16	33276.47	18359.19	15405.46
Personal family loan	2844.57	2504.61	3199.05	3977.04	6167.71
Personal family loan-other owners	303.6	0	0	0	1109.6
Business loan from family					
Business loan from owner					
Business loan FROM employee(s)	62.99	0	0	30.13	18.6
Other personal loan	578.56	15551.81	22743.28	1088.79	1349.39
Other personal funding	831.87	0	1773.05	1271.93	1819.4
Formal debt	33358.9	88526.29	130886.33	71897.51	109723.67
Personal bank loan	10647.69	14318.69	27701.75	20917.22	30832.99
Business credit card	1394.45	2250.87	1179.09	1638.85	2642.02
Other bank loan	1502.98	2835.18	3024.48	1635.72	5971.72
Business credit card-other owners	171.2	3.19	1090.01	145.25	405.34
Business credit cards	882.61	1337.27	4001.7	1283.75	1827.91
Bank business loan	10725.26	25059.47	33489.96	18094.84	38926.18
Credit line	3889.46	7998.63	5299.11	16884.33	2706.73
Other non-bank loan	2254.1	17940.34	27560.3	5477.01	13648.86
Government business loan	793.91	0	5582.89	796.8	1750.33
Other business loan	188.2	432.33	820.03	707.91	0
Other individual loan	263.07	15551.81	21132.94	663.08	1205.33
Other business debt	645.97	798.51	4.07	3652.76	9806.26
Total financial capital	83993.21	315386.75	549698.73	158338.66	381478.85
N	3974	81	61	271	103

Source: Kauffman Firm Survey Microdata. Sample includes only surviving firms over the 2004–2007 period, and firms that have been verified as going out of business over the same period. The original sample size in 2004 was 4,928

Table 10.6 Capital structure for high performing firms (2004 financing and 2007 outcomes)

	All firms	High tech > 100 K Rev	Low tech > 100 K Rev	High tech Employment > 5	Low tech Employment > 5
Owner equity	29567.36	64669.58	45200.86	92303.47	60959.2
Informal equity	1907.16	2834.91	1663.62	3382.84	2707.13
Formal equity	7628.91	34578.1	16425.04	75482.11	26929.49
Owner debt	3509.68	5053.35	3748.6	6598.7	4894.8
Informal debt	8021.2	9088.39	13092.03	10097.62	21275.48
Formal debt	33358.9	52902.68	59178.86	72780.53	87052.94
Total financial capital	83993.21	169127.02	139309.01	260645.27	203819.04
Owner equity	0.35	0.38	0.32	0.35	0.30
Informal equity	0.02	0.02	0.01	0.01	0.01
Formal equity	0.09	0.20	0.12	0.29	0.13
Owner debt	0.04	0.03	0.03	0.02	0.02
Informal debt	0.09	0.05	0.10	0.04	0.10
Formal debt	0.40	0.31	0.42	0.28	0.43
Total financial capital	1	1	1	1	1

Source: Kauffman Firm Survey Microdata. Sample includes only surviving firms over the 2004–2007 period, and firms that have been verified as going out of business over the same period. The original sample size in 2004 was 4,928

either patents or copyrights had a higher number on average, than high tech firms. Both high tech and low tech firms with intellectual property also had a higher number of employees on average than all firms in the data set. The same pattern held for firms surviving into 2007. Although a higher percentage of high tech firms had patents, copyrights, or trademarks, low tech firms had a greater number of patents and copyrights on average. As in 2004, firms with intellectual property had more employees than all firms suggesting a link between intellectual property, which can serve as a competitive advantage, and job creation.

Table 10.4 provides insights into the financing sources and strategies of technology-based firms. Consistent with prior research, the dominant sources of capital at startup for all firms in the Kauffman Survey were owner provided equity (35.2%) and external debt (39.7%). Alternatively, less than 10% of total financing came in the form of external equity (9.1%). Ten percent of firms in the total sample actually reported that they started with no financial capital.

For purposes of analysis, we divided technology-based firms into four different categories; high tech firms with high credit scores, low tech firms with high credit scores, high tech firms that used external equity, and low tech firms that used external equity. Our reasoning was that technology-based firms with high credit scores should be in a better position to attract external sources of debt. Because of the rigorous screening process typically associated with securing external sources of equity, we also reasoned that technology-based firms able to secure external equity would be those with the best prospects for success. Thus, these firms should be in a position to attract larger amounts of capital, both internal and external.

10 Sources of Financing for New Technology Firms

Our findings reveal that the financing sources used by low tech firms with high credit scores were roughly the same as for all firms in the sample as reported above. The dominant sources of capital were owner-provided equity (30.2%) and formal or external debt (45.4%). External equity represented only 7.9% of total financing. The finding is consistent with prior research on small firms and would seem to provide support for the Pecking Order theory. In the case of high tech firms, however, external equity played a much larger role. High tech firms with high credit scores obtained 40.8% of total financing from external equity. Conversely, they used much smaller percentages of both owner equity (20.7%) and external debt (28.1%). High tech firms that actually used external equity, used it satisfy over half of their financing needs (57.7% vs. 38.4% for low tech firms).

Table 10.4 also reveals that high tech firms were able to raise substantially larger amounts of both external equity and external debt at startup. High tech firms with high credit scores raised an average of $128,688 in external equity and $88,526 in external debt compared to $12,582 and $71,898 for low tech firms with high credit scores. High tech firms that used external equity raised an average of $317,298 in external equity and $130,886 in external debt, while low tech firms using external equity raised $146,397 and $109,724 respectively. It would seem obvious from these comparisons that starting a business in a high tech field enhances the firm's ability to attract external sources of capital, even at startup, when external sources tend to be limited. It is also noteworthy that technology-based firms in general, both high tech and low tech, raised substantially larger amounts of capital on average than all firms included in the Kauffman data set.

A more detailed breakdown of financing sources and amounts at startup is provided in Table 10.5. As in the case of Table 10.4, Table 10.5 reveals that high tech firms were much more successful in raising capital and, in particular, external sources of capital than all firms in the Kauffman data set. Although low tech firms with high credit scores raised twice as much capital as all firms ($158,339 vs. $83,993), high tech firms with high credit scores raised more than three times as much ($315,387 vs. $83,993). Correspondingly, high tech firms that raised external equity raised substantially more total financial capital on average than low tech firms that raised external equity ($549,699 vs. $381,479).

Table 10.6 provides insights into the initial capital structures of firms that (a) survived until 2007 and, (b) achieved a certain size level in terms of revenues and number of employees. For purposes of analysis, separate categories were created for high tech firms that achieved revenues in excess of $100,000 by 2007, low tech firms that achieved the same level of revenues, high tech firms with more than 5 employees by 2007, and low tech firms with more than 5 employees by 2007. Table 10.6 reveals that high tech firms with revenues in excess of $100,000 started with higher levels of owner equity (38.2%) and external equity (20.4%) and lower levels of external debt (31.3%) than either low tech firms with sales in excess of $100,000 or all firms in the sample. High tech firms with more than 5 employees by 2007 also started with higher levels of owner equity (35.4% vs. 29.9%), and external equity (29.0% vs. 13.2%), and lower levels of external debt (27.9% vs. 42.7%) than low tech firms. These results suggest a link between the firm's ability to attract external equity and its subsequent performance as measured by revenues and employment. As noted earlier, the screening process for obtaining external sources of equity is a rigorous one. Thus, it stands to reason that those firms that attract external equity are the firms most likely to succeed. It is also possible that firms having high levels of owner provided equity send a positive signal to external equity providers. Owners, as insiders, are in the best position to see the firm's longer term potential. If they are optimistic, they can signal their optimism by investing larger amounts of personal equity.

The comparisons presented in Tables 10.4 through 10.6 indicate that high tech firms have an advantage in terms of their ability to attract external equity in particular, and larger amounts of financial capital in general. It also appears that the owners of those firms are willing to seek out and use external sources of equity, even if it involves sharing ownership and control. The Pecking Order theory suggests that firms will choose to use internal sources of capital, followed by external debt, and then external equity. Further, prior research has suggested that the Pecking Order theory does a good job of explaining the financing choices of small and entrepreneurial firms (Coleman and Cohn, 2000; Guidici and Paleari, 2000). Our results suggest, however, that the Pecking Order theory may not do such a good job of explaining the financing behavior of new high tech firms, particularly higher quality firms. These results imply that those firms are able to attract larger amounts of external equity, and that their owners are actually more willing to use external equity rather than external debt. The Life Cycle theory of financing (Berger and Udell, 1998) contends that newer firms are informationally opaque and have a difficult time attracting external sources of financing. In contrast, our findings reveal that technology-based firms, particularly high quality firms and high tech firms, are adept at attracting substantial amounts of both debt and equity capital. We will explore these findings regarding capital sources and structure more thoroughly through the use of multivariate analysis.

10.6 Multivariate Analysis

Table 10.7 provides a probit analysis based on 2004 (startup) data in which various sources of debt and equity are used as the dependent variables. Thus, each probit model indicates the probability that firms in the sample will use the type of financing represented by the dependent variable. Dependent variables include (1) outside debt, (2) bank loans, (3) insider financing, and (4) outsider equity. Outside debt includes bank loans used for the business (both business and personal), lines of credit, business credit cards, government business loans, and other loans for the business. Bank loans include only personal and business bank loans used for the business. Insider financing includes both debt and equity provided by a parent, spouse, other family members, or employees. Finally, outsider equity includes angel, venture capital, or government equity financing. In total, these four different categories of financing provide an indication of the probability that firm owners are able to generate non-owner sources of financing. Independent variables include measures of firm

Table 10.7 Probit analysis: probability of financing

	Outside debt	Bank loans	Insider financing	Outsider equity
hightech	0.117***	0.0225*	0.155***	0.0458*
	(0.0307)	(0.0135)	(0.0329)	(0.0262)
lowtech	0.0885***	−0.00164	0.118***	0.0376***
	(0.0201)	(0.00755)	(0.0148)	(0.0143)
hours_own	0.00248***	0.000240*	0.00139***	0.00236***
	(0.000419)	(0.000134)	(0.000345)	(0.000290)
age_own	0.0117**	0.00396*	0.0107**	−0.00800**
	(0.00593)	(0.00231)	(0.00503)	(0.00404)
agesq	−0.000113*	−0.0000400*	−0.0000931*	0.0000609
	(0.0000629)	(0.0000238)	(0.0000534)	(0.0000433)
hsgrad	0.00872	0.0149	0.0519	−0.0968***
	(0.0726)	(0.0412)	(0.0685)	(0.0258)
somecoll	0.0354	0.0487	0.0560	−0.108***
	(0.0690)	(0.0422)	(0.0617)	(0.0343)
colldeg	0.0329	0.0401	0.0579	−0.130***
	(0.0696)	(0.0428)	(0.0630)	(0.0308)
graddeg	0.0444	0.0560	0.0934	−0.0928***
	(0.0722)	(0.0571)	(0.0698)	(0.0289)
work_exp	−0.00432***	−0.000403	−0.00336***	−0.00249***
	(0.000971)	(0.000325)	(0.000808)	(0.000737)
startup	0.00419	0.00323	0.0190	0.0105
	(0.0196)	(0.00657)	(0.0164)	(0.0139)
multiown	0.0599***	0.0320***	0.0486***	−0.0138
	(0.0203)	(0.00818)	(0.0173)	(0.0143)
dbscore	0.00206***	0.000143	0.00156***	0.0000556
	(0.000420)	(0.000135)	(0.000350)	(0.000297)
homebase_04	−0.0798***	−0.0335***	−0.0704***	−0.0608***
	(0.0199)	(0.00722)	(0.0165)	(0.0145)
intprop_04	−0.0106	0.0238**	−0.00200	0.0472**
	(0.0241)	(0.00958)	(0.0198)	(0.0192)
compadv_04	0.0432**	−0.00706	−0.000586	0.0133
	(0.0200)	(0.00728)	(0.0168)	(0.0145)
product_04	0.0449	0.00932	0.0346	−0.000510
	(0.0298)	(0.00893)	(0.0239)	(0.0214)
both_04	−0.0121	−0.0131	−0.00983	−0.00349
	(0.0299)	(0.00835)	(0.0239)	(0.0214)
black	−0.0560*	0.000388	−0.0421	0.0719**
	(0.0339)	(0.0133)	(0.0281)	(0.0284)
asian	−0.0161	−0.00786	−0.0298	0.0712*
	(0.0479)	(0.0124)	(0.0363)	(0.0408)
other	−0.0341	−0.0149	−0.0520	0.0750
	(0.0591)	(0.0174)	(0.0444)	(0.0555)
hispanic	−0.00972	−0.0186**	−0.0112	0.0771**
	(0.0430)	(0.00946)	(0.0349)	(0.0354)
female	−0.0283	−0.0175***	−0.0212	0.00877
	(0.0215)	(0.00639)	(0.0176)	(0.0157)
Observations	3751	3751	3751	3751

Standard errors in parentheses
*** $p < 0.01$, ** $p < 0.05$, * $p < 0.1$

and owner characteristics revealed by prior research to have an impact on capital structure. These include measures of owner characteristics such as age, education, experience, hours devoted to the business, gender, race, and ethnicity, and firm characteristics such as organizational structure and credit quality. Independent variables are also included to indicate whether or not the firm had some type of intellectual property or competitive advantage. Finally, there are dichotomous variables designating high tech and low tech firms. The excluded category is medium tech firms.

Table 10.7 reveals that both high tech and low tech firms had a significantly higher probability of using outside debt, insider financing, and outsider equity than medium tech firms. High tech firms also had a significantly higher probability of using bank loans. These findings suggest that high tech firms have an advantage over medium tech firms in terms of generating both internal and external non-owner sources of financing. Consistent with this, firms with some type of intellectual property also had a significantly higher probability of securing external financing in the form of bank loans and outsider equity. Our findings regarding the financing sources of high tech firms seem to contradict the Life Cycle theory which states that new firms have a difficult time attracting external sources of capital.

Other firm characteristics that had an impact on financing include measures of ownership structure and credit quality. Firms with multiple owners had a significantly higher probability of using outside debt, bank loans, and insider financing. Multiple owners may have more assets than can be used as collateral, and they also have a larger network of family members willing to provide internal equity. Conversely, home-based businesses had a significantly lower probability of using any of the four types of financing, possibly due to their smaller size and limited financing requirements. Not surprisingly, firms with higher credit scores had a greater probability of using outside debt. Firms with higher credit scores also had a significantly higher probability of using insider financing. This finding is consistent with the Pecking Order theory which states that firm owners prefer to use both internal equity and debt before turning to external equity. By doing so they are able to maintain control and avoid diluting their ownership position. High credit scores enable them to attract sources of external debt thus minimizing the amount of capital needed from external equity providers.

Table 10.7 reveals that a number of owner characteristics were associated with the probability of using various sources of financing. Firm owners who worked more hours had a significantly higher probability of using all four types of financing. This stands to reason, since the process of searching for and obtaining capital is a labor intensive and time consuming one. Older owners had a higher probability of using outside debt, bank loans, and insider financing. Conversely they had a significantly lower probability of using outsider equity. It is possible that older owners have had more time to develop contacts with providers of debt capital and potential sources of insider financing. Thus, consistent with the Pecking Order theory again, they prefer to use insider financing and outside debt rather than outsider equity. Similarly, Table 10.7 indicates that more highly educated owners were significantly less likely to use outsider equity as a source of financing, possibly because they are more aware of the risks associated with giving up control and diluting their ownership position. More educated owners may also feel that they have sufficient human capital to be able to manage the firm without the help of external providers of equity.

Table 10.8 provides the results of a regression analysis in which the ratios of outside debt, bank loans, insider financing, and outsider equity to total financial capital were used as the dependent variables. Whereas Table 10.7 provided an analysis of the probability that firms would use each type of financing, Table 10.8 provides an indication of the level of each type of financing used. As in the case of Table 10.7, the analyses provided in Table 10.8 is based on 2004 (startup year) data, and medium tech firms are the excluded category.

Table 10.8 reveals that high tech firms used a significantly higher ratio of outside debt, bank loans, and outsider equity than medium tech firms in the sample. Low tech firms also had a significantly higher ratio of outside debt and bank loans than medium tech firms. Although low tech firms had a significantly lower ratio of outside equity to total financial capital, the difference was not significant. These findings suggest that high tech startups have an advantage over other types of firms in attracting external sources of debt and equity. Consistent with this finding, firms with some type of intellectual property also financed with a higher percentage of outsider equity. These findings, again, would seem to contradict the Life Cycle theory of financing.

Other significant variables included measures of hours worked and organizational structure. Owners who worked longer hours used significantly higher ratios of bank debt and insider capital. Owners who work longer hours may be those who are most committed to the success of the firm. Thus, they are willing to commit not only human capital but also the financial capital of other family members. Firms with multiple owners were able to secure higher ratios of outsider debt, bank loans, and outsider equity, possibly because multiple owners have access to a wider network of external funding sources. Home-based businesses raised significantly lower ratios of all four types of capital, perhaps due to the limited nature of their needs as well as their limited prospects for growth and profits.

Measures of owner age, educational attainment, and industry experience were also significant. Older owners used significantly higher ratios of outside capital (outside debt, bank loans, and outsider equity) than the owners of all firms. It is possible that older owners, like multiple owners, have developed a network of external funding contacts and sources over time. Over the course of their careers, older owners may also have developed credibility with external funding sources. Table 10.8 reveals that educational attainment was associated with a lower ratio of insider financing. In this sense, education may serve as a signal of high human capital, making it easier to attract external rather than internal sources of financing. In keeping with this, firm owners that were more highly educated used a higher ratio of both bank loans and outsider equity although these differences were not significant. Interestingly, firm owners with more years of industry experience, another form of human capital, used significantly smaller ratios of both outside debt and bank loans, possibly due to prior bad experiences with debt. Not surprisingly, firms with higher credit scores used higher ratios of outside debt and bank loans.

Table 10.8 OLS Regressions of ratios of source of financing to total financing

	Outside debt	Bank loans	Insider financing	Outsider equity
hightech	0.0676***	0.0599***	0.00572	0.0240**
	(0.0186)	(0.0150)	(0.0120)	(0.0107)
lowtech	0.0589***	0.0652***	0.0153*	–0.00965
	(0.0125)	(0.00929)	(0.00838)	(0.00607)
hours_own	0.000523*	0.000348	0.000727***	0.00000210
	(0.000272)	(0.000228)	(0.000178)	(0.0000820)
age_own	0.00947***	0.00645**	–0.00740***	0.00340***
	(0.00351)	(0.00298)	(0.00277)	(0.000947)
agesq	–0.0000966***	–0.0000628**	0.0000622**	–0.0000338***
	(0.0000368)	(0.0000317)	(0.0000279)	(0.00000987)
hsgrad	–0.0119	0.0347	–0.152***	0.00198
	(0.0552)	(0.0398)	(0.0483)	(0.0113)
somecoll	–0.0237	0.0357	–0.148***	0.00918
	(0.0526)	(0.0377)	(0.0471)	(0.0105)
colldeg	–0.0346	0.0207	–0.160***	0.00757
	(0.0527)	(0.0376)	(0.0472)	(0.0109)
graddeg	–0.0209	0.0405	–0.156***	0.0125
	(0.0538)	(0.0386)	(0.0476)	(0.0118)
work_exp	–0.00131**	–0.00150***	–0.000479	–0.0000979
	(0.000650)	(0.000526)	(0.000394)	(0.000224)
startup	0.000781	0.00814	0.000368	0.00494
	(0.0129)	(0.0106)	(0.00840)	(0.00418)
multiown	0.0375***	0.0353***	–0.00174	0.0174***
	(0.0139)	(0.0117)	(0.00922)	(0.00505)
dbscore	0.00108***	0.000719***	0.0000362	–0.0000248
	(0.000292)	(0.000243)	(0.000192)	(0.0000979)
homebase_04	–0.0455***	–0.0296***	–0.0379***	–0.0171***
	(0.0131)	(0.0109)	(0.00931)	(0.00445)
intprop_04	–0.0261*	–0.0265**	0.0127	0.0127**
	(0.0150)	(0.0117)	(0.0111)	(0.00568)
compadv_04	–0.00972	–0.0104	–0.000125	–0.00190
	(0.0135)	(0.0110)	(0.00910)	(0.00452)
product_04	0.0141	0.0182	–0.00673	0.00611
	(0.0200)	(0.0168)	(0.0132)	(0.00712)
both_04	–0.00147	–0.00718	–0.00173	–0.0116*
	(0.0200)	(0.0170)	(0.0133)	(0.00695)
black	–0.0476**	–0.0385**	0.00166	–0.00823*
	(0.0211)	(0.0162)	(0.0144)	(0.00499)
asian	–0.0234	–0.00938	0.0673**	0.00701
	(0.0330)	(0.0279)	(0.0284)	(0.0145)
other	0.000789	–0.0000353	0.0210	–0.0111
	(0.0405)	(0.0366)	(0.0280)	(0.00790)
hispanic	–0.0299	–0.0146	0.0312	–0.0159***
	(0.0279)	(0.0232)	(0.0226)	(0.00479)
female	–0.0130	–0.00745	–0.000900	–0.0153***
	(0.0144)	(0.0117)	(0.00941)	(0.00389)
Constant	–0.0714	–0.136*	0.409***	–0.0523**
	(0.0993)	(0.0803)	(0.0802)	(0.0244)
Observations	3385	3385	3385	3385
R-squared	0.038	0.039	0.052	0.032

Standard errors in parentheses
***$p < 0.01$, **$p < 0.05$, *$p < 0.1$

In terms of differences by gender, women-owned firms used a significantly lower ratio of outsider equity than men. They also used lower ratios of outside debt, bank loans, and insider financing, although these differences were not significant. These findings suggest that, consistent with prior research, women-owned firms are more reliant of owner-provided sources of financing (Coleman and Robb, 2009). Possible reasons for the differences between women- and men-owned firms could be that women tend to start smaller firms, they may be more risk averse, or they may not have access to networks that could provide external sources of debt and equity.

Black-owned firms used a significantly lower ratio of outside debt, bank loans, and outside equity than all firms, while Hispanic-owned firms used a significantly lower ratio of outsider equity. It is noteworthy that Black-, Hispanic-, and Asian-owned firms all used a higher ratio of insider financing than all firms in the sample. This suggests that minority-owned firms, in general, are more dependent on financing from family members and other insiders rather than external sources of either debt or equity. These findings are also consistent with prior research indicating that minority-owned firms are less likely to use external sources of capital possibly due to the types of businesses they start, lack of access to formal providers of capital, and intentional or unintentional forms of discrimination (Coleman, 2002; Coleman, 2003; Robb et al. 2009b).

10.7 Summary and Conclusions

This research examines the sources and amounts of financing used by startup firms included in the Kauffman Firm Survey data. In particular, it was our intent to focus on the financing strategies of new technology-based firms. Our findings revealed that technology-based firms raised larger amounts of capital than all firms included in the sample. Further, both high tech and low tech firms raised larger amounts of non-owner financing than all firms. In the case of high tech firms, they were much more reliant on outsider equity than either low tech firms or all firms. Conversely, low tech firms were much more similar to all firms in their financing strategy in the sense that they relied primarily on owner-provided equity and external debt.

Multivariate analysis broadened our understanding of these discrepancies. We found that both high tech and low tech firms had a greater probability of using outside debt, insider financing, and outsider equity than medium tech firms. High tech firms also had a significantly higher probability of using bank loans than medium tech firms. These findings suggest that high tech firms, in particular, have an advantage in terms of their ability to seek out and attract non-owner sources of financing which can be used to fund operations, research and development, new products and services, and growth.

We also found that high tech and low tech firms were able to attract not only more sources of financing but higher levels of financing at startup. High tech firms used significantly higher ratios of outside debt, bank loans, and outside equity than medium tech firms, while low tech firms used significantly higher ratios of outside debt, bank loans, and insider financing. These are sources of non-owner financing that can be decisive in helping new firms survive and grow during the critical startup period.

Our findings seem to disprove the Pecking Order and Life Cycle theories, at least in the case of high tech firms. The Pecking Order theory states that firm owners prefer to use inside equity and outside debt to avoid diluting their ownership position and giving up control. Our results reveal, however, that high tech firms had a significantly higher probability of using both outside debt and outsider equity than medium tech firms. These results suggest that the owners of high tech firms are more open to using a number of different sources of financing to ensure firm survival, development, and growth. It appears that the owners of high tech firms are willing to trade off their concerns regarding dilution and control in return for larger amounts of external capital that will help them to achieve firm goals. By the same token, these results seem to refute the Life Cycle theory which states that newer firms are forced to rely on internal rather than external sources of capital. Our findings reveal that technology based firms raised substantial amounts of both external debt and equity, even in their startup year. To prove a point, high tech firm owners who used outside equity raised over five times as much capital in the startup year as all firms ($549,699 vs. $83,993). It would seem that external providers of capital are attracted by technology-based firms' prospects for growth and profits, even during the early stages of their existence.

Our results also revealed differences in the financing patterns of women and minority firm owners. Women were significantly less likely to use outside debt, bank loans, or insider financing than all firms. This finding is consistent with prior research indicating that women are more reliant on personal or owner-provided sources of financing than on external sources. Not surprisingly, women also had lower ratios of non-owner financing in the form of outside debt, bank loans, insider financing, and outsider equity. This pattern suggests the possibility of both demand and supply side constraints on women-owned startups. Prior research reveals that women start smaller firms than men and may have more limited financing requirements (Carter and Allen, 1997; Fairlie and Robb, 2009). Women may also be more reluctant to use external sources of financing, because they do not want to increase the riskiness of the firm, or alternatively, because they do not want to give up control. From a supply side perspective, however, some research contends that women use smaller amounts of external capital because they are excluded from the types of male-dominated angel investor and venture capital networks that typically provide it (Greene et al., 2001). These questions provide opportunities for further research on the financing strategies of women launching technology-based firms.

Finally, our findings revealed that, for the most part, minority firm owners were less likely to use external sources of financing. Further, when they did use external financing, they used significantly lower ratios of external sources of financing than all firms. Black-owned, Asian-owned, and Hispanic-owned firms did, however, use a higher ratio of insider provided financing revealing that family and other insiders play a greater role in starting minority-owned firms. Minority owners may develop these networks of insider financing because they are reluctant to approach external sources, or alternatively, because they have approached them and have been declined. Like women, minority firm owners may lack access to key networks that could provide them with links to external funding sources.

10.8 So What?

Our findings suggest that new technology-based firms demonstrate a different demand and supply pattern for sources of capital than firms in general. These results indicate that technology-based firms, and high tech firms in particular, are able to attract larger amounts of both external debt and external equity. This suggests that there is a potential supply of external capital if the firm can make a compelling case for growth or competitive advantage in the form of intellectual property. It also appears that the owners of high tech firms are more open to external sources of capital that will allow their firms to develop and grow. As noted above, they are willing to trade off their concerns for dilution and control in return for what they hope will be a smaller piece of a much bigger pie.

References

Audretsch DB (2002) The dynamic role of small firms: evidence from the U.S. Small Bus Econ 18:13–40
Audretsch DB, Lehmann EE (2004) Financing high-tech growth: the role of banks and venture capitalists. Schmalenbach Bus Rev 56(4):340–357
Berger AN, Udell GF (1998) The economics of small business finance: the roles of private equity and debt markets in the financial growth cycle. J Bank Finan 22:613–673
Bollingtoft A, Ulhoi JP, Madsen H, Neergaard H (2003) The effect of financial factors on the performance of new venture companies in high tech and knowledge-intensive industries: an empirical study in Denmark. Int J Manage 20(4):535–547
Bozkaya A, Van Pottelsberghe De La Potterie B (2008) Who funds technology-based small firms? Evidence from Belgium. Econ Innov New Tech 17(1/2):97–122
Brierley P (2001) The financing of technology-based small firms. A review of the literature. Bank Eng Q Bull 41(1):64–76
Carter NM, Allen KR (1997) Size determinants of women-owned businesses: choice or barriers to resources. Entrepreneurship Reg Dev 9:211–229
Coleman S (2002) The borrowing experience of black and hispanic-owned small firms: evidence from the 1998 Survey of Small Business Finances. Acad Entrepreneurship J 8(1):1–20
Coleman S (2003) Borrowing patterns for small firms: a comparison by race and ethnicity. J Entrepreneurial Finan Bus Vent 7(3):87–108
Coleman S, Cohn R (2000) Small firms' use of financial leverage: evidence from the 1993 National Survey of Small Business Finances. J Bus Entrepreneurship 12(3):81–98
Coleman S, Robb AM (2009) A comparison of new firm financing by gender: evidence from the Kauffman Firm Survey data. Small Bus Econ 33:397–411
Colombo MG, Grilli L (2007) Funding gaps? Access to bank loans By high-tech start-ups. Small Bus Econ 29:25–46
Fairlie RW, Robb (2009). Gender differences in business performance: evidence from the Characteristics of Business Owners Survey. Small Bus Econ 33:375–395
Freear J, Wetzel WE Jr (1990) Who bankrolls high-tech entrepreneurs? J Bus Vent 5:77–89

Greene, PG, Brush CG, Hart MM, Saparito P (2001) Patterns of venture capital funding: is gender a factor? Vent Capital 3(1):63–83

Guidici G, Paleari S (2000) The provision of finance to innovation: a survey conducted among Italian technology-based small firms. Small Bus Econ 14(1):37–53

Hadlock P, Hecker D, Gannon J (1991 July) High technology employment: another view. Mon Lab Rev 114:26–30

Hogan T, Hutson E (2005) Capital structure in new technology-based firms: evidence from the Irish software sector. Global Finan J 15:369–387

Hustedde RJ, Pulver GC (1992) Factors affecting equity capital acquisition: the demand side. J Bus Vent 7(5):363–374

Lerner J (1999) The government as venture capitalist: the long-run impact of the SBIR program. J Bus 72(3):285–318

Manigart S, Struyf C (1997) Financing high technology startups in Belgium: an exploratory study. Small Bus Econ 9:125–135

Modigliani F, Miller MH (1958) The cost of capital, corporate finance and the theory of investment. Am Econ Rev 48(3):261–297

Moore B (1994) Financial constraints to the growth and development of small high-technology firms. In: Storey DJ, Hughes A (eds) Finance and the small firms. Routledge, New York, NY, pp 112–144

Myers SC (1984) The capital structure puzzle. J Finan 39(3):575–592

Myers SC, Majluf NS (1984) Corporate financing and investment decisions when firms have information that investors do not have. J Finan Econ 13:187–221

Robb A, Ballou J, DesRoches D, Potter F, Zhao Z, Reedy E (2009a) An overview of the Kauffman Firm Survey. Kauffman Foundation, Kansas City, MO

Robb A, Fairlie R, Robinson D (2009b) Financial capital injections among new black and white business ventures: evidence from the Kauffman Firm Survey, Working Paper

Westhead P, Storey DJ (1997) Financial constraints on the growth of high technology firms in the United Kingdom. Appl Finan Econ 7:197–201

Chapter 11
Do Male and Female Loan Officers Differ in Small Business Lending? A Review of the Literature

Andrea Bellucci, Alexander Borisov, and Alberto Zazzaro

Abstract In this chapter we review the academic literature on the role of loan officers in the loan origination process and lending relationships with small businesses. In particular, we focus on a recent stream of research which recognizes that loan officers – with their behavior, character and even emotions – are a key factor affecting the outcome of bank-firm relationships.

JEL Classification G21, G32, J16

11.1 Introduction

It may be surprising to professional bankers, but it has only been recently recognized in the economic literature that loan origination and bank relationships with small enterprises are strongly influenced by the personality, disposition and behavior of loan officers. Information on new loan applicants and client small firms is in the hands of loan officers at local bank branches. A large part this information is tacit, non-codifiable and can be fully understood only by those who are present in the socio-economic context where borrowers operate. In this view, the quality of granted loans and the accuracy of their pricing, as well as the forgone profit of denied loan applications, crucially depend on the unobservable effort spent by these loan officers on collecting and interpreting soft and hard information on actual and potential borrowers. Since this effort is costly and loan officers' interests might not be aligned with those of bank's senior managers (or shareholders), the former may strategically reveal the proprietary information they collect, in order to influence the distribution of resources and power within the bank organization and/or to maximize

A. Zazzaro (✉)
Dipartimento di Economia, Università Politecnica delle Marche, and Money and Finance Research Group (MoFiR), Piazzale Martelli 8,
60121 Ancona, Italy
e-mail: a.zazzaro@univpm.it

their prospects of internal career (Milgrom and Roberts, 1990; Scharfstein and Stein, 2000; Milbourn et al., 2001; Agarwal and Wang, 2009; Hertzberg et al., 2010). Anticipating this, banks routinely design monetary and non-monetary incentives for loan officers by trading-off the inducement to exert effort in collecting exclusive information and the deterrence of moral hazard behavior due to loan officers' informational rents.

On the top of this, a critical part of the loan officer's job is relational, meaning that he/she makes decisions through interpersonal interactions with specific borrowers often on the basis of limited information and cognitive capacity. Intuitional, emotional, behavioral and cultural factors drive the loan officers' assessment of borrower's creditworthiness, complementing (sometimes, even reversing) information from financial statements (Buttner and Rosen, 1988; McNamara and Bromiley, 1997; Lipshitz and Shulimovitz, 2007).

In fact, many of the factors that influence loan officers' behavior have proven to be gender-specific, or at least more pronounced for one gender than the other. For example, a common finding in the economic and psychological literature is that women tend to be more risk-averse and less self-confident than men (Byrnes et al., 1999; Croson and Gneezy, 2009). There is also evidence that women make slower career advancements than men and are less likely to accept jobs away from their family (Walker and Fennel, 1986). On the other hand, women are typically less sensitive to competitive incentives than men (Gilligan, 1982; Croson and Gneezy, 2009). Men and women also seem to respond to the sex of the other party involved in the transaction in different ways (Eckel and Grossman, 2001; Ben-Ner et al., 2004; Dufwenberg and Muren, 2006). For such reasons, female loan officers could be inclined to use stricter criteria when deciding upon loan applications in order to avoid defaults and maximize the probability of internal career. On the other hand they might be less sensitive to incentive and display a greater sense of solidarity with borrowers.

In the wake of these considerations, a number of papers have recently focused on the lender's gender, asking whether perceptions of borrowers' creditworthiness significantly differ between male and female lenders (Wilson et al., 2007; Ravina, 2008; Barasinska, 2009); whether the average default rates on loans handled by female lenders are statistically lower and whether women respond to incentives differently than men (Agarwal and Wang, 2009; Barasinska, 2009; Beck et al., 2009); whether loan contract terms vary systematically with the loan officer's gender (Bellucci et al., 2010).

In the following pages, we provide a review of this new strand of literature. In particular, in Sect. 11.2 we examine theoretical arguments and empirical evidence on why loan officers matter, while in Sect. 11.3 we discuss reasons why female loan officers could behave differently than their male counterparts and present recent empirical evidence on whether lenders' gender is relevant for loan origination, quality (riskiness) of granted loans and their contract terms. In Sect. 11.4, we draw conclusions and some indications for future research.

11.2 Why Loan Officers Matter?

Banks operate in credit markets through a network of branches where loan officers are called to make decisions upon applicants' financing requests on the basis of policy guidelines established by the bank at the central level. Regardless of the lending technologies adopted, loan officers' decisions on lending applications and contracts are crucial for the success of both their banks and customers.

11.2.1 Theory

11.2.1.1 Information and Moral Hazard

Making decisions on loans is plagued by two fundamental information asymmetries. The former originates from the borrowers who have more information on their capacity and willingness to repay the loan. For a large part this information is soft, "hard to quantify" (Berger and Udell, 2002), and socially embedded. It requires an outlay of time and effort by those who are in charge of the loan approval process. In such circumstances, it would be optimal for a bank to delegate both loan origination and monitoring activities to its local loan officers who have a detailed knowledge of the particular social and economic context and a privileged access to information about local borrowers (Aghion and Tirole, 1997; Dessein, 2002). However, there is a second source of information asymmetry – internal to the bank organization – and it works against the formal delegation of loan decisions to local officers. The energy loan officers devote to assess a loan applicant's quality, as well as their ability to distinguish good borrowers from bad ones, is only imperfectly self-documentable and not directly observable by supervisors (loan reviewers) at the upper layers of the bank (Garicano, 2000; Milbourn et al., 2001; Novaes and Zingales, 2004). Therefore, a key trade-off banks face is between information production and communication costs. Greater decision-making authority left to loan officers increases their incentive to produce information on borrowers and the likelihood that worthy credit requests will be approved. But it also leads to greater information rent of loan officers and higher communication costs that must be incurred in order to limit moral hazard and adverse selection.

To address this trade-off, banks provide loan officers with monetary and non-monetary career-related incentives. To the extent that loan officers are the depositary of unobservable information and their efforts cannot be monitored by the principal, input or output-based contracts can mitigate moral hazard problems and allow for an optimal allocation of risk. This possibility is explicitly investigated by two recent contributions by Agarwal and Wang (2009) and Inderst (2009) who analyze the effects of piece-rates compensation contracts on loan officers' screening and loan origination decisions.

Agarwal and Wang (2009) assume that a risk-neutral loan officer can observe the quality of loan applicants with a certain probability which increases with the unobservable effort spent on screening. Loan officer's compensation depends on the amount of loan granted but, in addition to that, defaulted loans have negative consequences on the loan officer's career prospects. For loan officers with greater career concerns, piece-rate contracts increase effort spent on collecting information and assessing loan quality. In contrast, if loan officers are not career-concerned or if monetary incentives to book loans are very high, the number of approved loans increases, but the screening effort and the average loan quality decrease. In addition, the lower the capacity to process soft information, the greater the monetary incentive needed to promote loan officer's effort in screening applicants.

Inderst (2009) assumes that loan officers have to spend effort to generate new loan applications and that they may or may not be called to use soft information at the loan-approval stage according to the lending technology adopted by the bank. The compensation scheme offered by the bank comprises a fixed part, independent of both the origination and approval of a loan, and a fee part contingent on whether a loan is approved. The bank also arranges a loan-review technology that allows it to observe the quality of the loan officer's decision with a certain probability. Consistent with Agarwal and Wang (2009), if the bank allows loan officers to use soft information, more high-powered compensation contracts lead to less strict loan standards by the bank. However, the model also suggests that if loan officers are less sensitive to competition and find it costly to search for new customers, banks should provide them with high monetary incentives at the loan-approval stage in order to induce them to exert effort at the loan-origination stage. In this case, the bank is more likely to adopt a hard-information lending technology by depriving loan officers of any active role at the loan-approval stage.

Hertzberg et al. (2010) focus on banks' rotation policy which, by reassigning tasks among loan officers, operates as a disciplinary device and promotes reliable information disclosure about borrowers' quality. If loan officers are certain to stay in the same branch during their career, they have incentives to conceal bad news about borrowers in order to preserve their reputation of good screeners and to enhance their prospects of career advancement. In contrast, if loan officers rotate across bank branches, they anticipate that the new loan officers who are going to enter their current position will disclose all bad loans made in past since they are not responsible for them. Therefore, loan officers in charge would prefer to self-report any negative information on borrowers' repayment capacity, thus demonstrating their honesty and passive-monitoring skills. Rotation, however, may also have negative effects for the bank. First, frequent turnover may destroy valuable soft information accumulated by loan officers. It may also generate risk aversion and short-termism on the part of loan officers who respond by over-lending to well-known borrowers and investing in safe, but less profitable, short-term projects (Hirschleifer and Thakor, 1992; Palley, 1997; Berger and Udell, 2002).

11.2.1.2 Emotion, Stereotypes and Confidence

Economic literature on loan officers assumes that they are fully rational and selfish agents, making decisions on the base of real, although noisy and not verifiable, information concerning the quality of applicants and their investment projects. However, the reality is that loan officers make decisions on specific individuals and not on impersonal projects or abstract entrepreneurs. Loan officers are engaged in "emotional labor": for example, they have to "suppress their feelings of sympathy for defaulters in order to collect money or seize household items for sale" (Dixon et al., 2007). This implies that behavioral, emotional, moral and cultural factors assume a crucial role in the loan-approval decisions of loan officers.

Organizational and psychological research on decision-making behavior has acknowledged the importance of non-rational factors for a long time. Intuition and emotion, for example, have been considered by many authors as a primary source of error in judgment formation (Bonabeau, 2003). Others, however, have taken a more positive view on impressions and "gut feelings", by considering these factors as a valuable source of information, especially for experienced decision makers in repeated transactions (Lipshitz and Shulimovitz, 2007). McNamara and Bromiley (1997) also argue that the cognitive process followed by loan officers when they make decisions on risk is influenced by their perceptions and by the context in which they operate. For example, the likelihood of loan officers overrating a borrower is positively affected by historical factors like the duration of the relation between the bank and that borrower or by the past successes achieved by the bank branch. In addition, a fads-and-fashions effect can influence loan officers who "may prefer to lend to firms in exciting or innovative industries even if industry performance indicators suggest otherwise" (McNamara and Bromiley, 1997, p. 1070).

Furthermore, loan officers are frequently called to make decisions in contexts characterized by numerous loan alternatives, very dissimilar from each other, and each described by many, possibly inconsistent cues. In such environment, loan officers have incentives to reduce cognitive processing by eliminating some of the alternatives through non-compensatory decision behavior, in which a high score on one dimension is not used to balance for low scores on other dimensions (Tversky, 1972; Biggs et al., 1985).

Finally, the risk assessments loan officers assign to borrowers are affected by the perceptions and stereotypes they form about the borrowers' entrepreneurial capacity and trustworthiness (Buttner and Rosen, 1988; Carter et al., 2007), and by the degree of confidence they attribute to the acquired information and to their own judgment capacity (Danos et al., 1989).

11.2.2 Evidence

11.2.2.1 Information and Moral Hazard

The existence of a trade-off between the effective selection of loan applicants and the information rent left to loan officers – that is between the reliability of the information produced in the lending relationship and the reliability of the information communicated to loan reviewers – is corroborated by many pieces of empirical evidence.

First of all, to the extent that loan officers' effort in searching for and screening of applicants is unobservable, banks are used to introducing compensation- and career-related incentives in order to align loan officers' interests with their own and to limit moral hazard problems. Agarwal and Wang (2009) investigate how incentive compensation affects small business lending at a major commercial bank in the United States. Starting from 2005, this bank introduced a new incentive compensation system for half of its loan officers, while the other half of lenders continued to be paid on a fixed wage basis. Consistent with the predictions of their model we previously described, the empirical analysis confirms that the adoption of incentive compensation has a two-sided effect: it increases loan origination but also induces loan officers to book riskier loans with a greater amount of soft information. More specifically, Agarwal and Wang find that the approval rates of the treated group of loan officers increase by 47%, the number of granted loans by 44% and the average loan size by 45%. At the same time, however, they also find that the average default rate of loans approved by lenders on incentive pay increases by 24%, while the time spent on each loan application decreases by 21%. Moreover, loan officers with greater career concerns are less likely to book a loan and the loans they book have lower default probability.

Apart from monetary incentives, banks may use rotation policy of loan officers in order to induce them to refuse new loans to unhealthy firms and not to conceal bad news on borrowers. The effect of reassigning tasks among loan officers on moral hazard in communication within the bank is the focus of the Hertzberg et al. (2010). They test three hypotheses: (1) the predictive power of internal ratings on the probability of a loan entering default in the next 12 months increases when the rotation of the loan officer assigned to the borrower becomes imminent, (2) the debt of client firms is more sensitive to the internal risk rating during high rotation quarters; (3) the average internal rating attributed to client firms is lower during low rotation quarters. Hertzberg et al. confirm all three hypotheses using data from a large multinational U.S. bank operating in Argentina. Central to the analysis are the 3-year loan officer rotation rule followed by the bank and the monthly communication of risk ratings completed by the bank's loan officers.

The incentive effect of rotation policy is also confirmed by Ferri (1997) who shows, using Italian data, that the average time a loan officer spends in a branch is negatively associated with the size of the bank and therefore, with the importance of agency problems. However, loan officer turnover also leads to a loss of valuable soft information accumulated during the relationship and deters loan officers from investing resources in the production of such information. In this vein, Scott (2006), using firm-level data for a large sample of U.S. small businesses, shows that an increase in the frequency of loan officer turnover is associated with greater likelihood of the firm being turned down on its last loan application. Uchida et al. (2009), look at a sample of Japanese small businesses and find that the production of soft information increases in the lack of turnover of the loan officer serving the firm in the past 3 years. Finally, Liberti (2004), using the same data set as Hertzberg et al. (2010), finds that empowering loan officers in making lending decisions increases the effort they devote to screening and monitoring of borrowers, and improves the performance of the bank. However, as Udell (1989) shows, such beneficial effect of delegation tends to be counteracted by the greater resources that the parent bank devotes to loan reviewing activities.

11.2.2.2 Behavioral Factors

The importance of behavioral factors for loan officers' decisions and credit access of small businesses has been verified in a number of psychological and organizational studies. Lipshitz and Shulimovitz (2007), for example, report results from in-depth interviews of fourteen loan officers at a large Israeli bank showing that credit decisions are strongly influenced by impressions, "gut feelings" and emotional intuitions. McNamara and Bromiley (1997) show that risk-rating errors made by loan officers are affected by organizational pressure for profitability and by cognitive factors, e.g. loan officer's excitement about borrower's industry prospects.

Andersson (2004) provides experimental evidence on the effects of experience on lending decisions. He investigates the information-acquisition processes used by 61 individuals with different amount of expertise with the most experienced group in the sample consisting of 23 senior loan officers. The starting point of the analysis is previous research in psychology which has documented that experts are more efficient in their search processes as they seem to acquire less but more relevant information (Camerer and Johnson, 1991; Davis, 1996). In contrast to these studies, Andersson reports that senior loan officers tend to acquire more cues across all the information categories considered. However, the senior loan officers do not behave differently from junior loan officers. In addition to that, Andersson cannot find evidence of greater consensus on risk assessment across experienced loan officers compared to novices.

Finally, there is evidence that loan officers attribute risk to loan applicants on the basis of personal perceptions and stereotypes of entrepreneurial capacity. Carter et al. (2007) show that, besides financial statements, loan officers use a wide range of criteria to form their opinion about loan applicant's creditworthiness. Danos et al. (1989) show that loan officers achieve high levels of confidence early in the lending process, and when making their final lending decision tend to ignore information which is not consistent with their early opinion and judgment. Other studies use survey-based evidence derived from loan officers' responses to questionnaires. They focus on how risk and loan approval are affected by the reliability of applicants' financial statements and the personal degree of tolerance for ambiguity of the decision-maker. The results are mixed. Johnson et al. (1983) find that the level of attestation of firms' financial statement (no attestation, compilation, review and audit) does not affect the decision to lend. Wright and Davidson (2000) show that the effect of auditor type on loan officers' risk assessment is statistically insignificant, even though the latter influences both the likelihood of loan approval (negatively) and the charged interest rate (positively). Moreover, they show that loan officers who are more tolerant to ambiguity tend to attribute a greater probability of default to loan applicants. This complements the results reported by Tsui (1993) that tolerance per se does not affect loan approval and interest rate decisions. In contrast,

Bandyopadhyay and Francis (1995) find that higher levels of attestation are associated with a higher probability of approval of a loan application. Schneider and Church (2008) find that a negative judgment on the effectiveness of a firm's internal controls expressed by the auditors decreases the probability that loan officers will extend credit.

11.3 Why Should the Gender of Loan Officers Matter?

11.3.1 Gender in Decision-Making

The extant literature in economics and psychology has advanced various reasons as to why the gender of agents with decision-making power may influence the outcome of economic transactions. A non-exhaustive list includes differences between men and women with respect to risk attitude, overconfidence, social preferences, tolerance for inequality, negotiation skills, information processing, experiencing of emotions, competitiveness and career patterns.

11.3.1.1 Risk Taking and Overconfidence

There is extensive evidence from different fields of research that the gender of a decision-maker is associated with his/her risk propensity and overconfidence. Byrnes et al. (1999) provide a meta-analysis of 150 articles published in major psychological journals finding that women are, on average, significantly more risk averse than men. However, they also suggest that gender differences in risk-taking tend to be conditional on the particular context or task under study. Economic studies broadly confirm that females exhibit both greater risk aversion and lower overconfidence, even after controlling for other factors associated with risk attitude (Eckel and Grossman, 2008b; Croson and Gneezy, 2009). Most of the economic evidence is experimental, coming out of abstract gambles or games of financial decision-making played in the laboratory. Some experiments provide support for the existence of unconditional gender gap in risk preferences. Powell and Ansic (1997), for example, find that females are less risk-seeking than males irrespective of problem framing or degree of ambiguity. Similarly, Eckel and Grossman (2008a), looking at financial decision-making behavior, find that women are more risk-averse than men in both abstract and contextual designs. Others, however, suggest that risk-taking differences depend on whether lotteries are framed as gains (where women are more risk-averse than men) or losses (where the opposite holds) and that differences disappear when men and women are called to make decisions in contextual frames (Schubert et al., 1999).

Besides providing experimental evidence, research in economics and finance has also studied whether risk-preferences in actual financial decision-making differ between women and men. For instance, Jianakopolos and Bernasek (1998) utilize the Survey of Consumer Finances to analyze allocation of risky assets in portfolios held by individuals. They show that, relative to single men, single women exhibit higher relative risk aversion. Sunden and Surette (1998) study observed choices made by individuals with respect to their defined contribution plans. Their findings are consistent with women being less likely to allocate retirement funds in stocks and more likely in bonds. Bernasek and Shwiff (2001) also analyze the determinants of the proportion of a pension plan invested in stocks, focusing on differences between males and females. The results of their study imply that women are more conservative investors than men.

Psychologists show that some of the factors behind the lower risk attitude of women are gender differences in instinctive and emotional reactions to risk (Loewenstein et al., 2001), in perceptions of probability of adverse events (Lerner et al., 2003) and especially in the degree of confidence in the rightness and success of their own decisions. For example, Estes and Hosseini (1988) provide experimental evidence on the determinants of confidence with respect to investment-related tasks among security analysts, institutional investors, shareholders and general business people. They conclude that women are significantly less confident in their investment decisions than men even after controlling for other relevant variables such as experience and investment amount. Lundberg et al. (1994) conduct an experimental study by asking students to identify their confidence in answers they give to test questions. Thus, the authors focus on a specific rather than general context. Confirming the existence of differential degree of overconfidence in men and women, the authors conclude that females do not necessarily lack confidence but it is males who have too much confidence, especially in the cases when wrong. Rather than following the experimental approach, Barber and Odean (2001) focus on actual trading made by individual investors and broadly confirm that women are less overconfident than men. The authors document that men trade more often than women and the increased trading volume leads to lower net returns.

11.3.1.2 Social Preference and Gender Pairing

Another major reason of gender bias in decision-making is that men and women often attach different weight to the payoffs of others in their own preferences. As put by Croson and Gneezy (2009), women are often considered to be more "other-regarding" than men. They also differ from men with respect to generosity and willingness to help. Eagly and Crowley (1986), for example, compile a meta-analytic study of more than 170 published articles and conclude that males end up helping others more frequently than females. The authors also hint at the role of gender-pairing: men are significantly more likely to help women than other men, while women are equally likely to help. Salminen and Glad (1992) also focus on gender pairing in helping by studying whether men and women are more likely to help a person of the opposite sex. However, they find no support for this claim.

Gender differences in generosity are often the focus of experimental economic analysis. Eckel and Grossman (1998) study the oft-mentioned claim that women are more socially-oriented or selfless than men in a dictator game, in which players are called to propose a split of a given sum of money with another person who cannot refuse the proposal. The authors consistently find that, in a setting of anonymity, women are willing to give a larger share of their own resources to others. Dufwenberg and Muren (2006) also find that females give slightly more than males. They also show that the donations are lower and less frequent when they are made publicly and that men donate from 27 to 50% more to women than to other men. Eckel and Grossman (2001) study giving behavior in an ultimatum game with face-to-face contacts, where the proposer receives a positive payoff only if the responder accepts the proposal. Once again, they find that women's proposals are more generous and that women are satisfied with the initial proposal more often. They also find that men accept more frequently proposals coming from women than from other men (chivalry effects), while women almost never reject the proposal of other women. The hypothesis that women exhibit greater generosity and solidarity is rejected by Ben-Ner et al. (2004). They find that women tend to give slightly less than men and that the difference is driven by the cases in which women are asked to give to other women.

Finally another interesting piece of evidence on gender differences in social loafing is provided by Karau and Williams (1993). They perform a meta-analysis of 78 studies which analyze the tendency for individuals to exhibit less effort when working collectively. Their results suggest that females might be less likely to free-ride, and hence, more likely to work for the benefit of the group.

11.3.1.3 Negotiation Skills

If females and males follow different bargaining tactics and norms or have different propensity to initiate negotiations, the bargaining outcome could be affected by the gender of the participants. A meta-analytic exploration of more than 20 published articles collected by Stuhlmacher and Walters (1999) indeed finds that on average men tend to negotiate significantly better outcomes than women. By conducting interviews with more than 200 students about negotiation strategies, Kaman and Hartel (1994) confirm that males and females follow different bargaining styles, with men being more focused on active strategies like starting a negotiation to get the highest salary possible or making a higher counter offer in response to the initial offer made by the company, while women being more likely to rely on traditional self-promotion like emphasizing the relevance of their own education for the required task or their willingness to be engaged in different tasks. Gerhart and Rynes (1991) analyze salary negotiations in a sample of graduating students and show that even though men and women have similar propensity to bargain for high salary, the outcome of such bargaining, i.e. the salary that the applicant eventually accepts, varies substantially with gender. A possible explanation advanced by the authors is that men use more effective bargaining tactics or use the same tactics more skillfully. In contrast, Small et al. (2007) confirm the presence of gender-differences in negotiation propensity despite the lack of differences in actual negotiation performance. The main driver of the observed asymmetry seems to be framing: gender differences exist in situations framed as opportunities for negotiation on compensations but not in situations framed as opportunities to ask for more money. The finding is consistent with women being more likely to follow a norm of politeness.

11.3.1.4 Information Acquisition and Reporting

Gender can interact with decision-making if men and women acquire and process information in different ways, forming different judgment with respect to the same issue. Brown et al. (1980) explore gender-based differentials in cognitive activity by focusing on qualitative differences in perception and memory. Their study shows that, consistent with gender differences in information processing, masculine words are better recalled by males, whereas feminine words by females. Sex differences in information processing strategies are also documented by Darley and Smith (1995). In an experimental setup, they ask men and women to listen to subjective and objective advertising claims for either a low-risk or moderate-risk product and rate their perceptions about the claims in terms of perceived credibility and purchase intention. They find that women tend to be more comprehensive information processors who consider both objective and subjective aspects giving them different importance according to the product riskiness. In contrast men are more selective and tend to focus on single cues regardless of the risk attached to the product. In a study of the association between gender-driven differences in information processing and performance of accounting students, Chung and Monroe (1998) find that females are more inclined to rate disconfirming information as important. On the contrary, males are more likely to rate confirming information as important. More related to the tasks performed by a typical loan officer, Graham et al. (2002) explain gender differences in investment strategies by differences in information-processing styles: they suggest that males might be more likely to focus on expected returns, while women would be more likely to incorporate the risk dimension along with other secondary information. Interested in the use of accounting information, Smith (1999) also suggests that gender is important characteristic with an impact on accounting-based decisions. Finally, Powell and Ansic (1997) show experimentally that women tend to adopt strategies which avoid the worst-case alternative, while men are significantly more likely to focus on the best-case alternative.

Gender differences are also found in the propensity to misreport. For example, Karlan and Zinman (2008) conduct a survey on borrowing behavior of first-time applicants for expensive consumer credit in South Africa, showing that nearly half of the respondents underreport their recent borrowing activity, but women tend to "cheat about borrowing" more frequently than men. Interestingly to our end, the authors also show that the lying incentives of the respondents depend on the surveyor's gender: misreporting is most likely in the cases when female borrowers are interviewed by men.

11.3.1.5 Stereotypes and Perceptions

Recent research in psychology and management has documented that males and females form different stereotypes of successful entrepreneurs or managers and perceive financial matters in different ways. Gupta et al. (2009) study whether entrepreneurs are perceived to have mainly masculine or feminine traits and show that both genders ascribe more masculine characteristics to the entrepreneurial image, even if women are more likely to attribute female traits to the ideal entrepreneur type. Similarly, Duehr and Bono (2006), find that male students rarely consider manager characteristics as feminine, and this stereotype is rather persistent over time. More generally, Miller and Budd (1999) provide evidence that occupational sex-role stereotypes can be detected at a very early age and that male students are more likely to form such stereotypes. A study by Kray et al. (2001) shows that women are more concerned about stereotypes and more susceptible to stereotype threats, especially if they perceive a task as being diagnostic of their ability.

11.3.1.6 Competitiveness

There is further robust evidence that men and women behave differently under competition and that they have different sensitivity to competitive incentives. Gneezy et al. (2003) run a series of experiments and conclude that women might be less effective than men in certain competitive environments. In particular, the authors document that women are not less effective than men in non-competitive or in single-sex contexts but tend to exhibit inferior performance when facing competition by males. Shurkhov (2009), however, suggests that it is not competition per se that affects the gender gap in performance but time pressure. The author finds that, if time pressure is reduced, women can outperform men even in competitive environments by increasing both the quality and quantity of their output. Men tend to focus on quantity at the expense of quality. Niederle and Vesterlund (2007) hint that any observed performance under competition might be due to differential willingness to compete. In their study, the authors show that men are more likely to select competitive environment even though their performance in such environment is not superior. Overall, the authors conclude that women tend to shy away from competition. A similar perspective emerges from the meta-analytic study of Karau and Williams (1993). As the authors argue, men are often described in the literature as more likely to follow competitive concerns, while women are associated with cooperative ones.

11.3.1.7 Career Patterns and Discrimination

Different career patterns and societal roles between men and women or concerns with gender-based discrimination within organizations and in the external labor market could strengthen the effect of the decision-maker's gender on the outcome of the actual decision. For example, following the classical Becker's (1985) argument, the greater responsibility of women for child care and housework could have implications for their occupational/career choices and earnings. Studies in organizational science also indicate that gender is an important criterion for task and/or authority assignment within companies. Walker and Fennell (1986), reviewing studies on gender-based role differentiation, report that men are more likely to be assigned to more instrumental and influential tasks, while women are more often in passive and cooperative roles. Wright et al. (1995) study various determinants of the gender gap in workplace authority in seven countries. The analysis reveals that a gender gap in authority exists in each of the countries: women are less likely to be in the formal authority hierarchy, to have sanctioning power or to participate in organizational policy decisions. Research in economics has also provided extensive evidence of gender-based discrimination in the labor markets. As Darity and Mason (1998) state in their review of the literature, one of the major causes of gender disparity in the American economy is discriminatory treatment of women in the labor market.

11.3.2 Gender in Lending Decisions

Applied to the context of lending decisions, the factors outlined in the previous section make it clear why the gender of the loan officer matters for the origination and shaping of a loan contract.

If male loan officers exhibit higher risk tolerance and/or overconfidence, projects of similar risk could be funded by them, while rejected by their female colleagues. Alternatively, female lenders could extend credit but only if stricter contract terms and requirements are ensured. In contrast, social preferences may have ambiguous effect on female and male decision-making in the lending context. If female loan officers have more solidarity with borrowers, they could apply less stringent loan-approval criteria than male loan officers. However, social preferences and gender-pairing between loan officer and borrower could significantly loosen or tighten decisions on loan approval and contract terms depending on whether solidarity, chivalry or envy sentiments prevail. In addition, loan contract terms depend on the negotiation ability of the two transacting parties and, as we saw, this ability might be gender-specific. Furthermore, the loan officer's gender may be a crucial element in lending transactions if male and female lenders search for information and process the information they acquire in different ways. For example, to the extent that women make decisions taking into account both formal and informal pieces of information, female loan officers might be more inclined to process soft information and decide upon small, informationally opaque borrowers. Alternatively, female loan officers could reach better credit decisions if they are superior at identifying crucial cues or they have a tendency to assess borrowers' creditworthiness more thoroughly. In addition, male and female loan officers can make biased decisions on loan applications presented by male and female entrepreneurs depending on the stereotype of successful businessperson they hold. Finally, gender differences in propensity to compete and career concerns could make the severity of the agency problems between the bank and its loan officers, as well as the appropriate design of internal incentive structures, gender-specific.

Given the pervasiveness and importance of these factors in the loan decision-making process, it is rather surprising that the gender of the loan officers has long been overlooked in the existing banking literature. Apart from studies that introduce the gender of the loan officer as a control variable in more general regression models of lending behavior, papers which explicitly focus on how and why loan officer's gender affects the loan approval strategy and the terms of the loan contract are rare. For the sake of our presentation, we classify the existing evidence along the lines of our theoretical discussion on why loan officer's gender matters. Therefore, the findings of some papers will be discussed in different subsections according to the specific gender factor they analyze. For studies that simply control for the loan officer's gender, we make an attempt to infer the factors consistent with the evidence presented, even beyond what the authors suggest. Table 11.1 summarizes research objectives, variables, methodology and results of the empirical studies focusing on the gender differences in lending decisions.

11.3.2.1 Risk Taking, Overconfidence and Information Processing

Three recent papers focus on whether gender-based differences in risk taking, overconfidence and information processing are associated with the outcome of the lending process in terms of loan performance and contract terms.

Beck et al. (2009) study how the gender of the loan officer who approves and services a loan application affects the subsequent loan performance defined as the probability that the loan will be in arrears for more than 30 days. The authors use a proprietary dataset of loans granted by a microcredit lender in Albania over the period 1996–2006. The overall conclusion of the study is that loans screened and monitored by female lenders tend to perform better, being 4.5% less likely to become problematic. The authors advance several explanations for this pattern. One of them is the existence of different degrees of risk-aversion and/or overconfidence between lenders of different gender. If female lenders are less willing to take risk, they should be more restrictive in their approval decisions. To address this hypothesis, the authors analyze how loans granted by male and female lenders differ in terms of ex-ante observable risk measures. In contrast to the risk-aversion hypothesis, they find that, if anything, female lenders are associated with more risky borrowers rather than less risky ones, and they do not seem to reject loan applicants more often compared to their male colleagues.

Another explanation for the superior performance of the loans underwritten by female lenders investigated by the authors is that female lenders might have better hard-information processing skills. To address this conjecture, Beck et al. focus on the rejection/approval decisions by male and female lenders and show that, based on observable factors, female loan officers do not seem to use different screening strategies. This insight is also formally confirmed by an econometric test (Chow test) for equality of the coefficients in the two sub-samples (male loan officers vs. female loan officers) that does not indicate any statistically significant difference. In sum, Beck et al. do not find support for the notion that female lenders are more risk-averse or possess different information processing skills with respect to information based on observable features of the borrower. However, the authors suggest that female loan officers might have better information processing skills with respect to

11 Do Male and Female Loan Officers Differ in Small Business Lending?

Table 11.1 Loan Officer's gender: a summary of the existing evidence

Authors	Research objective and variables	Methodology	Factors driving gender differences	Gender differences in lending decisions
Agarwal and Wang (2009)	Loan approval rates Loan performance – default rates	Logit model	Career concerns (less)	F > M
Alesina et al. (2008)	Loan contract terms – interest rate	Ordinary Least Squares (OLS) Panel random-effects model	Gender-pairing	F > M
Barasinska (2009)	Loan funding – participation by female lenders Loan performance	Logit model	Risk/overconfidence Prudence	F < M F > M
Bellucci et al. (2010)	Loan contract terms – interest rate, collateral, credit availability	Ordinary Least Squares (OLS) Probit model	Risk/overconfidence Gender-pairing	F > M F ≧ M
Beck et al. (2009)	Loan performance – arrear probability	Probit model	Risk/overconfidence Career concerns Gender-pairing	F < M F < M F < M
Black et al. (2000)	Loan contract terms – overcharge	Tobit model	Bargaining skills	F < M
Buttner and Rosen (1988)	Loan officers' perceptions – similarity between men/women and successful entrepreneurs	Interviews/t-tests	Stereotypes/perceptions	F < M
Carter et al. (2007)	Loan assessment criteria and application processes	Verbal protocol/χ^2-tests	Information acquisition/decision criteria	F ≠ M
Ravina (2008)	Loan funding – participation by female lender Loan contract terms – interest rate	Probit model Tobit model	Gender-pairing Perception	F > M F > M
Wilson et al. (2007)	Loan officers' perceptions – constructs held for men/women	Repertory grid/t-tests	Stereotypes/perceptions	F ≠ M

unobservable, soft-information factors pertaining to the character and nature of the loan applicant.

Rather than focusing on ex-post loan performance, Bellucci et al. (2010) study the relevance of loan officer's gender for the shape of the loan contract in terms of interest rate, collateral and credit availability. The authors use a proprietary dataset of credit lines granted to more than 7000 sole proprietorships by a major Italian bank during the years 2004–2006 to analyze whether and how price of credit, incidence of collateral and probability that a borrower exceeds the credit limit allowed by the bank using the costly option to overdraw funds vary with the loan officer's gender. The underlying motivation is that if female lenders are more risk averse than male lenders, loans approved by the former should be characterized by stricter contract terms. Controlling for a large number of borrower characteristics, nature of the bank-borrower relationship and conditions in the local credit market, the authors show that the gender of the loan officer does not affect the loan contract terms for the average borrower. Bellucci et al. (2010) also provide insights as to whether male and female lenders process information differently in different information environments. The authors use the length of the bank-borrower relationship as a proxy for the amount of information available about the loan applicant. In particular, borrowers with longer relationship with the bank should be characterized by lower opacity to the lender. The analysis reveals that the association between the gender of loan officer and the shape of the loan contract depends on the information environment in which the transaction takes place. For new and un-established borrowers, the probability of overdrawing costly funds when all loan officers at the lending branch are women is almost 15% higher than when all loan officers are men. The gender gap disappears for borrowers with longer relationships with the bank. This finding is consistent with the idea that men and women behave differently in different information contexts: the gender effect is important when a borrower is less transparent but disappears once sufficient information is accumulated over time. It is in the former case, when female lenders tighten credit terms.

Rather than analyzing the behavior of trained professionals such as bank loan officers, Barasinska (2009) investigates the importance of lender's gender in person-to-person lending transactions. The author uses a sample of more than 37,000 bids for loans made by more than 4,200 lenders on more than 2,400 applications in the period March, 2007 to October, 2009 on the German web-platform Smava.de. She advances two hypotheses based on risk preferences, over-confidence and information-processing. The overconfidence hypothesis states that female lenders are more likely to finance less risky loans. The prudence hypothesis argues that, due to their superior information-processing skills, females will form loan portfolios which over-perform over time. The author studies the probability that a female lender will finance at least part of a loan and shows that female lenders are more likely to participate in loans with lower interest rates and longer maturity. The only borrower-related characteristic which influences the incidence of female financing is borrower risk. However, in contrast to the overconfidence argument, Barasinska finds that female lenders are more likely to take part in loans requested by riskier borrowers.

A major drawback of the previous studies is that they cannot directly measure the information-processing skills and strategies of the decision-makers. The studies by Andersson (2004) and Schneider and Church (2008) try to address this issue by directly measuring the strategies and processes followed by decision-makers. Although they do not explicitly focus on the existence of gender-based differences, both studies find no evidence of gender gap in the information acquisition processes. Andersson finds that on-the-job experience influences neither male nor female loan officers, while Schneider and Church find that the impact of negative internal auditing reports on loan officers' risk assessment of applicants is the same regardless of their gender.

In summary, the extant literature presents evidence on gender differentials in risk-taking, overconfidence and information processing which is at best inconclusive. Papers which study outcomes of the lending process provide evidence that women might be more likely to fund riskier borrowers but the contract terms are not systematically different between male and female lenders. Studies which focus on information acquisition and behavior of men and women in different information environments show that information-processing does not differ by gender when the context is constant. On the other hand, the outcome of the transaction might depend on the information context.

11.3.2.2 Stereotypes and Perceptions

Buttner and Rosen (1988) conduct a survey of 106 loan officers (60 male and 46 female) to investigate if they perceive men and women applicants differently along various dimensions believed to characterize successful entrepreneurs. In particular, the authors focus on leadership, autonomy, propensity to take risks, readiness for change, endurance, lack of emotionalism, low need for support, low conformity, and persuasiveness. The authors first document that men are generally seen as closer to successful entrepreneurs than women. Men are ranked higher than women along 6 of the characteristics. The findings of the study also reveal that male loan officers perceive a larger gap between the attributes which describe successful entrepreneurs and the attributes of women. Compared to their male colleagues, female loan officers are more likely to rate women higher along attributes such as autonomy, endurance and low need for support. The characteristic of successful entrepreneurs that truly distinguishes the perceptions of male lenders from those of their female counterparts appears to be leadership. Thus, the evidence supports the existence of differential perceptions and/or stereotypes by male and female lenders. Buttner and Rosen, however, do not study if these perceptions affect the actual lending behavior of the officers.

An attempt to fill this void is made by Carter et al. (2007) who, by focusing exclusively on the criteria and processes followed by male and female loan officers in their lending decisions, complement the analysis of Buttner and Rosen (1988). Using a sample of 35 loan officers from a major British bank, Carter et al. show that the relative importance of certain assessment criteria used by the loan officers in their decision-making processes is gender specific. In particular 3 out of 18 loan assessment criteria are found to be significantly different at the 95% confidence level across male and female loan officers. Additional 5 criteria are found to be different across the two groups at the 90% confidence level. The former set includes criteria such as marital status, need for a personal meeting and borrower commitment. For instance, female loan officers are more likely to consider the marital status of the applicants or the need to meet them personally, while male loan officers are more likely to consider the commitment of the borrower. Male lenders are also more likely to discuss positive comments about the application and to consider the past experience, education and finances of the borrowers. Conversely, female loan officers are more likely to discuss the need for more information about the applicant. Besides gender-based differences in lending criteria, the authors also document gender gap with respect to the lending processes the loan officers focus on. The authors show that male and female loan officers differ along 7 out of 13 elements of the lending process. For instance, male lenders are more likely to focus on the general lending process and their own "gut instinct" about the transaction, while female lenders are more likely to consider the general terms of the contract, the business plan of the applicant, and the size of the request. Overall, the analysis presented by Carter et al. shows that male and female loan officers use different criteria in their lending decisions and focus on different aspects of the lending process.

In a related study which investigates differences in perceptions between male and female lenders, Wilson et al. (2007) focus on the constructs – defined as basic contrasts/distinctions between members of two groups – used by male and female bank loan officers when deciding upon female and male loan applicants. Using a survey of 35 loan officers (19 male and 16 female) from a major bank in UK, the authors hypothesize and test three different gender-based patterns in perceptions: (1) no gender difference, (2) unsystematic differences, and 3) systematic differences. In most of their analysis, the authors show either no gender difference or no systematic gender difference. Hence, the study concludes that female lenders are as likely as their male colleagues to draw gender distinctions.

Finally, interesting insights into how feelings and emotions drive the decisions of female and male lenders are offered by Ravina (2008). In this study, the author uses lending which takes place on the specialized web-site Prosper.com in the United States in order to investigate whether male or female lenders are more susceptible to their perceptions by analyzing who lends to more beautiful borrowers or borrowers who visually appear more creditworthy. Consistent with female lenders being more susceptible to emotions, the author shows that women are more likely to lend to beautiful borrowers or to creditworthy-appearing ones. However, once controls for income and other borrower characteristics are introduced, the importance of lender's gender loses its significance. Moreover, the effect seems to be driven by solidarity for both male and female lenders: an indicator variable for cases where borrower and lender have the same gender is highly significant. Overall, it seems that solidarity affects both men and women in their decisions to grant credit to the, ex-post worse, beautiful borrowers. Women do not seem to be more sensitive to their perceptions, once all factors affecting a lending decision are considered. Furthermore, in line with the lack of gender gap in perceptions, the lending behavior of females towards black borrowers does not seem to differ substantially too.

In sum, the early evidence on the formation of stereotypes and perceptions of male and female lenders is consistent with the existence of gender-based gap along these dimensions. The more recent studies however, fail to detect systematic gender differences in this area. Hence, further research is needed in order to reach a conclusion.

11.3.2.3 Social Preference and Gender Pairing

The importance of the social preferences of lenders and the possibility that gender-pairing effects are driving the decisions of male and female loan officers have been treated in a number of papers.

Partial evidence comes from Alesina et al. (2008) who focus on the question of gender discrimination in access to credit. By using a large dataset on overdraft facilities to sole proprietorship firms in Italy, they show that, all else equal, female entrepreneurs pay higher interest rate than their male counterparts. Since male and female entrepreneurs do not seem to differ significantly in terms of risk, the authors' conjecture is that the discrimination against females is taste-based. Even though Alesina et al. do not have information on the gender of the loan officer handling a particular loan, they do recognize its importance. The authors suggest that, if what they find is indeed taste-based discrimination, banks with female representatives on their boards might be more likely to make efforts to avoid it. The underlying reasoning is that banks with female board members might be more sensitive to the issue of discrimination and understand the concerns of female borrowers better. Reported regression results suggest that interest rates charged by banks with at least one female director tend to be lower on average. However, the authors do not find evidence that the presence of female directors decreases gender-discrimination effects as the beneficial effect of women on the board of the bank does not occur predominantly to female borrowers.

A drawback in the analysis conducted by Alesina et al., at least with respect to gender-pairing, is that the authors do not have information on the loan officer who prepares the contract. Bellucci et al. (2010) alleviate this issue by using the proportion of female lenders at each bank branch and sub-sample analysis of loans granted at branches with male only and female only lenders. The authors study the importance of gender pairing not only for price of credit but also for other contract terms such as collateral requirements and credit limit. Consistent with gender-specific differences in social preferences and gender-pairing – chivalry/subjection and solidarity effects in particular – female lenders tend to charge male borrowers lower interest rates but request collateral from female borrowers less often.

Beck et al. (2009) further improve on Alesina et al. (2009), and Bellucci et al. (2010) by incorporating information on the gender of the very loan officer who approves and monitors a loan. The analysis of Beck et al. (2009), however, complements that in the other two studies by focusing on loan performance rather than the terms of the contract. In particular, Beck et al. find that the positive effect on loan performance associated with female loan officers previously discussed is particularly pronounced when the borrower is also female. The authors suggest cultural affinity as possible explanation, i.e. individuals of the same gender could be better at understanding each other.

Further evidence on the role of gender-pairing in person-to-person lending is presented by Ravina (2008). The author advances the importance of gender-pairing in lending because, as she puts it, "similarity breeds trust". In other words, lenders of the same gender as the borrowers could feel more solidarity with them and be more likely to fund these loans or to grant larger amounts. The evidence on gender-based similarity, however, does not fully support this argument. On the one hand, similarity seems to affect neither bid incidence nor offered amount because the coefficient on indicator for same gender is negative but statistically insignificant. A negative coefficient would be consistent with presence of chivalry rather than solidarity among lenders and borrowers of the same gender. On the other hand, the author finds contrasting results when she studies the proportion of lenders with the same gender as the borrower. In this case, gender-based similarity increases the probability that a loan is funded and the percent of funding but does not affect the interest rate.

Barasinska (2009), who also looks at person-to-person lending on the web, fails to detect any evidence of gender pairing effects as the probability of female participation among the lenders who respond to a borrowing bid is independent of the bidder's gender.

Overall, the extant literature on gender-pairing and social preferences provides some evidence that these factors could drive the shape of loan contracts and their performance ex-post. The results of studies based on bank lending seem to be most consistent with gender-based solidarity and cultural affinity, while the evidence from interpersonal lending is mixed.

11.3.2.4 Negotiation Skills

Despite its importance, the impact which negotiation skills and strategies have in the lending context has remained largely unexplored. An interesting exception is Black et al. (2000) who investigate mortgage lending practices by using proprietary data from a major lending institution in the United States. The focus of their analysis falls on the use of overages – the difference between the price at which a loan closes and the minimum price acceptable to the lending organization. The authors hypothesize that the gender of the loan officer might be an important determinant of the amount of overage as it could be related to the bargaining skills of the decision-maker. Consistent with male loan officers being tougher negotiators and/or possessing better negotiation skills, the authors conjecture that male lenders should impose higher overages than their female colleagues. However, the reported results are mixed and depend on the loan purpose. When a mortgage is used by the borrower to finance the purchase of a new estate, male loan officers tend to charge significantly higher overages. In contrast to this case, male and female lenders close contracts at similar overage amounts when the loans are used for the refinancing of existing mortgages.

Overall, the evidence on gender-based differences in terms of negotiation skills and strategies in the context of bank lending is rather limited. Hence, more research in this area would enable us to better understand the role and importance of this factor.

11.3.2.5 Career Concerns and Competitiveness

Finally, Agarwal and Wang (2009) provide some interesting results on gender gaps in career concerns and differential degrees of competitiveness between male and female lenders. As previously discussed, the authors investigate how incentive compensation and competition affect small business lending at a major commercial bank in the United States. In passing, the authors provide evidence which suggests that the effect of the new scheme is gender-dependent. Consistent with the idea that men respond more to competitive incentives, the authors show that the new incentive scheme almost doubles the gender gap in approval rates – from almost 4% difference in approval rates to almost 11% difference – but also increases the default rates of loans approved by female lenders over proportionally – from 0.8% differential between male and female lenders to negative 0.05%. As an explanation for the documented gender effect, the authors argue that female loan officers are more likely to have distorted incentives because they have shorter career spans and fewer career concerns. Thus, they are more likely to approve riskier loans. Although the authors do not acknowledge this directly, this finding could also be consistent with the notion that females are less effective than their male colleagues in competitive environments and thus competition has a detrimental effect to their performance.

Once again, further research along this dimension is needed if one wants to judge the importance of factors such as competition and career concerns more thoroughly.

11.4 Conclusion

Loan officers are not only the conduit of bank policies and operations in credit markets but also the central element of the interaction between small businesses and lending institutions. They are also at the heart of two important problems of information asymmetry pertinent to banking: the asymmetric information between banks and loan applicants and the moral hazard within the banking organization itself. Until recently, the economic literature considered loan officers as rational agents with unlimited information-processing capacity. In this review, we provide a brief overview of a more recent stream of literature which recognizes that lending decision could be affected by the behavior, character and even feelings or emotions of loan officers. Our focus falls on gender-based factors which could affect the tasks performed by the loan officers. Different degrees of risk-aversion and overconfidence between man and women might result in male and female loan officers reaching different lending decisions. Social preferences and gender-pairing, to the extent that they differ across the genders, might also lead to gender-specific outcomes of lending. Negotiation skills, stereotypes and perceptions, career concerns and discrimination have also been shown to vary with gender and hence are important. The extant literature for most of these factors is scarce. Thus, these factors remain topics important for future research.

References

Agarwal S, Wang FH (2009) Perverse Incentives at the Banks? Evidence from a Natural Experiment. Federal Reserve Bank of Chicago working paper 2009–08 http://www.chicagofed.org/digital_assets/publications/working_papers/2009/wp2009_08.pdf

Aghion P, Tirole J (1997) Formal and real authority in organizations. J Polit Econ 105:1–29

Alesina A, Lotti F, Mistrulli P (2008) Do women pay more for credit? Evidence from Italy, NBER working paper, No. 14202

Andersson P (2004) Does experience matter in lending? A process-tracing study on experienced loan officers' and novices' decision behavior, J Econ Psychol 25:471–492

Bandyopadhyay S, Francis J (1995) The economic effect of different levels of auditor assurance on bankers' lending decisions. Can J Adm Sci 12:238–249

Barasinska N (2009) The role of gender in lending business: evidence from an online market for peer-to-peer lending, DIW Berlin working paper

Barber B, Odean T (2001) Boys will be boys: gender, overconfidence, and common stock investment. Q J Econ 116:261–292

Becker G (1985) Human capital, effort, and the sexual division of labor. J Labor Econ 3:S33–S58

Bellucci A, Borisov A, Zazzaro A (2010) Does gender matter in bank-firm relationships? Evidence from small business lending. J Bank Finan 34:2968–2984

Berger A, Udell G (2002) Small business credit availability and relationship lending: the importance of bank organizational structure. Econ J 112:F32–F53

Beck T, Behr P, Guettler A (2009) Gender and banking: are women better loan officers?, working paper. Available at http://papers.ssrn.com/sol3/papers.cfm?abstract_id=1443107

Ben-Ner A, Kong F, Putterman L (2004) Share and share alike? Gender-pairing, personality, and cognitive ability as determinants of giving. J Econ Psychol 25:581–589

Bernasek A, Shwiff S (2001) Gender, risk, and retirement. J Econ Iss 35:345–356

Biggs S, Bedard J, Gaber B, Linsmeier T (1985) The effects of task size and similarity on the decision behavior of bank loan officers. Manage Sci 31:970–987

Black H, Boehm T, DeGennaro R (2000) Overages, mortgage pricing, and race, working paper. Available at http://papers.ssrn.com/sol3/papers.cfm?abstract_id=417440

Bonabeau E (2003) Don't trust your gut. Harv Bus Rev 5:116–123

Brown A, Larsen M, Rankin S, Ballard R (1980) Sex differences in information processing. Sex Roles 6:663–673

Byrnes J, Miller D, Schafer W (1999) Gender differences in risk taking: a meta analysis. Psychol Bull 125:367–383

Buttner E, Rosen B (1988) Bank loan officers' perceptions of the characteristics of men, women and successful entrepreneurs. J Bus Vent 3:249–258

Camerer C, Johnson E (1991) The process-performance paradox in expert judgment: How can experts know so much and predict so badly? In: Ericsson KA, Smith J (eds) Towards a general theory of expertise: prospects and limits. Cambridge Press New York, NY, pp 195–217

Carter S, Shaw E, Lam W, Wilson F (2007) Gender, entrepreneurship, and bank lending: the criteria and processes used by bank loan officers in assessing applications. Entrepreneurship Theory Pract 31:427–444

Chung J, Monroe G (1998) Gender differences in information processing: an empirical test of the hypothesis-confirming strategy in an audit context. Account Finan 38: 265–279

Croson R, Gneezy U (2009) Gender differences in preferences. J Econ Lit 47:448–474

Danos P, Holt D, Imhoff E Jr (1989) The use of accounting information in bank lending decisions. Account Org Soc 14:235–246

Darity W, Mason P (1998) Evidence on discrimination in employment: codes of color, codes of gender. J Econ Perspect 12:63–90

Darley W, Smith R (1995) Gender differences in information processing strategies: an empirical test of the selectivity model in advertising response. J Advert 24:41–56

Davis J (1996) Experience and auditors' selection of relevant information for preliminary control risk assessment. Audit J Pract Theor 15:16–37

Dessein W (2002) Authority and communications in organizations. Rev Econ Stud 69:811–838

Dixon R, Ritchie J, Siwale J (2007) Loan officers and loan 'delinquency' in microfinance: a Zambian case. Account Forum 31:47–71

Duehr E, Bono J (2006) Men, women, and managers: are stereotypes finally changing? Pers Psychol 59:815–846

Dufwenberg M, Muren A (2006)Generosity, anonymity, gender. J Econ Behav Org 61:42–49

Eagly A, Crowley M (1986) Gender and helping behavior: a meta-analytic review of the social psychological literature. Psychol Bull 100:283–308

Eckel C, Grossman P (1998) Are women less selfish than men?: Evidence from dictator experiment. Econ J 108:726–735

Eckel C, Grossman P (2001) Chivalry and solidarity in ultimatum games. Econ Inq 39:171–188

Eckel C, Grossman P (2008a) Forecasting risk attitudes: an experimental study using actual and forecast gamble choices. J Econ Behav Org 68:1–17

Eckel C, Grossman PJ (2008b) Men, women and risk aversion: experimental evidence. In: Plott C, Smith V (eds) Handbook of experimental economic results, Volume 1. Elsevier, New York, NY, pp. 1061–1073

Estes R, Hosseini J (1988) The gender gap on Wall Street: an empirical analysis of confidence in investment decision making. J Psychol 122:577–590

Ferri G (1997) Branch manager turnover and lending efficiency: local vs. national banks. BNL Q Rev 50(March):229–247

Gilligan C (1982) In a different voice: psychological theory and women's development. Harvard University Press, Cambridge

Garicano L (2000) Hierarchies and the organization of knowledge in production. J Polit Econ 108:874–904

Gerhart B, Rynes S (1991) Determinants and consequences of salary negotiations by male and female MBA graduates. J Appl Psychol 76:256–262

Gneezy U, Niederle M, Rustichini A (2003) Performance in competitive environments: gender differences. Q J Econ 118:1049–1074

Graham J, Stendardi E Jr, Myers J, Graham M (2002) Gender differences in investment strategies: an information processing perspective. Int J Bank Market 20:17–26

Gupta V, Turban D, Wasti S, Sikdar A (2009) The role of gender stereotypes in perceptions of entrepreneurs and intentions to became an entrepreneur. Entrepreneurship Theory Pract 33:397–417

Hertzberg A, Liberti JM, Paravisini D (2010) Information and incentives inside the firm: evidence from loan officer rotation. J Finan 65:795–828

Hirschleifer D, Thakor A (1992) Managerial conservatism, project choice and debt. Rev Finan Stud 5:437–470

Inderst R (2009) Loan origination under soft- and hard-information lending, University of Frankfurt working paper. Available at http://www.imfs-frankfurt.de/documents/WP_2009_27_Inderst.pdf

Jianakopolos N, Bernasek A (1998) Are women more risk averse? Attitudes toward financial risk. Econ Inq 36:620–631

Johnson D, Pany K, White R (1983) Audit reports and loan decisions: actions and perceptions. Audit J Pract Theor 2:38–51

Kaman V, Hartel C (1994) Gender differences in anticipated pay negotiation strategies and outcomes. J Bus Psychol 9:183–197

Karau S, Williams K (1993) Social loafing: a meta-analytic review and theoretical integration. J Pers Soc Psychol 65:681–706

Karlan D, Zinman J (2008) Lying about borrowing. J Eur Econ Assoc 6:510–521

Kray L, Thompson L, Galinsky A (2001) Battle of the sexes: gender stereotype confirmation and reactance in negotiations. J Pers Soc Psychol 80:942–958

Lerner J, Gonzalez R, Small D, Fischhoff B (2003) Effects of fear and anger on perceived risks of terrorism: a national field experiment. Psychol Sci 14:144–150

Liberti JM (2004) Initiative, incentives and soft information. How does delegation impact the role of bank relationship managers? London Business School, Mimeo

Lipshitz R, Shulimovitz N (2007) Intuition and emotion in bank loan officers' credit decisions. J Cogn Eng Decis Mak 1:212–233

Loewenstein G, Weber E, Hsee C, Welch N (2001) Risk as feelings. Psychol Bull 127:267–286

Lundberg M, Fox P, Puncochar J (1994) Highly confident but wrong: gender differences and similarities in confidence judgments. J Educ Psychol 86:114–121

McNamara G, Bromiley P (1997) Decision making in an organizational setting: cognitive and organizational influences on risk assessment in commercial lending. Acad Manage J 40: 1063–1088

Milgrom P, Roberts J (1990) Bargaining costs, influence costs, and the organization of economic activity. In: Alt J, Shepsle K (eds) Perspective on positive political economy. Cambridge University Press, Cambridge, pp 57–89

Milbourn T, Shockley R, Thakor A (2001) Managerial career concerns and investments in information. Rand J Econ 32:334–351

Miller L, Budd J (1999) The development of occupational sex-role stereotypes, occupational preferences and academic subject preferences in children at ages 8, 12 and 16. Educ Psychol 19:17–35

Niederle M, Vesterlund L (2007) Do women shy away from competition? Do men compete too much? Q J Econ 122:1067–1101

Novaes W, Zingales L (2004) Bureaucracy as a mechanism to generate information. Rand J Econ 35:245–259

Palley T (1997) Managerial turnover and the theory of short-termism. J Econ Behav Org 32: 547–557

Powell M, Ansic D (1997) Gender differences in risk behavior in financial decision-making: an experimental analysis. J Econ Psychol 18:605–628

Ravina E (2008) Love & loans: the effect of beauty and personal characteristics in credit markets. New York University working paper. Available at http://ssrn.com/abstract=1101647

Salminen S, Glad T (1992) The role of gender in helping behavior. J Soc Psychol 132:131–133

Scharfstein D, Stein J (2000) The dark side of internal capital markets: divisional rent-seeking and inefficient investment. J Finan 55:2537–2564

Schneider A, Church B (2008) The effect of auditors' internal control opinions on loan decisions. J Account Public Pol 27:1–18

Schubert R, Brown M, Gysler M, Brachinger H (1999) Financial decision-making: are women really more risk-averse? Am Econ Rev 89:381–385

Scott J (2006) Loan officer turnover and credit availability for small firms. J Small Bus Manage 44:544–562

Shurkhov O (2009) Gender differences in output quality and quantity under competition and time constraints: evidence from a pilot study. Wellesley College working paper. Available at: http://ssrn.com/abstract=1515794

Small D, Babcock L, Gelfand M, Gettman H (2007) Who goes to the bargaining table? The influence of gender and framing on the initiation of negotiation. J Personal Soc Psychol 93:600–613

Smith M (1999) Gender, cognitive style, personality, and management decision-making. Manage Account 77:18–22

Stuhlmacher A, Walters A (1999) Gender differences in negotiation outcome: a meta-analysis. Pers Psychol 52:653–677

Sunden A, Surette B (1998) Gender differences in the allocations of assets in retirement savings plans. Am Econ Rev 88:207–211
Tsui J (1993) Tolerance for ambiguity, uncertainty audit qualifications and banker's perceptions. Psychol Rep 72:915–919
Tversky A (1972) Choice by elimination. J Math Psychol 9:341–367
Uchida H, Udell G, Yamori N (2006) Loan officers and relationship lending. RIETI Discussion paper
Udell G (1989) Loan quality, commercial loan review and loan officer contracting. J Bank Finan 13:367–382
Walker H, Fennell M (1986) Gender differences in role differentiation and organizational performance. Annu Rev Sociol 12:255–275
Wilson F, Carter S, Tagg S, Shaw E, Lamz W (2007) Bank loan officers' perceptions of business owners: the role of gender. Br J Manage 18:154–171
Wright M, Davidson R (2000) The effect of auditor attestation and tolerance for ambiguity on commercial lending decisions. Audit J Pract Theor 19:67–81
Wright E, Baxter J, Birkelund G (1995) The gender gap in workplace authority: a cross-national study. Am Soc Rev 60:407–435

CPSIA information can be obtained at www.ICGtesting.com
Printed in the USA
LVOW030543220911

247352LV00007B/18/P